What Leaders Are Saying

"Sam, it's time for you to quit taking courses in spiritual formation and start teaching them. Your project needs to be published."

– **Dr. Eugene H. Peterson,** Translator of *The Message;* author of *Leap Over a Wall: Earthy Spirituality for Everyday Christians; Christ Plays in Ten Thousand Places: A Conversation in Spiritual Theology;* Sam's spiritual formation teacher in the Doctoral program at Fuller Theological Seminary

Dr. Sam, this book is timely for our age. Let me say, I have been to combat in the Global war on Terror and witnessed the discipline Soldiers exhibit. Discipline keeps them alive on the battlefield. They have been trained in their Warrior Tasks and Drills. This book illustrates the imperative disciplines of the soul that are needed for our combat with the terrorist kind of evil forces that threaten to destroy our faith and witness. We can win this spiritual warfare if we apply these *Keys to Spiritual Formation.*

– **Tommy W. Fuller**, Chaplain (GEN, Ret.). Command Chaplain, Mississippi National Guard and Camp Shelby. Author's Brother-in-Law. *"Pro Deo Et Patria."*

This is not a book that can be read quickly or casually. You must read it with a desire to be changed from the inside out. The stories reflect the pastor's heart – the pastor who learned to hear what hurting people were unable to say. Read it and allow your mind to be transformed by the Word of God until the Word becomes your life.

— **Mary E. Fuller,** Attorney at Law; Ordained Minister, Church of God (Anderson, IN)

Dr. Sam Bruce is a talented, gifted servant of the church who for years has demonstrated a living Gospel through a dynamic life of learning and daily application of the principles of God's Word. However, with the release of *Spiritual Formation: Forming Our Inner Lives and Relationships with God . . . Transforming Our Outer Lives and Relationships with Other People*, Dr. Sam lets us all in on the secret of his life of devotion and passion for the Lord. *Spiritual Formation: Forming Our Inner Lives and Relationships with God . . . Transforming Our Outer Lives and Relationships with Other People* is an amazing visual of a man's life devoted to pursuing a real relationship with the Messiah. As you read it you will not only learn how to incorporate the many principles and exercises of Spiritual Formation into your own life, but you will also see how one man did it. Unlike so many other textbooks, this one demonstrates as well as instructs! A great read, a greater experience!

— **Pastor Mitch Burch;** Evangelist & State Pastor/Overseer; West Virginia Ministries of the Church of God (Anderson, IN)

"Pastor Bruce, you are the watchman of my soul. You are responsible for helping me make it to heaven." (I interpreted that to mean that she considered it my responsibility to help her keep her spiritual formation in order so she could "finish well" and make it to heaven. However, I learned much about the reality of the power of spiritual formation in the life of this faithful saint.)

– **Lillian "Grandma" Perry**, former parishioner; Mother-in-law of Rev. Floyd Tunnel, Former pastor of Fourth Street Church; Great Grandmother of Sandie Patti

The word intimacy comes from three Hebrew words meaning: to know, to be known and to be caringly involved. Intimacy with the Almighty is a deep desire within every individual. It is the deep hunger of the human spirit. You will find insight, instruction and inspiration within Dr. Bruce's writing that will give you tools for developing intimacy with God. He has written out of his own intimacy with his heavenly father. You will be challenged and encouraged as you apply the biblical truths. You will discover intimacy with God is possible through *Spiritual Formation: Forming Our Inner Lives and Relationships with God . . . Transforming Our Outer Lives and Relationships with Other People.*

– **Dr. Claude Robold**; Former Pastor New Covenant Church, President of the Board, Mid-America Christian University, College & Seminary Classmate.

Sam, I only wish I could have been exposed to a fraction of what you have written in this helpful and practical resource. I predict your book *Spiritual Formation: Forming Our Inner Lives and Relationships with God . . . Transforming Our Outer Lives and Relationships with Other People* will become a classic in many religious and Church circles for both ministers and lay persons. Your writing skills are reminiscent of a capable surgeon - who invites us to expose the inward illnesses of our souls to the sharp scalpel of God's Word; the gentle touch of God's hands; and the spiritual disciplines of the Holy Spirit.

> – **Dr. Alvin Lewis,** Ph.D., M.Div.; Senior Pastor, Central Community Church of God; former National Director of Family Life and Adult Ministries, Board of Christian Education - Church of God (Anderson, IN)

Spiritual Formation: Forming Our Inner Lives and Relationships with God . . . Transforming Our Outer Lives and Relationships with Other People is a refreshing spiritual formation guide for the minister's inner person. Pastors and other ministers often operate within a different paradigm than the congregation. Dr. Sam brings a fresh awareness of the need for a lifelong discipline of spiritual formation that is sure to capture the hearts of those who read this book. The use of *Forming Our Inner Lives and Relationships with God . . . Transforming Our Outer Lives and Relationships with Other People* is brilliant when we truly hear what Proverbs 4:23 says, **"Guard your heart above all else, for it determines the course of your life."** I rejoice that Dr. Sam's book is available to this generation of ministers (and everyone else!) who need what each chapter presents. Well done Dr. Sam!

> – **Rev. Dr. Bettie L. McCarty**, Pastor, Lighthouse Church of God Credentials Chair, Mississippi Ministries of the Church of God

Dr. Sam, I want to thank you for teaching me about spiritual formation. It was probably one of the most demanding courses I ever took, but it is the one I turn back to most often for reminders of what can keep me and my relationships and ministries strong, fulfilling, effective, and healthy. The most effective thing I learned was prayer journaling – you had us journal through the Psalms. I know that if I am not spending *that* time with the Lord, then my spiritual life is not what it needs to be. Journaling is one of my *love languages with the Lord.*

> – **Rachel Whetstone Mosher**, former Spiritual Formation Student, Mid-America Christian University; Worship Minister, Shartel Church of God, Oklahoma City OK.

In This book my good friend, Dr. Sam Bruce, has written a classic on spiritual discipline. For any serious Christian, who desires to grow spiritually, this is a must-read book. Sam has demonstrated the living out of these spiritual disciplines that are so evident in his own life. God has gifted Sam and his wife, Sandie, with great musical talent. You can be assured that every word has the Holy Spirit's anointing.

> – **Victor P. Smith**, Victor P. Smith Co.; President, Here's Life Mission to Africa; Co-Founder, Mission Mississippi (a racial reconciliation movement); Owner, Maranatha Christian Stores, Jackson, MS; Rotary Club of Jackson.

Dr. Sam Bruce is a pastor to many searching to understand the ways of God and His purpose for their lives. Additionally, he is a friend to all who know him through Christian fellowship. Because of his obedience to listen to God, *Spiritual Formation: Forming Our Inner Lives and Relationships with God . . . Transforming Our Outer Lives and Relationships with Other People* is a powerful guide in shaping or transforming our inner life. I am blessed to call him my friend.

> – **Charles Doty**, President, CEO, Lextel Manufacturing, LLC

Through the twenty years I have known Sam and Sandie Bruce, reliability comes to mind. Sam's public prayers are as though God is directly talking through him to me. His ever-present gentleness, care and attention, especially to Sandie, and to others is God inspired. Only when we all get to heaven will we understand the positive impact Sam has had on our life. Why should we expect anything else from his book *Spiritual Formation: Forming Our Inner Lives and Relationships with God . . . Transforming Our Outer Lives and Relationships with Other People* than a similar successful conclusion? During my thirty-three years with the worldwide Dale Carnegie Training organization, I learned that our clients expect results. Participants who read and study Sam's book and make real life applications can expect meaningful God-inspired results.

— **Wes Holsapple**, Owner, Manager, Instructor: Dale Carnegie
Training, Jackson, MS; Wes Holsapple Realty: licensed
Commercial Real Estate Broker in Alabama and Mississippi

SPIRITUAL FORMATION

Forming
Your Relationship
with God

Transforming
Your Relationships
with People

Dr. Sam Bruce

7710-T Cherry Park Dr, Ste 224
Houston, TX 77095
(713) 766-4271

Cover design: Teresa Granbury, www.HarvestCreekGraphics.com

Printed in the United States

ISBN: xxxxxxxxx

My Life Purpose Power Prayer

"Eternal God . . . Creator of the Universe . . . Maker of My life . . . Your life repeated in my life, Lord. I want to become the holy JesusFollower person of God You designed me to be.
Empower me, *Lord, by Your Son – as clay in Potter's Hands – to become all You created me to be.*
Energize me, *Lord, by Your Spirit – as gold in Refiner's Fire – to accomplish all You call me to do.*
Enliven me, Lord, by Your Love – as one who's been transformed – to bring all you call me to love and lead home to You.
Enkindle me, *Lord, by your Presence – as one who grows through spiritual formation, to be a person wholly committed to You . . . Amen."*

Making this prayer part of your regular prayer times can be the launching pad for your continual *Spiritual formation: shaping our inner lives and relationships with God in ways that transform our outer lives and relationships with other persons.* We accomplish this by becoming *People Inundated by the Word, People Immersed in Prayer, and People Ignited by Worship which shape us into People Infused with God.*

When God finds those, who will covenant to live in this Life Purpose Power Prayer . . . He has found those through whom He can work as His Holy Conduits to transform the world of those He calls them to love and lead through their ministries. Lord, forge me into that person! "Oh, Yes!"[1]

– Wisdom Sketches from Proverbs of Dr. Sam 3:23[2]

---

1   Eugene Peterson's translation of "Amen" in *The Message*: "Oh, Yes!"
2   Bruce, Dr. Sam. *WisdomSketches* from Proverbs of Dr. Sam: The Book of Wisdom from a Wise Ol' University Professor. Florence, MS: Unpublished. Come to the Waters Be Refreshed! Ministry & Music Resources, Sam& Sandie Bruce Ministries, drsambruce@aol.com www.bruceministries.net

"This book should be in the hands of every Christian and written in their hearts. God has inspired you and the pages throughout your book reflect your passion and love for the Lord. You are a conduit for holiness and this masterful, inspired work causes one to read, re-read, study, reflect, practice and interiorize its content. I agree with all the responders about this book. It is priceless, timeless, so steeped in Scripture and God centered. Through your holy lifestyle you exude God's love and goodness by your life, your ministry, your book, and your deep, authentic spirituality. This is a book that I will continue using in my personal spiritual growth and prayer life. It has helped me to become a better religious Sister so I cannot thank you enough for this treasured gift from a treasured friend."

– **Sister M. Dorothea**, President, Ret. St. Dominic Medical Center, Jackson, MS. Fellow Rotarian with Dr. Sam

Contents

Acknowledgements

I am forever grateful to God for His awesome kindness and generosity shown through giving Dr. Walter and Dr. Lois Bruce to me as my parents. Although they did not use the words *spiritual formation* to describe the process of becoming *JesusFollowers*, they simply modeled it 24/7, and taught it in ways that made it attractive, not only to me, but also to my sister Mary Bruce Fuller and my brother Bill Bruce (both of whom are dynamic *JesusFollowers* and special friends).

And Sandie . . . the girl I fell in love with the first day I met her – my best friend and partner in ministry. A living model of the spiritually-formed life – a true *JesusFollower* whose love and life are a legacy of *Christ in you* for all who know her.

The legacy continues in our daughters – the joy of our lives – Janelle Bruce -Bond and Janette Bruce-Bock who are passing the *JesusFollower* spiritual formation principles to their families, friends and colleagues. They and their families are a testimony to the power of generational spiritual formation, and we thank God for them every day.

My deep gratitude goes to Dr. Eugene Peterson, my spiritual formation teacher at Fuller Theological Seminary, who had an awesome, life-transforming impact on my life and ministries. He was more than a teacher; he was a model of the principles of spiritual formation. As mentioned earlier, he wrote on my grade sheet: *"Sam, it's time for you to quit taking courses in spiritual formation and start teaching them. Your project needs to be pub-*

lished." Those 22 words planted a dream in my heart that is being fulfilled in this book, as well as in the spiritual formation courses I have been teaching in colleges, churches and service clubs across the nation for many years. My prayer is that as you read these pages, you also will listen for the *gentle whispers of God* (1 Kings 19:12 NIV) shaping the dreams He and you want to fulfill in your life.

Foreword

Are there "holes" in your spiritual formation? Many Christian leaders are in trouble today. Sadly, those who follow them may be in more trouble. Almost daily we hear of another leader's moral failure or dropout. Why? How can this be? In a great many cases, today's Christian leaders came to Christ in their late teens or early twenties; many were literally "saved off the streets" during the Jesus Movement. Although having little or no biblical foundation for life, because of their newfound joy, excitement for Christ, their charismatic personalities and innate leadership abilities, they were quickly released and encouraged to give public testimonies of their salvation. This often led to Bible College and some to seminary where they learned about the Bible, the written Word, and how to present it. However, many were never exposed to the Living Word and how to relate to Him. The bottom line is that they were never shown "the bottom line." Some have struggled silently throughout their ministries; others have soared in the eyes of men; yet they are desperately lacking in terms of a true living relationship with Christ. Spiritual formation hasn't occurred.

My friend, Dr. Sam Bruce, long-time pastor and Christian educator, has responded to this virtual vacuum by providing *Spiritual Formation: Forming Our Inner Lives and Relationships with God . . . Transforming Our Outer Lives and Relationships with Other People*. In it, he has distilled the issues of spiritual formation and laid them out in a step-by-step format which he and his wife Sandie teach in their popular spiritual formation retreats. This marvelous book, *Spiritual Formation: Forming Our Inner Lives and Relationships with God . . . Transforming Our Outer Lives and Relationships with Other People*, will fill in the "holes" in your spiritual formation, and lead you through the process of establishing a relationship with Christ that will reshape your inner life – your intimacy with the King; and transform your outer life – your relationships with others. This is the key to abundant life!

 – Eddie Smith: Best-selling author, internationally-known conference speaker, owner/CEO WorldwidePublishingGroup.com, Co-founder and President of www.USPrayerCenter.org

Introduction

Those who have read my book and those who have taken one or both of my bachelor and master courses in spiritual formation (built around the Word of God and this book) through Mid-America Christian University (Oklahoma City OK) and Wesley College (Florence MS) have testified that God used their experiences to deeply renovate and transform their spiritual lives and relationships with God and other people. Walking with our Lord on His path into this Portal of Spiritual Formation often leads us into His awesome *Holy Ground Crossing Points*.

A *Holy Ground Crossing Point* is a God-Moment where our impossibilities intersect with God's Possibility Factor – His *3/20 Immeasurably More Principle* (Ephesians 3:20). A Holy Ground Crossing Point is where our dreams, desires, visions, relationships, needs, heartbreaks, potentials and victories intersect with God's presence, power, plans, and provisions. Faithful application of these *JesusFollower Life Principles* is a path to growth in dynamic spiritual depth, leadership skills, and holy success in all you do. SO! Please open your spirit, mind, and emotions to our Lord's presence and message to you personally as you listen carefully, hear clearly, apply diligently, and follow purposefully His leadership. And pray . . . pray my **Life Purpose Power Prayer:** *"Eternal God . . . Creator of the Universe . . . Maker of My life . . . Your life repeated in my life, Lord. I want to become the holy JesusFollower person of God You designed me to be.* **Empower me**, *Lord, by Your Son – as clay in Potter's Hands – to become all You created me to be.*

Energize me, *Lord, by Your Spirit — as gold in Refiner's Fire — to accomplish all You call me to do.* *Enliven me*, *Lord, by Your Love — as one who's been transformed — to bring all you call me to love and lead home to You.* *Enkindle me*, *Lord, by your Presence — as one who grows through spiritual formation, to be a person wholly committed to You . . . Amen."*

God's awesome best to you as you walk with Him into His Portal of *Holy Ground Crossing Points!*

About the *Small Voice* Picture

I was given the special privilege of speaking for Spiritual Emphasis Week at Gulf-Coast Bible College (now Mid-America Christian University) the last year it was on the Houston, Texas, campus. One of the students was from the Philippine Islands. Before coming to college, he had worked as an artist in the Philippine Mint. Dr. Donald Brumfield, the Christian Education teacher, asked him to draw this caricature of me during chapel. They presented the original pen and watercolor picture to me as an appreciation gift at the end of the week. In the caption the artist picked up on the words, *"Always listen to the small voice of God . . ."* from a message I did about Elijah, when he was in the cave feeling forsaken and alone. After he had heard and felt the windstorm, the forest fire, and the earthquake, and he got still and listened, he heard **a still small voice** (1 Kings 19:12 KJV); **a gentle and quiet whisper** (1 Kings 19:12 MSG) and it was the voice of God.

That caricature is one of my most cherished possessions to this day, and it hangs beside my desk as a reminder that my source of power as a Christian leader comes only as I *"Always listen to the small voice of God . . ."* The event, as only God could have planned, happened in the early days of my personal learning and beginning to grow in spiritual formation. It was the first sharing time about the biblical principles of spiritual formation other than in my own church. God was overwhelming my heart with wonder, showing me the need and power of *living in tune* with my Lord Jesus which would keep me *living in harmony* with those He calls me to love and lead through my ministries.

As you read through the following pages – many of which are from *My Journal*, written in response to that *small voice of God* as I read His word, prayed, observed others who *listened to the small voice of God*, and sensed deep transformation in my inner being – imagine that you and I are walking together on a forest trail with Jesus walking between us. Listen to His *gentle and quiet whisper*, His *still small voice* as He draws you into His intimate, life-transforming presence. Let Him make whatever changes are necessary to empower you to become all He created you to be, and to accomplish all He calls you to do. The little caricature will appear at the beginning of each chapter as a reminder to *"Always listen to the small voice of God . . ."* just as it does me whenever I see it. If you will do this, your life will never be the same. Your life and ministry will be empowered in ways you never dreamed possible. As you listen, in response, pray the following words from a song I wrote on my wooded prayer trail as I listened to the *small voice of God* while quoting 2 Thessalonians 1:11-12: **"With this in mind, we constantly pray for you, that our God may count you worthy of his calling, and that by his power he may fulfill every good purpose of yours and every act prompted by your faith. We pray this so that the name of our Lord Jesus may be glorified in you, and you in him, according to the grace of our God and the Lord Jesus Christ."**

Glorify Your Name in Me
(2 Thessalonians 2:11-12)

Lord, bring me closer, closer than I've ever come before to You.
Lord, plunge me deeper, deeper than I've ever been before in You.
Lord, take me higher, higher than I've ever soared before with You.
Lord, send me farther, farther than I've ever gone before for You.

Lord, glorify Your name in me;
Oh Lord, glorify Your name in me;
Lord, please glorify Your name in me,
And my name in You.

Lord, lead me closer; and deeper; and higher; and farther
Than I've ever dreamed before.[3]

---

3   Words & Music © by Samuel K. Bruce, 2004. For a copy of the music: 601-955-3176 or drsambruce@aol.com

Prelude

When Eugene Peterson (professor in my doctoral program at Fuller Theological Seminary) sent my grade for the *Spiritual Formation Course*, after reading my papers and projects, he wrote a note on the grade sheet: "Sam, it's time for you to quit taking courses in spiritual formation and start teaching them. Your project needs to be published." My project for the Spiritual Formation course at Fuller Theological Seminary was the curriculum for our *Christian Growth Groups* at Fourth Street Church of God, Madera, California, where I served as Senior Pastor for twenty-one years. Those lessons were the beginning stages of my dissertation at Fuller, which has served as the foundation of the spiritual formation courses I have taught across the years, as well as for this book. Within a few months after Peterson's comments, to my surprise, the Lord opened an invitation for me to begin adjunct teaching the Spiritual Formation Course at Mid-America Christian University. I now have written and teach the online Spiritual Formation Course at Mid-America Christian University. *Spiritual Formation: Forming Our Inner Lives and Relationships with God . . . Transforming Our Outer Lives and Relationships with Other People* is the text for that course. As President of Wesley College, I developed and taught the Spiritual Formation Course there. Little did I know then that I would be teaching these principles today in churches and on college campuses throughout the United States and around the world (through online courses). It is awesome to watch God's plan unfolding across the years, as we allow Him to shape our lives. I have felt privileged to have a small part in training men and women for ministry as they follow God's plan for their lives.

In 2003, God surprised us with the call for Sandie and me to leave Wesley College, where I served as president for twelve years, to go full time with *Sam & Sandie Bruce Ministries*, of which I am president. In addition to our extensive national preaching and music ministry, I teach the principles of spiritual formation and ministry in churches, camps, and retreats, as well as in the online education programs at Mid-America Christian University. Talk about multiplying your ministry to another level—the online education system allows me to teach people around the world, no matter where I am in other ministry, if I have internet access! Only God could have dreamed that He could take the principles of spiritual formation He began in a small child many years ago and multiply them through the lives of people across this nation and around the world. But then He has a way of doing that when people allow Him to *form their inner lives and relationships with God in ways that will transform their outer lives and relationships with other people.*

You will discover that this book is written, not in a typical "textbook style," but in a more conversational or relational style. These lessons had their beginnings in my own life in a time of seeking to take my relationship with God to a deeper level. As I entered a fresh covenant with God through the His Word, prayer, and worship, He provided me with the opportunity to study spiritual formation under Dr. Eugene Peterson, as mentioned above. That experience provided me the accountability of studying and practicing disciplines of spiritual formation through studies in the Word, Scripture memory, prayer, worship, journaling, personal spiritual retreats, and reading a host of books on spiritual formation. These lessons in spiritual formation grew out of my dissertation for the doctoral program at

Fuller. It is my sincere desire that as you read them, they will serve as catalysts for your personal spiritual formation or transformation. I hope that in these studies you will listen for the leadership of our Lord to make your own covenants with Him about taking your relationship with Him to a higher level, and in turn to lead the people to whom you minister in the same direction.

One of the titles we considered for this book was *Firewall: Keys to Spiritual Formation*. My publisher suggested it after reading the manuscript. We like that title but felt it might not make sense to those who are not yet "computer literate." However, *Firewall* is a good description of the disciplines of Spiritual formation, which I define as *Forming Our Inner Lives and Relationships with God . . . Transforming Our Outer Lives and Relationships with Other People.* Spiritual formation is not intended to replace our studies in Bible, theology, church growth, counseling, Christian education, or academic disciplines. Rather, I see it as like the Operating System on a computer.

The Operating System is what enables all other programs to function appropriately and effectively. Without the Operating System none of the programs like Microsoft Word, PowerPoint, Excel, and Internet Explorer will function. The Operating System runs in the background, and, when it works correctly (we know it does not always work correctly!), it is supposed to keep everything working smoothly and effectively. The biblical disciplines of Christian spiritual formation configure (set up, design, or arrange the parts of something for a specific purpose) the only God-designed Operating System that can keep us steady, effective, and online for a lifetime of ministry. The foundational disciplines of spiritual formation – particularly becoming *People of the Word* (studying, memorizing, meditating), *People of Prayer* (regular practice of personal, intercessory, family, and corporate prayer), and *People of Worship* – shape us as *People of God*.

These indispensable, life-transforming disciplines build all the *firewall* protection that is needed to shield our God-designed Operating System from the virus, spyware, and phishing assaults and other attacks that Satan, the world system, circumstances, temptations, and other people can use to trip us up, to tear down our relationships, to torpedo our dreams, or to topple our ministries. Phishing refers to the practice of a website placing a *cookie* on your computer which tracks what software you have and how you use your computer. This helps the company know what kind of advertising to send you to make offers for you to buy their products. The *firewall* protects your computer from phishing kinds of cookies. The *firewall of the disciplines of Spiritual Formation* is what provides the kind of protection around our inner world described by Proverbs 4:23 (NLT): **"Guard your heart above all else, for it determines the course of your life."**

Even though we did not use the title *Firewall – Keys to Transformed Living*, the book is filled with *Keys to Transformed Living*. What is a key? How does it fit into this book subject? A key is a small piece of metal that will lock or unlock a door. A key is a lever or a valve that is pressed when playing a musical instrument like a piano, flute, or trumpet. It is a lever on an electrical switch that makes or breaks an electrical circuit. It is a list of symbols used to read and understand a map so you can follow them to reach your destination. A key can also be a principle used to bring success in an activity or business. When you *key into* a principle or another person, it enables you to be connected or in harmony with that principle or person. To be *keyed up* can mean you are nervous, tense, anxious, or excited about an opportunity, challenge, or a person you anticipate meeting.

Each of these definitions of a *key* is descriptive of various principles of spiritual formation. Again, even though we did not use the title *Firewall – Keys to Transformed Living* as the title for this book, the biblical principles shared on its pages are really *keys* that will unlock the doors to a deeper and more intimate relationship with our Lord and with other people that He brings into our lives. These *keys of spiritual formation* are like the electrical switch that connects a light bulb, a machine, or even a whole city with the source of power that enables it to function smoothly and efficiently. The *keys of spiritual formation* enable us to *key into* the Person, power, purpose, and provisions that God makes available to those who make it their ambition to become all He created us to be and to accomplish all He calls us to do. When we *key into* THAT plan of God for our lives, we are empowered to live in harmony with Him and His awesome purposes for our lives, relationships, ministries, and jobs.

Personally, I get *keyed up* when I realize that the Creator God invites me into a personal relationship with Himself, and I experience all the emotions involved in this concept. I am sometimes nervous, tense, and anxious because I know I can never, on my own, live up to His expectations. But I am always excited, enthused, and eager because I know He can renovate, transform, equip, and energize in ways I never dreamed possible as He shapes me into that person, He created me to be so He can energize me to achieve all He asks me to do.

The keys – principles – of spiritual formation are like the symbols used to read and understand the directions on a map that enable us to arrive at our intended destination. The keys of becoming *people of the Word, people of prayer, and people of worship* will guide us toward the goal of becoming people of God. Those are the keys that can open the doors to a kind of *holy success* in achieving that close, intimate relationship with God that our hearts so deeply desire.

As you enter this study of *Spiritual Formation: Forming Our Inner Lives and Relationships with God . . . Transforming Our Outer Lives and*

Relationships with Other People, please make these words of my song your prayer: *"Lord, lead me closer, and deeper, and higher, and farther than I've ever dreamed before. Lord glorify Your name in me, and my name in You."*[4]

Having served many years as pastor, Bible college president, Credentials Committee member, and counselor to many people in various ministries, I have witnessed too often the tragic fall of many church leaders (lay and professional) who failed because they did not maintain the protection of the interior world with the firewall kind of virus protection in the spiritual disciplines. They left themselves vulnerable and unprotected, and when a virus-like temptation or pressure came they had not enough power or desire to resist.

I have often told my students I can guarantee that if they do not incorporate the Christian biblical spiritual disciplines, we learn in a study like this, sooner or later they will experience a major hard drive crash in their lives—a fallout, burnout, rust-out, or wimp-out that will ruin their lives and sideline their ministries and hurt a lot of people. In the wake of such lost battles are hard drive crashes that lead to disconnected marriages, devastated spouses, disillusioned congregations, destroyed lives, and disabled ministries.

Everybody loses when leaders fall in this way. Sometimes we may feel like the man who said in a testimony meeting, "I feel like a Pepsi that has been left out of the refrigerator for several days with the lid off, the fizz has gone out of my life!" That is graphic description of the condition of our lives when we neglect those important life-energizing disciplines of Christian biblical spiritual formation, which we will study in this book.

I am sometimes asked why I have such a passion for teaching the principles of Christian biblical spiritual formation. Is it because I studied

---

4   The words are the bridge in my song *Glorify Your Name in Me, which is given in full later in the book. You may order a copy, along with the track, at* <u>drsambruce@aol.com</u> or <u>601-845-8693.</u>

spiritual formation under Eugene Peterson? He did have a great influence on my life. Is it because spiritual formation was the concentration of my doctoral dissertation at Fuller Theological Seminary? My life was deeply strengthened by everything I learned in that process. Is it because I have taught spiritual formation in churches, camps, and college campuses for over 20 years? That has enriched my personal life immensely.

However, these are not the driving influences in my passion for teaching spiritual formation. It comes from seeing the light come on in people's lives when they begin to come alive spiritually in ways never before experienced as they start to learn and practice the spiritual disciplines that renovate, transform, and empower their lives, relationships, and ministries. People who have been disillusioned with dull, dry, drab Christian experience begin to overflow with the joy of walking with God on new levels. Many who have been derailed by overwhelming temptations, devastated by destructive habits, disillusioned by broken relationships, or detained by a lack of a vital relationship with God have experienced the awesome protective power of the firewall provided by the spiritual disciplines. They discover that there is more than the tiring monotony of shoddy, shallow, mask-wearing, unfulfilling spirituality they have seen personally and in other persons.

As I crisscross this country in ministry, I regularly meet former students (and other participants) of spiritual formation courses who tell me something like, "I want to thank you for teaching me about spiritual formation. It was probably one of the most demanding courses I ever took, but it is the one I turn back to most often for reminders of what can keep me and my relationships and ministries strong, fulfilling, effective, and healthy." Comments like that are more exciting to me than hitting a grand slam home run, striking out three batters in a row, achieving a hole in one, climbing to the top of a mountain, running seven miles, or catching a five-pound bass. This is true because the results of teaching spiritual forma-tion last a lot longer – for eternity.

Student Comments

The following are a few comments from former students that illustrate the reason for my continued passion for teaching spiritual formation.

This is a great class. I wish I had (taken) this a long time ago. I have been in college for one year, and this is one of the most practical classes I have had. The material is excellent and easy to use. It has been good for me to take this class after just completing "Biblical Life and Witness." This should be taught to new Christians, regardless of their age. Of course, twelve-year-olds should be introduced to this in a different way, but I believe they can grasp the concepts.

In the area of spiritual disciplines my life has been and still is lacking. I am not as disciplined as I should be. My biggest excuse is time. When I was told this class was being offered this summer, I decided to take it. I am glad I did. The class changed my life. The Lord showed me the areas that have been lacking, and He is showing me how to become disciplined again. My spiritual disciplines are changing for the better, and I am excited at what God is going to do in my life and my family. He is helping me to change our family devotion time which is lacking at the present time. This class gives me a new perspective on God that I have never had before.

The whole experience was something I would not give up. I am so thankful that I was given this experience. It has changed my life. It has changed the way I spend my quiet time and the way I look at the blessings from God, with a new perspective. I plan to continue journaling. I have learned that I can express myself better now than I could before. This is a neat and wonderful experience, and I am so glad that we have men like Dr. Sam who can impart their knowledge to others to help us with our daily walks with the Lord.

In a book report on Henri Nouwen's *Making All Things New*, one student wrote: The last thing that really spoke to me from this book was setting our hearts on God. "A spiritual life requires human effort." This means we do not get our spiritual lives by simple osmosis. We must work at it. Sometimes I think we do not fully understand this. So many people believe that once they are saved that is all that is necessary. I do not believe this. Spiritual life takes discipline. "The practice of spiritual discipline makes us more sensitive to the small, gentle voice of God. A spiritual discipline sets us free to pray, or to say it better, allows the Spirit of God to pray in us." I have not been taking a lot of this seriously until now. Through reading and journaling for this class, I have learned to fine-tune my spiritual discipline so that my whole life is more disciplined, productive, and my communication [with God] is now at a higher level than ever before.

Comments like these keep kindling my passion for teaching the principles of Christian biblical spiritual formation to men and women, to equip them for effective Christian ministry. As stated earlier, this will possibly be one of the most demanding classes you will take during your college years. It will also be one of the most important classes, for those who aspire to do the work of ministry long-term will need the strength of the spiritual disciplines to enable them to remain faithful to God and to their calling. Those who fail in the spiritual disciplines will usually fall short, give up, or experience a moral, ethical, or relational breakdown that can ruin or seriously hamper lifelong ministry.

Dig Deep Wells in Spiritual Formation

As you read *this book*, I encourage you to *"dig deep wells"* in spiritual formation, for this will provide an unending supply of spiritual refreshment and stamina as you pursue your God-given callings for life and ministry. I believe that if you will see this book as God's appointment for you to grow and stretch in your relationship with Him, it will be a life-transforming time for you that will enrich your ministries and relationships with other persons.

It will take intentional disciplining of yourself to persevere in making your personal spiritual formation a priority, and deliberate persistence in learning and practicing the spiritual disciplines to the best of your ability. This will pay great spiritual, mental, emotional, relational, and ministry dividends for the rest of your life.

Speaking of doing your best work in personal spiritual formation, think about this: suppose I was diagnosed with a brain tumor, and I went to see the neurosurgeon that was going to surgically remove it. And while I was in consultation with him, I looked up and saw his impressive diploma in neurosurgery. Suppose I said to him, "Hey, doc, what kind of grade did you get in neurosurgery?" If he answered (as I have heard many ministerial students say), "Aw, I did just enough work to slide by with a 'C'!" I would be looking for another neurosurgeon, because I want the best possible surgeon to be working inside my brain. The ministries you and I are involved in (whether lay or professional, full-time or part-time) are more important and have longer lasting consequences than the most intricate neurosurgery you can imagine. The people God entrusts into our ministries deserve our best training and care. Let's do our best!

Please join me in prayer that, as we together study and learn to practice some life-empowering, ministry-energizing Christian biblical disciplines of spiritual formation, God will renew, refresh, and revive us and all those God calls us to love and lead in our ministries.

I pray that studying these principles will be an awesome experience as you allow God to challenge and change you at the deepest level of your life. When God comes knocking at the entrance of your spirit, click on the *firewall* button that says, "*Allow access from this Website*"! His is a protected website, and you will be enriched as you allow Him entrance.

Better yet, here is another way of thinking about it. When the Norton Antivirus Technician was helping me solve some computer issues, she asked me to connect to a website called *Remote Access* and to allow her to take over the controls of my computer. As I surrendered my computer to her control, I watched my cursor move across the screen as she made all the necessary changes, downloaded, and installed the latest version of Norton Protection System. When I disconnected from *Remote Access* my computer was working better than ever before.

As you study the Word, pray, journal, and worship, learn and prac-tice the disciplines of *Spiritual Formation: Forming Our Inner Lives and Relationships with God . . . Transforming Our Outer Lives and Relationships with Other People* and allow God, through His Holy Spirit, to have *uncon-ditional access* to the control room of your life to make whatever changes are needed. Allow Him to install in your spirit a new *Operating System* that will be empowered by the spiritual disciplines which are *keys to spiritual formation*. This relationship will provide the *firewall protection* of our Lord Jesus Christ and His Holy Spirit from all inner and outer forces that would seek to destroy your relationship with God and weaken your witness to other persons. As you do this, your inner life will be empowered, and your ministries will be energized in ways you have never yet dreamed possible! And remember, *always listen to the small voice of God!*

God's Best to You!

PART 1

INTRODUCTION TO SPIRITUAL FORMATION

Chapter 1

Overview of Spiritual Formation

Spiritual Formation: Forming Our Inner Lives and Relationships with God . . . Transforming Our Outer Lives and Relationships with Other People, is the primary setting in which the shaping of who we are, what we become, and ultimately, what we do takes place. That **"inner being"** (Ephesians 3:16), as Paul describes it, is the control center of our personal lives as well as our relationships with God and with other people. The writer of Proverbs must have had this principle in mind when he wrote, **"Above all else, guard your heart, for it is the wellspring of life"** (Proverbs 4:23). This highlights the paramount importance of giving serious, consistent attention and care to the inner person, the interior spiritual world which regulates the outer world of activities and relationships. If our inner lives and our relationships with God are not in order, it will be impossible to keep our outer lives and relationships with other persons in order.

Spiritual formation is *the process of God's giving Himself to us (in Jesus Christ, by the Holy Spirit, through the Word), and our giving ourselves to God (in submission, obedience, prayer, worship, and spiritual disciplines).* This is

3

what fashions us into people of God, as He speaks to us through His Word, giving directions, instructions, and challenges. We respond by saying, "Yes, Lord, let this happen in me; shape me, mold me, fill me, empower me, use me; I am Yours; Your will be done in my life." As we walk along the path of spiritual formation with our Lord, He gradually shapes us into people of God. In spiritual formation, God is taking His place at the control center of our lives. As we allow Him the freedom to do this, we develop more and more one desire: that God should have absolute control of our lives. This is the process of shaping people of God, which is the result of shaping people of the Word, people of prayer, and people of worship.

Disciplines of Spiritual Formation

The disciplines of spiritual formation provide the infrastructure for empowering the inner being and fashioning dynamic interpersonal relationships. I believe that all other spiritual disciplines such as fasting, spiritual direction, solitude, and fellowship (and many others) can be viewed as the tools we use for incarnating the disciplines of the Word, prayer, and worship. Those disciplines provide the curriculum for our training in spiritual things and in interpersonal relationships, as well as the internal fortitude needed to bear up under the strains of life and to stand victoriously in Christ. The disciplines furnish us with an effective communication system between God and us, and between us and other persons. As an integral part of the infrastructure of our lives, the disciplines provide the foundation on which the inner spiritual life and the outer relational life are built. They are the avenues along which we walk, with the Word of God serving as the road map which guides us safely to our destination of becoming people of God.

The Discipline of the Word

The underpinning for all the spiritual disciplines is the Bible, the Word of God, which has proven in the test of time to be the only dependable foundation for all life. The Word of God is the only foundation on which to structure our spiritual formation—both in the inner being and in the outer relationships and circumstances. It is the only dependable foundation on which to build a lasting ministry—a ministry that will glorify God and build the Kingdom of God. Any other foundation is like shifting "sand"—"human tradition and the basic principles of this world," which will erode and disintegrate.

The Discipline of Prayer

While the Word of God is the foundation for our spiritual formation, prayer is the key to releasing the power of the Word to transform our lives and to focus on our requests and the needs of others. Prayer is our response to God's speaking to us through His Word.

This is the reason it is so important to combine prayer with the reading of the Bible. As we study the Holy Scriptures, we discover how people of faith have prayed in the past and how God answered their prayers. This shows us how God wants to relate to us and answer our prayers as well. When we read the Bible, we discover many patterns for our prayers. More importantly, when we pray based on the Word of God, we discover the God of the Bible Himself—listening, understanding, caring, responding, helping, encouraging, giving answers—communicating with us through His **"living and enduring Word"** (1 Peter 1:23b). When we pray according to the Word of God and the promises He gives us in the Word, we can come boldly before the throne of grace, expressing our needs to God through the intercession of the Holy Spirit, with the confident expectation that God will certainly hear and respond to our requests.

Prayer unleashes the power of the Word to transform our lives, to regroup our thoughts, to reveal God's game plan, to replenish our energies, and to move ahead in confidence and victory as we follow the guidance of our Lord. Prayer, in many ways, is like any other discipline in which we might participate: the more we practice, the better we get.

The Discipline of Worship

Worship ushers us into the presence of the Creator God, whose purpose is to transform us by the **"renewing of our minds"** (Romans 12:1-2), spirits, emotions, and relationships. Worship like this sets the climate for the removal of negative viewpoints, divisive attitudes, dissenting opinions, critical comments, and complaining spirits. It brings spiritual revival into the lives of worshipers. Such things happen when people determine to worship the Lord in a spirit of love, unity and oneness of purpose.

I am convinced that worship is at the heart of spiritual formation, both individually and corporately. As Christian people we exist to worship God. Unless worship is given top priority in our lives, we have no basis for an enduring life of meaning and purpose. All our ministry, activities, and work should be results of our relationship with God in worship.

True worship sets a person, a family, a church, a college, or a nation in a right relationship with God. Such an alliance with God positions everything else in proper perspective: goals, motives, service, ministries, activities, interpersonal relationships, priorities, and decisions. When an individual determines to become a person of the Word, a person of prayer, a person of worship, then he or she is shaped into a person of God. Worship gathers up all the other spiritual disciplines to give them cohesiveness, symmetry, and balance.

The reason this is true is that in worship our focus is first on God rather than on our needs or on our relationships with other persons. Worship places God at the center of our spiritual formation. Genuine spiritual formation is the result of our relationship with God through His Word and prayer.

It is precisely at the point of worship that Satan launches his most powerful attacks because he knows that he can neither stand against, control, defeat, or detour the person, family, church, business, or nation that practices a lifestyle of worship and spiritual formation. Genuine spiritual formation flows out of true worship, as we worship God simply because He is worthy of our worship, praise, adoration, submission, and service. Satan knows that he is a defeated foe when God is the central focus of our worship. He loses control over us when our worship centers on what God has done in Christ and what He continues to do in our lives and relationships through the ministry of the Holy Spirit. Satan has no power over us when we truly practice a lifestyle of worship.

As we become people of the Word, people of prayer, and people of worship, we discover that we are being shaped into people of God. Living in the Word, in prayer, and in worship consistently are three facets in the process of cultivating an intimate relationship with God, which is the purpose of spiritual formation.

The Discipline of Intentionality

One of the propelling forces in spiritual formation is what I have labeled as "the spiritual discipline of intentionality." This has to do with the basic direction of our lives, the goal of our hearts, and the controlling attitude of our minds. I have heard people who were caught in moral or ethical lapse say something like, "Oh, I did not intend to lie. I did not intend to become involved in an adulterous relationship. I did not intend to cheat on the test." Sometimes they really mean, "I did not intend to get caught."

When we say, "I did not intend to do a certain thing," it is almost as though we are leaving the door open for us accidentally to fall into sin, to be driven to failure or falsehood by other persons or circumstances. It is the mentality that says if we are victimized, then it is not our fault. Therefore, we feel that we should not have to pay the consequences of our actions. However, as we live in the disciplines of spiritual formation, we gain a more positive stance toward the intentions of our hearts. Instead of saying, "I did not intend to do a certain thing," we should say, "I intend not to do something." Rather than saying, "I did not intend to fail to do God's will," we should say, "I intend to succeed in doing God's will." This attitude removes the victim syndrome. As we focus on the will, purposes, and resources of God through the spiritual disciplines, God and we take charge of the temptations, circumstances, opportunities, and desires "to make them obedient to Christ."

There are three *Key Elements of Intentionality* which, when consistently practiced, enable us to pursue the disciplines of spiritual formation. These elements are the bare necessities, without which the spiritual life is incomplete at best and virtually impossible at worst. Yet when intentionally practiced consistently, these elements form the supporting framework for spiritual vitality, energy, faithfulness, and endurance. Those elements are discipline, priorities, and balance.

Key Element of Intentionality: Discipline

The first *Key Element of Intentionality* is discipline. Most people cringe when they hear the word discipline, yet without it our lives will be characterized by inconsistency, powerlessness, fragmentation, ineffectiveness, and discouragement. Since our inner world is always with us, and the outer world is always clamoring for attention, it is easy for us to ignore the inner world for long periods of time while trying to take care of all the outer challenges, problems, relationships, and involvements of our lives. It seems that we hardly ever have the time to cultivate a rich, personal relationship with God. We continue putting off the spiritual disciplines of the Word, prayer, and worship—neglecting the interior world—until a crisis arises, and we discover we have little or no resources with which to face it. It takes great discipline and self-control to consistently shape the inner life and relationship with God in a way that will transform the outer life and relationships with other persons. Yet, this is the most valuable work we can do, for it sets the tone for all our lives and relationships. The undisciplined spiritual life is the source of failure and frustration in the lives of many Christian leaders, while the disciplined spiritual life can be a source of success and fulfillment.

Key Element of Intentionality: Priorities

Another *Key Element of Intentionality* is keeping our priorities in proper order. Since we can never do everything there is to be done, and we can never satisfy all the people around us all the time, it is important that we prioritize our opportunities so that we take care of first things first, and that we accomplish the most important tasks.

It takes discipline to set our priorities straight according to God's plan for us. When we are arranging our priorities, we maintain balance by placing God in the center of our lives, relationships, decisions, and activities. When we view both the telescopic universe in the heavens and the microscopic universe within the very fabric of matter and life, we see God, in His creative activities, as the God of balance, precision, and order. He is the God of dependability and predictability. When we live in covenant relationship with Him, according to the directions and insights of His Word, then we can expect his blessings, leadership, guidance, protection, and provision for all facets of life. When we step outside the boundaries of that covenant relationship, then we subject ourselves to the attacks of Satan, along with the whims of people and circumstances. Practicing the spiritual disciplines and arranging our priorities around God's priorities produce balance in our lives, our family relationships, our ministries, our vocations, and our leisure times. This is living in Kingdom authority, which Jesus interpreted as **"seeking first God's kingdom and His righteousness"** (Matthew 6:33). The consequence of prioritizing our lives in this way is that **"all these other things will be given to us as well"** (Matthew 6:33). That is the balanced life.

Key Element of Intentionality: Balance

The balanced life produced by practicing the spiritual disciplines empowers us to enjoy all facets of life, including our families, ministries, vocations, and leisure time. The balance between the spiritual disciplines and arranging our priorities around God's plans for us maintains our relationship with the Lord. The balanced life is like the oil in an engine that keeps it running smoothly and consistently and protects it from burning out. Rather than burning out, our lives can be like that bush in the desert that was burning but not being consumed. We are ablaze for God, yet we do not burn out, stress out, or rust out. This is the balance that enables us to enjoy our relationship with God and that empowers our relationships with other persons.

Renovated: Changed into People of God!

As God and we intentionally develop disciplined, prioritized, balanced lives, we discover ourselves becoming people of the Word, people of prayer, and people of worship. This process renovates us from the inside out and changes us into people of God through spiritual formation, *shaping our inner lives and relationships with God in a way that transforms our outer lives and relationships with other persons.*

Chapter 2

Praying Out of the Word (Journaling)

One of the most effective and rewarding methods of Bible study and prayer that I have discovered is what I call praying out of the Word. By this I mean reading meditatively and prayerfully a portion of Scripture, and then praying back to God the insights, requests, promises, intercessions, and praises that come from that section of the Word. I find that this is a way to lift my spirits when I am discouraged, discover hope for impossible situations, find guidance for difficult decisions, realize comfort for those who are hurting, and gain the resources necessary to meet my needs and the needs of others for whom I am praying.

A Pattern for Journaling

The process I use for praying out of the Word is the spiritual discipline of journaling. Many of my journal entries are responses (what the passage says to me; how it applies to my life, situation, ministry, etc.) and prayers based on the Scripture passages I was reading or quoting that day. Sometimes I write a story or illustration that relates to the Scripture passage. Often, I personalize the Scriptures passages, simply praying God's Word and promises back to Him in the first person. This I do in faith that the Word God has planted in my heart and mind, or which I read in the Bible, will connect with the Word in God's heart. This gives me direction and opens the door to God's resources for my life and for the situations and circumstances I face. I am especially blessed by going back through my journal and praying the prayers I have written there. Some of the entries describe answers to prayer, interaction with people, reactions to what I am reading in books, particularly books that have to do with spiritual formation or spiritual leadership. It is encouraging to see that many of those prayers have been answered, and it also helps me keep in perspective the struggles and blessings I am experiencing today, as I realize how God has worked in my life in the past. This gives me confidence that God is at work in my life now and will continue to be at work in my behalf in the future.

A few of the entries are songs that I wrote, based on Scripture passages I was reading or quoting. Some of them are simply a listing of Scripture passages quoted or read during my morning *Quiet Time*, on the days when there was not time for other reading or reflective praying or journal writing. However, almost every day of my life includes at least some Scripture quotation and prayer time.

Journaling has become for me a powerful tool for prayer, Bible study, worship, and my personal walk with God. As I write my prayers in response to Scripture passages that speak meaningfully to me, I discover that I express to God, more clearly and honestly than ever before, my feelings, longings, joys, excitements, hurts, frustrations, heartaches, disappointments, plans, and desires. After writing a prayer, I usually read it out loud to God, as a prelude to the remainder of my prayer time. I find that this practice enhances my prayer time.

When I am in the *journaling mode,* I guard against thinking about preaching and teaching for the benefit of other people. This is a time to concentrate on the vertical relationship between God, His Word, and me. Therefore, I usually write the original entries in the first and second persons, keeping the thoughts and interaction within the vertical relationship between God and me.

As I read through past journal entries, I often find that what I have written fits situations that come up later. I sometimes share them with individuals who are struggling and in need of a pattern to help them pray. When I was developing the lesson plans for the Christian Growth Groups in the church I pastored, I used some of my journal entries as models for prayer or reflective meditations to stimulate persons' hearts for their own prayer and meditation times.

Diary or Journal

There is a difference between recording events in a diary and the discipline of journaling. A diary records events as they happen. The spiritual discipline of journaling is recording the interaction between God, His Word, and us (*shaping our inner lives and relationships with God*), and then recording the interaction of God in us with other persons (*in a way that transforms our outer lives and relationships with other persons*).

Since I have practiced journaling for several years now, it has become a significant part of my spiritual formation and discipline. My time spent in prayer and journaling helps prepare me for the various ministries in which I am involved by giving me insight, strength, energy, stamina, direction, wisdom, encouragement, and help that I would not have had otherwise. It is not uncommon for God to remind me in my QuietTime of significant ways to change others' lives.

My journal entries are important to my spiritual discipline because they reflect much of my spiritual formation and growth as I study the Word. They have had a powerful shaping influence on my whole life and ministry. I am deeply grateful for having been introduced to this meaningful tool for communicating with God and for formulating my responses to His Word and activities in my life.

Covenants with God

The discipline of journaling is a good means for recording the covenants we make with God. It is good to make covenants with Him, but if we forget them, broken covenants can hinder our spiritual formation and growth. The discipline of writing the words is also a means of recording them more permanently in our hearts, which enhances our sensory perceptions. We first think the concepts in our minds, then we formulate the thoughts that we write on paper; next, we see what we have written. Then we can read them out loud and hear what we and God have discussed. In this way God's promises and our responses are recorded indelibly in our minds, spirits, and emotions, reinforcing the formation of our hearts. There are wonderful precedents for this throughout Scripture. Exodus 17 records the story of Israel's defeat of the Amalekites, under the leadership of Joshua and Moses: **"Then the Lord said to Moses, 'Write this on a scroll as something to be remembered and make sure that Joshua hears it, because I will completely blot out the memory of Amalek from under heaven.' Moses built an altar and called it The Lord is my Banner"**

(Exodus 17:14-15). Writing down God's promise served as a reminder forever after of the victory He gave the people of Israel over their enemies that day. This written promise would give them courage to face their enemies in the strength of the Lord in the future.

Regarding the Ten Commandments, God said to Moses,

> **"Fix these words of mine in your hearts and minds; tie them as symbols on your hands and bind them on your foreheads. Teach them to your children, talking about them when you sit at home and when you walk along the road, when you lie down and when you get up. Write them on the doorframes of your houses and on your gates, so that your days and the days of your children may be many in the land that the Lord swore to give your forefathers, as many as the days that the heavens are above the earth"** (Deuteronomy 11:18-21).

Writing the Ten Commandments, first on the stone scrolls, and then on the symbols on their hands and foreheads, and on the door frames of their houses and on their gates, would enable the people to remember them. They would serve as a written record to teach to their children and grandchildren. This is a good example of the value of the written word as a means of learning and remembering. The discipline of journaling is also a method of learning and remembering.

Journaling through the Psalms

I especially enjoyed journaling through the Psalms because the Psalmist experienced the same emotions, struggles, joys, fears, frustrations, anger, cursing and blessing, depression, victories, insecurities, attacks from inner sins and outer foes, defeats, and victories that are common to us all. I have discovered that the Psalms are good prayer starters. I have also learned that there are times when I have difficulty getting started, when prayers do not flow easily. The Psalms often are catalysts for my prayers. They provide a pattern for prayer that usually leads to a fulfilling and meaningful time with my Lord. Regarding the value of the Psalms for guiding us in our prayers, Eugene Peterson says,

The psalms, more than anything else in the church's life, are God's provision for [our] needs, stimulating and shaping the prayers of Christians. They do not do our praying for us—they cannot be mechanized into a prayer wheel—but they get us praying when we don't feel like it, and they train us in prayers that are honest and right. They are both an encouragement to pray and patterns of prayer. They represent the experience of men and women who have prayed in every conceivable circumstance across thirty centuries.[1]

Next Step: Begin

Once we learn the value of the spiritual discipline of journaling, the next step is to begin. A good way to begin journaling is to pick a Scripture passage, an attribute of God, or a directive from the Word to a particular character trait. You could read through the Psalms. Then, simply think about whatever you have chosen to focus your mind on. Continue to resist distractions: those renegade thoughts and plans that bombard your mind and that demand activity, time, and energy. Discipline your mind to stay in focus on the chosen subject. Picture every aspect of it. Repeat it several

---

1   Peterson, E. H. (1979). *A Year with the Psalms. Waco, TX: Word Books.*

times, emphasizing a different word each time. Think about the meaning of that word. Look for ways that the passage applies to your personal life. Envision yourself partaking of the part of it that applies to you personally. Write your thoughts in your journal. If you do not have a journal, this would be a good time to begin one.

After you have spent some time doing this, you can return to your daily life with a new perspective and a fresh confidence, acting on the reality of spiritual truths planted deeply in your mind and spirit. Obey the directives you have received. Discipline yourself to follow the guidelines you received in your meditation and journaling time. Periodically read through your journal entries as reminders of God's grace, guidance, and help in times of need to give you assurance of His promises for the present and future. Peterson says that according to the Psalms, God is the pivotal center of life. Other persons, events, or circumstances are third parties[2]. When we realize that God is the center of everything, we can view our lives through the lens of His wisdom, knowledge, insight, and resources, and know that nothing we face is beyond the scope of His ability to sustain, enlighten, comfort, heal, and give victory in every episode of life.

Keeping the Gems of Insight

This is why the spiritual discipline of journaling is so important. It is so easy for us to lose those gems of insight that come to us when we are meditating on the Word and praying, but when we write them down in our journals, we preserve them for future blessing and use. When I first began journaling, I discovered that it did not always come easily, but as I kept practicing and disciplining myself, it began to flow more easily.

---

2   Peterson.

My encouragement to those who wish to explore the heights and depths, length and breadth of sheer adventure and sublime fulfillment in the journey of spiritual formation is that you begin simply and prayerfully, listening to God as He speaks through His Word. Then write down the insights, promises, and directions that come. You will be pleasantly surprised at the blessing and joy that you will experience as you communicate with our Lord through His Word and prayer. Perhaps you could write a prayer, or how you feel about that part of the Word. As God speaks to you, then tell Him the intents, questions, and desires of your heart.

Journaling as a Tool for Spiritual Formation

Tools enable us to accomplish tasks, create various necessities and extravagances, and do things we could not achieve without them. Peterson writes, "Prayers are tools, but with this clarification: prayers are not tools for doing or getting, but for being and becoming. Prayers are tools that God uses to work His will in our bodies and souls. Prayers are tools that we use to collaborate in His work with us."[3] Journaling is also a tool for spiritual formation and growth. It is an exceptionally important and influential implement for Forming Our Inner Lives and Relationships with God . . . Transforming Our Outer Lives and Relationships with Other People. This is the reason for my earlier statement that when I am in the journaling mode, I guard against thinking about preaching and teaching for the benefit of other people. This is a time to concentrate on the vertical relationship between God, His Word, and me.

---

3   Peterson, E. H. (1989). *Answering God: The Psalms as Tools for Prayer.* New York, NY: *Harper & Row.*

Journaling as a Quiet Stream of Deep, Inner, Spiritual Refreshment

Henri Nouwen's *Genesee Diary* was one of the most helpful examples and encouragements for my beginning the life-changing journey up the avenue of journaling. He wondered, as he was deciding to lay down his normal work of writing and ministry to spend a year in a Trappist Monastery to reflect and regroup his own perspective on life, ministry, and spiritual formation, "Is there a quiet stream underneath the fluctuating affirmations and rejections of my little world? Is there a still point where my life is anchored and from which I can reach out with hope and courage and confidence?"[4] I have found that quiet stream of deep, inner, spiritual refreshment in practicing the discipline of journaling.

PRAYER RESPONSE

Lord God, as I practice the spiritual discipline of journaling, may I find that "quiet stream" of deep, inner, spiritual refreshment, renewal, and refurbishment, as I interact with You through Your Word and prayer. Enable me to remember and fulfill the covenants I make with You, to recall the promises You make to me, to reminisce with joy about the answered prayers, to reflect with confidence for the future on the met needs, as I record the times spent with you. May my journal entries serve as points where my life is anchored, and from which I can reach out with hope, courage, and confidence in Your continued ministry in and through my life.

As I record our times together, enable me to get up and go back into the activity of life with new a perspective and a fresh confidence, acting on the

---

4   Nouwen, H. J. (1976). *The Genesee Diary: Report from a Trappist Monastery.* Garden City, NY: Image Books, Doubleday & Co.

reality of spiritual truths planted deeply in my mind, emotions, and spirit. Help me to obey the directives I receive from You, and to discipline myself to follow the guidelines I am given in my meditation and journaling time. From time-to-time, as I go back and read through the journal entries, may I use them as reminders of Your grace, guidance, and help in times of need to give me assurance of Your promises for the present and future. Keep me in an environment in which You are the pivotal center of life, and other persons, events, or circumstances are third parties. Plant deeply within my inner being the realization that You are the center of everything: my existence, relationships, struggles and triumphs. Allow me to view everyone and everything through the lens of Your wisdom, knowledge, insight, and resources, and to know that nothing I face is beyond the scope of Your ability to conquer, sustain, enlighten, comfort, heal, and give victory in every episode of my life. In the name of the One who draws me into close communion with You, my Lord Jesus Christ, I pray. Amen.

Chapter 3

Excerpts from My Journal

Listening, Praying, Learning, Living in the Life-Transforming Word of God

Following are some excerpts from *My Journal.* I share them, not as the only way to do journaling, but as illustrations of one adventurous explorer's pursuit of God's gracious invitation to spiritual formation – the shaping of my inner life and relationship with God in ways that transform my outer life and relationships with other people. I invite you to join with me in the exciting and fulfilling journey of prayerfully meditating on the Word of God, then writing your responses and prayers. As you do this, you will be touched, transformed, and energized spiritually, mentally, emotionally, and relationally. I encourage you use these journal entries of mine as models for developing your own personalized style of meditating and journaling in the Word. For more information, please see previous chapter, **Praying Out of the Word (Journaling).**

➤ **My Appointment with God**

Wait upon the Lord;
never consider it a waste of time.
When God speaks to your heart,
He can in one second
do far greater things
than you can do in an entire year.
Wait upon the Lord
and you will see great things accomplished (Cho, 1984).

Today, in the beginning stages of my spiritual renewal journey, I write the following words in response to comments by Paul Yonggi Cho and Don Postema in a splendid devotional guidebook, *Space for God*. This is my personal covenant to make regular appointments with God, to spend quality, intimate, personal time with Him. Postema said, *"Making space for God takes some discipline. At first it may sound like one more thing you 'have to do' in your already hassled life. But, as you know, it takes discipline to do anything well, and it is no different with prayer. We make appointments with everyone. Maybe we should make appointments with God."* [5]

My Covenant with God

My Appointment with God:
Now that this time has been set,
this covenant made,
Guard it carefully,
use it wisely.

---

[5] Postema, D. (1983). *Space for God: The Study and Practice of Prayer and Spirituality.* *Grand Rapids, MI: Board of Publications of the Christian Reformed Church. 158.*

For herein you will discover
inner depth
spiritual strength
reflective insight
power for living
love for giving
peace for coping
insight for growing
As you create space for God in your life.

Creating space for God makes spiritual life possible. It brings sanctification – living a life for God in our world which is the goal of spiritual formation. This happens through prayer – which is based on the realization that I belong to God and thus live my life saying thanks to God. This encourages me to truly know God, to enjoy Him forever, and in the process to touch life at a deep level.

PRAYER RESPONSE

Lord, this is my covenant with You, to set regular appointments – priority times – with You. I want to walk with You in an unbroken relationship of intimacy and friendship that will transform my inner life as well as my relationships with other persons. I ask for Your help in keeping this covenant of love and commitment to You as the center of my life. Please shape me as a man of God according to the pattern You had when You created me. Then enable me to accomplish all you call me to do in your strength and timing. I am Yours, my Lord. Amen.

The Artist of My Life

The world doesn't need more busy people, maybe not even more intelligent people. It needs "deep people" – people who are deep in the relationship with their God; people who not only want their lives to be filled, but full and fulfilled; people who are in touch with the One who is "a greater Artist than all other artists . . . who made neither pictures not statues nor books; but loudly proclaimed that He made . . . living men, immortals!"[6] The world needs people who will allow time for God to recreate them, shape them, mold them, fill them, and touch them as an Artist who is making something beautiful of their lives.

PRAYER RESPONSE

O Lord, I truly want You to be The Artist of my life – remolding, reshaping, refilling, recreating me. Help me to live in depth. Bring my spirit into close touch with Your Spirit. May I learn the true meaning of sanctification – living my life for God in my world. Better yet, live Your life in me, Lord. Transform all my relationships: with You, my family, my church family, my friends, myself. Lord, I want to know You and serve You better. Since I belong to you, I want my life to be one continuous
  "Thank You,"
  "Praise You,"
  "Bless You,"
  "Glorify You."
  I love You, Lord, and
  I'm glad to be Your child.
  Amen!

---

6   Postema, D. (1983). Paraphrased. *Space for God: The Study and Practice of Prayer and Spirituality. Grand Rapids, MI: Board of Publications of the Christian Reformed Church. 17.*

Praying in the Shadow of a Monument to a Boll Weevil[7]

"I know the plans I have for you," declares the Lord, **"plans to prosper you and not to harm you, plans to give you hope and a future."** Jeremiah 29:11 (NIV)

Those verses have been a theme of my life and ministry. At the age of 20, following my sophomore year of college, I felt I was educationally prepared to take on the invitation to pastor a country church in the backwoods near the Florida/Alabama state line – what a precious group of *JesusFollowers* they were! I was bi-vocational, having to work at carpentry, plumbing, and electrical work, while also trying to keep up my pastoral ministries. Within a few months, I felt like a juggler, trying to balance it all, and became discouraged, disillusioned, and ready to quit the ministry. I lived alone in a mobile home near Enterprise Alabama, home of *The Monument to a Boll Weevil.* For many years cotton had been the major crop that made the farmers wealthy, but an infestation of boll weevils destroyed cotton crops and bankrupted the farmers. Someone introduced the farmers to a new crop, peanuts, which the farmers planted in place of cotton. Boll weevils do not eat peanuts. They left them alone, and the people made more money off peanuts than cotton. As a result, city leaders erected a huge statue holding a giant boll weevil up to the sky, as the plaque beneath it says, "In profound appreciation of the Boll Weevil and what it has done as the herald of prosperity, this monument was erected by the citizens of Enterprise, Coffee County, Alabama." The county was catapulted into

---

7   Bruce, Dr. Sam (2010). A *WisdomSketch from Proverbs of Dr. Sam: The Book of Wisdom from a Wise Ol' University Professor. Florence, MS: Unpublished, in process. Come to the Waters Be Refreshed! Ministry & Music Resources, Sam & Sandie Bruce Ministries,* drsambruce@aol.com www.bruceministries.net

unprecedented new hope, new wealth, and new life because of the pesky, destructive boll weevil.

Not far from that monument to a giant boll weevil – symbol of new life – I like to say, "in the Shadow of a Monument to a Boll Weevil," as a lonely, disillusioned, ready-to-give-up-and-quit young pastor, I was home alone one day, feeling a bit like Moses on the back side of the desert. I knelt by the couch and began to pray. I said something like, *"God, I'm tired of playing ministry games, tired of playing church, tired of playing Christian. Today, I declare before You that I want to get all the way in with You, or I want to get out. I'm at the end of myself; at the end of sloppy ministry and sloppy living. I want You to become Lord of my life, my ministry, and every other part of me."* And there, on that day, almost in the shadow of the *Monument to a Boll Weevil,* symbol of a new beginning and new life for farmers, I erected in my heart a new monument. Since then, the Cross of Jesus Christ has been my *Monument to a New Life,* the beginning of an unbelievable lifetime of ministry. God said, **"You will seek me and find me when you seek me with all your heart"** Jeremiah 29:14 (NIV). That day God became the Senior Partner of my life and ministries and my life has never been the same! Within 2 months I enrolled in Gulf-Coast Bible College; met my wife; and earned bachelor, master, and 2 doctor of ministry degrees. God catapulted me into a lifetime of ministry that has included a 21-year pastorate; Bible college president; and now, *Sam & Sandie Bruce Ministries* – national and international ministries of preaching, music, teaching online courses for Mid-America Christian University, leadership training, Spiritual Formation & Leadership retreats; National Guard Marriage Retreats; Director of a 125-member community choir and orchestra, and others. All this brings fresh meaning to my theme verse, **"I know the plans I have for you," declares the Lord, "plans to prosper you and not to harm you, plans to give you hope and a future."** Jeremiah 29:11 (NIV)

This puts it into perspective: *"When God finds a person who will place as his priority a life of intimate, personal, dynamic fellowship with Him, He directs His power, guidance, and wisdom into and through that person. God has found a person through whom He can change the world."* [8]

Prayer: *Lord, that's where I want to live, placing as my priority a life of intimate, personal, dynamic fellowship with You, so You can direct Your power, guidance, and wisdom into and through me – a person through whom You can change the world of those You call me to love and lead through my ministries if You wish. Amen.*

Lord, Tune Me to Your A-note – Key to Living in Harmony with God's Plans

"Dear friend, listen well to my words; tune your ears – [your head and heart and hands and habits in loyalty] – to my voice." Proverbs 4:20 (MSG/DSP[9])

"The word from our Lord for *ears* can mean *turning one's heart (mind) in a certain direction* and *being loyal*,"[10] which describes for me a great picture of living in tune with God and in harmony with other people. It reminds me of one of my all-time favorite stories about the Conductor of the Philadelphia Philharmonic Orchestra who stepped up to the podium before a large elite audience one night and said that before the concert began, he wanted to read a letter he had received that week, and it went something like this: *"Mr. Conductor, Sir, I am an old sheepherder out in the hills of Montana; and I listen to your orchestra over the radio every Saturday*

---

8   Leroy Eims, *Be the Leader You Were Meant to Be* (Wheaton, IL: Victor Books, 1975), 19.
9   DSP: Dr. Sam's Paraphrase of a Scripture Passage
10   From Warren Baker and Eugene Carpenter, *The Complete Word Study Dictionary – Old Testament*, (Chattanooga, TN: AMG Publishers, 2003), WORDsearch CROSS e-book, Under: "â€❹× Ö ×˜Ö ×"â€Ž".

night. I love to play along with you on my old violin; but my old violin has gone out of tune and it's hard to play in harmony anymore. So, Sir, next Saturday night, just before your orchestra begins to play, could you please ask the head violinist to play the A-note so I can tune to it and play along in harmony once again?" Well, when the conductor turned back to the orchestra and signaled, not only the head violinist, but the whole orchestra played the A-note in perfect tune so the old sheepherder could tune his old violin and play in harmony once again.

I heard a preacher tell that story in a Camp-meeting in northern Florida at a time when I, as a young college-age minister, was deciding whether to continue in ministry or not. This happened within a few days of my story about *"Praying in the Shadow of A Monument to a Boll Weevil"* (above). God transformed my life through that story and set me on a tune-up path that started a fresh fire in my heart and kindled a new vision for ministry in my spirit that has empowered and energized me ever since. In my mind I sat down beside the old sheepherder and re-tuned my life with God's purpose, plans, and provisions that have carried me on an unbelievable path of ministry with my awesome Lord ever since! I do not know the original source of this story; I do not even remember the preacher's name; but I remember well how it spoke to my heart and transformed my life! It opened the doors of my heart to all the awesome plans of God that have followed for the rest of my life! And my continuing prayer is: "Lord, Tune Me to Your A-note – that I will live in Harmony with your desires for my life."

I suggest that when our lives go out of tune and we turn to God for His A-note to tune – through His Word, prayer, and worship – our ears – *our Heads, our Hearts, our Hands, and our Habits in loyalty*[11] – to His voice, His Holy Spirit is there with the Word of God to tune us up by His love and

---

11   Equipping our *Heads, Hearts, and Hands* for ministry and service is part of the Mid America Christian University results of our Mission Statement. Our *Habits* represent the disciplines of spiritual formation that enlighten, engage, empower and equip our Heads, Hearts, and Hands to accomplish our ministries and service to those we are commissioned to love and lead.

grace so we can live and minister in tune with Him and His plans for us. The quality of loyalty here is demonstrated in the response of Jonathan's servant to King David when they were headed into battle, "Do all that you have in mind," his armor-bearer said. "Go ahead; I am with you heart and soul." 1 Samuel 14:7 (NIV) That's being in tune with each other, and it's what God asks of us. The Proverb writer gives the process and results of A-Note Living: Always Keep my message in plain view. Concentrate! Learn it by heart! Those who discover these words live, really live; body and soul, they're bursting with health. Keep vigilant watch over your heart; that's where life starts. Proverbs 4:21-23 (MSG) Our will must be in tune with God so that we allow the desires of His heart to become the desires of our hearts. And then He can give us the desires of our hearts – that's In Tune A-Note Living! And that keeps us living in the power of "Spiritual Formation: shaping our inner lives and relationships with God [in tune with God] in ways that transform our outer lives and relationships with people [in harmony with other persons]. Lord, Tune Me to Your A-note – the Key to Living in Harmony with Your Plans. Make it true in me, Lord! And in all those You call me to love and lead! Yes!

My precious Lord, this is my commitment of loyalty to You; as I listen well to Your words and tune my ears – my Head, my Heart, my Hands, and my Habits – to Your voice, bring me in tune with your dreams, visions, and plans for my life and ministries. Enable me to keep vigilant watch over my heart; let Your in-tune re-harmonized life start in me and spread out to those You call me to love and lead! Use me as You wish, I am with You heart and soul. Amen! Bless you! ~Dr. Sam

Prayer for Freedom: Who Sets Your Boundaries?[12]

"I know the plans I have for you," declares the Lord, "plans to prosper you and not to harm you, plans to give you hope and a future." Jeremiah 29:11 (NIV)

I walked into a funeral home office, where I saw a large saltwater aquarium with colorful exotic fish. My eyes landed on what looked like a six-inch shark. It was. The funeral director explained that it was a white shark. He said sharks adapt to their environment. This one would grow no longer than six inches in the aquarium. In the ocean, it could grow up to twenty-five feet long. I thought, as I watched it swimming continuously from end to end with a restless passion, "How sad! That shark's environment determined its maximum size. Five pieces of glass glued together limited the fulfillment of the shark's potential! Born to be a magnificent creature fathoming the depths of oceans yet confined to a four-foot aquarium."

I pictured people who allow their boundaries to be determined by environment, circumstances, negative-thinking, power-hungry, controlling people; low self-image, memories of failure always playing on the screen of your mind, laziness, and a myriad of dream-destroying, potential-robbing attitudes.

That little shark didn't have a choice. The only way he could fulfill his potential was if someone reached in and took him out of the aquarium and released him in the ocean. God can reach into your imprisonment, and lift you out, and place You in the ocean of His love, power, and resources. He promised: **I know the plans I have for you, plans to prosper you and not to harm you, plans to give you hope and a future** (Jeremiah 29:11).

---

12   © Bruce, S. K. (2010). *Your Life Repeated in My Life: Story Devotions for ChristFollowers. Florence, MS: Unpublished, in process. Come to the Waters Be Refreshed! Ministry & Music Resources, Sam & Sandie Bruce Ministries,* drsambruce@aol.com www.bruceministries.net

Don't let circumstances, other people, fear of failure, poor self-esteem, the way you look, or anything else set the boundaries for your life and ministry. God says, **Call upon me; come and pray to me, I will listen to you. You will seek me and find me when you seek me with all your heart. I will be found by you, and will set you free.** (Jeremiah 29:12-14) That prayer that will release you to fulfill your God-given potential and set you free to be the winner He created you to become through His power and creativity! Just in case you don't understand who you are in Christ, saturate your inner spirit with this *Proverb of Dr. Sam*: *Learn a lesson of wisdom from a Wise Ole' Instructor* :-): Live in the power of this awesome promise from God: **See, I am doing a new thing! Now it springs up; do you not perceive it? I am making a way in the desert and streams in the wasteland . . . to give drink to my people, my chosen, the people I formed for myself that they may proclaim my praise.** Isaiah 43:19-21 (NIV) He is worthy of our praise; and He makes us worthy to proclaim His praise; to represent Him, witness for Him, touch peoples' lives with His life transforming love and power! He makes us worthy to be outstanding success stories. Don't ever forget that each of us is a person of *extreme worth* and *extravagant value* to our God – You, [your name], are a person of *extreme worth* and *extravagant value* to our God. We are all *King's Kids!* Jesus proved how valuable we are to Him when He went up on the cross, stretched out His arms, and said, "This is how much I love you!" What an awesome, wonderful, perfect way to put a *finale* onto His life . . . No!

This is, in fact, the *prelude* – just the beginning – of the fresh new things God is planning as a result of what Christ did for us on that cross! Hear Him say triumphantly, **"You are my people, my chosen, the people I formed for myself that you may proclaim my praise."** So, don't ever let anyone tell you, and don't ever believe that you are inferior, a failure. You are a valuable *King's Kid!* Live in the triumphant joy of this fact and spread it to others: you are a person of *extreme worth* and *extravagant value* to our God – Yes! You, [your name], are a person of *extreme worth* and *extravagant value* to our God! :-) (Proverbs of Dr. Sam 2:23). Jesus says, "Get up, pick up your brokenness, failure, hopelessness and give them to Me. Walk into My healing, wholeness, joy, and incredible love like you've never dreamed possible." Pick up every dream for your life, every heart's desire, every longing in your spirit, everything you want to do, and place them in the Master's hands, and pray:

*Lord, please set me free from the boundaries people, circumstances, and I have placed on me. Show me the awesome plans you have for me. "By Your power, fulfill every good purpose of mine and every act prompted by my faith."*13 *Set me free to fulfill my God-given potential. Heal and restore me in my spirit, mind, emotions, body, and relationships. Thank You! Amen!*

Alone Before God

In Luke's Gospel, Jesus talked about the consequences of being too busy to spend adequate time with the Master. It is easy to give excuses, but in the end, failure to spend quality time with Him shortchanges us in the formation of our inner beings, thereby shortchanging our outer lives. Here are the words of our Lord:

> **Jesus replied: "A certain man was preparing a great banquet and invited many guests. At the time of the banquet, he sent his servant to tell those who had been invited, 'Come, for everything is now ready.' But they all alike began to make excuses. The first said, 'I have just bought a field, and I must go and**

---

13 2Thessalonians 1:11 (NIV)

see it. Please excuse me.' Another said, 'I have just bought five yoke of oxen, and I'm on my way to try them out. Please excuse me.' Still another said, 'I just got married, so I can't come.' The servant came back and reported this to his master. Then the owner of the house became angry and ordered his servant, 'Go out quickly into the streets and alleys of the town and bring in the poor, the crippled, the blind and the lame.' 'Sir,' the servant said, 'what you ordered has been done, but there is still room.' Then the master told his servant, 'Go out to the roads and country lanes and make them come in, so that my house will be full. I tell you, not one of those men who were invited will get a taste of my banquet'" (Luke 14:16-24).

The following prayer from *My Journal* is based on Luke 4:14, 42; 5:16; 6:12; 14:16-24; and Mark 1:29-45. It is an example of the kind of commitment needed to make time for the disciplines of spiritual formation—time spent alone with God in prayer and in His Word.

Alone Before God

Busyness—misplaced priorities
   rob me of my greatest
   power,
   joy,
   blessing,
   inner strength.
Yet this does not leave room for
   laziness,
   sluggishness,
   procrastination.

It means I must pause to
    listen,
    reflect,
    open myself to God . . .
    His promptings,
    His way,
    His will.
I develop a receptive attitude of mind,
    letting myself go,
    hearing my deepest longings,
    sharing them with God,
    realizing what life is about,
    penetrating reality –
    making a space for God in my life
    through prayer,
    by His word,
    with quiet contemplation.
There I discover
    an awareness of what holds the world together –
    my true identity,
    my mission,
    my relationship with God.
Just as Jesus needed to listen to God,
    so do I!
    I need to come away
        from people,
        from my work,
        and the hectic places where I am needed
    to be
        refreshed,

replenished,
rejuvenated,
and to be emptied of all that
distracts,
distorts,
disrupts,
So that I can be
full,
fulfilled,
at the depth of my inner being.
As the artist of my soul,
under the guidance of the Master Artist,
I need to develop
a deep insight into reality,
a capacity to see beneath the surface
of nature and people,
an awareness that uncovers a spiritual vitality in
my world – myself –
and points toward God.
The source of this is in my becoming
a truly contemplative
and prayerful person,
developing in my inner world:
a capacity for seeing deeply into reality,
an ability to pay attention to what is beneath the surface,
a willingness to concentrate long enough to catch a vision.
Jesus,
in His aloneness before His Father,
found His source of power.

There, I also must find mine!
Amen. (Bruce, 2008)

My Covenant Responsibility for You

This passage from 1 Samuel 12:23-24 describes the kind of covenant responsibility we have to each other in the Body of Christ for intercessory prayer and for caring for one another. It says, **"As for me, far be it from me that I should sin against the Lord by failing to pray for you. And I will teach you the way that is good and right. But be sure to fear the Lord and serve him faithfully with all your heart; consider what great things he has done for you."**

In these verses, I see four responsibilities that we have to one another regarding intercessory prayer, and our ministry to one another which grows out of such prayer.

Pray for You

Samuel said, **"As for me, far be it from me that I should sin against the Lord by failing to pray for you"** (1 Samuel 12:23a).

It is a privilege for me to go the Throne of God in intercessory prayer on your behalf. I want God's best for you, and if I want it for you, I must ask, in faith, believing that God wants to give you His best. There is no greater privilege or responsibility that we Christians have than intercessory prayer. Yet, God never fails – every time I go to Him on your behalf, He always sends me away with some blessing for myself, as well as meeting your needs.

Teach You

Samuel said, **"And I will teach you the way that is good and right"** (1 Samuel 12:23b).

The Word is my source for teaching you God's truths. In that Word, God has given us everything we need for living life in the way He wants us to live – **the way that is good and right.** Yet, more than just teaching you abstract ideas and vague concepts, the best way I can teach you is by the example of my life of faith, trust, and dependence on God. As I let Him lead me, I become equipped to lead you.

Admonish You

As one who loves you, and who is interested in your growth and maturity in the Lord, I am called by God to challenge you to live a life of reverence and respect, an attitude of worship, glorifying God in all you do. Samuel said, **"Be sure to fear the Lord and serve him faithfully"** (1 Samuel 12:24a). I should encourage you to be faithful to Him, for in your faithfulness lies God's opportunity to give you His greatest blessings. His promises to His chosen, faithful ones are unending.

Remind You

During those times when you feel discouraged or inadequate, I am called to remind you of how God has blessed you in the past. Samuel said, **"Consider what great things He has done for you"** (1 Samuel 12:24b). Such reminders will enable you to realize that, just as he has blessed you in the past, He has all the resources needed to bless you in the present and future.

I am thankful that God has given these words of instruction and encouragement. They show how we can minister to one another through intercessory prayer.

PRAYER RESPONSE

My precious Lord, this kind of prayer is not easy. It is difficult to follow through with a commitment to pray for others, for I often face more difficulties and setbacks of my own than I can handle. Yet it is true that when I enter deeply into the needs, hurts, and concerns of others, I begin to find my own needs, hurts, and concerns being met, healed, and fulfilled. For when I bring other persons before Your throne, I am led into Your healing presence where I can be touched at the very center of my being.

Since Your heart, Lord, is "large enough to embrace the entire universe," certainly there is room there for me and for those You have entrusted to my care.

This being true, my Lord, then enable me to open my heart to Your great heart of love and compassion. Help me to develop more and more into an intercessory prayer warrior, placing before Your throne of mercy the people You have given me to lead. Make me effective in this, for this is the most important work I can do. Help me to **"pray in the Spirit on all occasions, with all kinds of prayers and requests. [And] with this in mind [help me to] always keep on praying for all the saints."**[14] Empower me Lord, so that "whenever I open my mouth, words may be given me so that I will fearlessly make known the gospel for which I am an ambassador."[15] Enable me to "pro-

---

14 Ephesians 5:18.
15 Ephesians 6:19.

claim it clearly as I should."[16] May I always "wrestle in prayer" for those for whom You have given me responsibility that they "may stand firm in all the will of God, mature and fully assured."[17] And whatever I do, help me to work at it with all my heart, as working for the Lord, not for men, since I know that I will receive an inheritance from the Lord as a reward. It is the Lord Christ I am serving![18] May I never forget this. In the name of the One who is my Strength, my Help, my Shield and my Source – my Lord Jesus Christ, I pray. Amen.

In a study I did in Ephesians I found 39 times it says "InChrist," "Through Christ," etc. Reviewing all those occurrences, I discovered The ABC's of being InChrist. There is at least one InChrist concept for each letter of the alphabet. The next journals are from that collection.

X - *InChrist* God Xeroxes Us[19]

"Surely you heard of him and were taught in him in accordance with the truth that is in Jesus . . . to put on the new self, created to be like God in true righteousness and holiness" Ephesians 4: 21, 24 (NIV)

The letter "X" (which is the first letter in the Greek word for Christ!) represents that *InChrist* God *Xeroxes* us: "Put on the new self, created to be like God in true righteousness and holiness." Ephesians 4:2 (NIV) Put your face on a copy machine and push the copy button (Be sure to close your eyes first!). What prints out? A likeness of your face. If you keep

16 Colossians 4:4.
17 Colossians 4:12.
18 Colossians 3:23-24.
19 © Bruce, S. K. (2010). *Your Life Repeated in My Life: Story Devotions for JesusFollowers. Florence, MS: Unpublished, in process. Come to the Waters Be Refreshed! Ministry & Music Resources, Sam & Sandie Bruce Ministries,* <u>drsambruce"aol.com</u>

your eyes open, you might not see the picture for a while due to all the spots in your eyes from the bright copy machine light! As *JesusFollowers*, we were created to be like God, *Xeroxed* – an image of His *likeness: His true righteousness and holiness reproduced in us.* When people see us – who we are and how we act – they should see *the likeness of Christ in us.* There is a chasm between Christians-in-name-only (church members who are not *JesusFollowers*) and true *JesusFollowers*. Having grown up in a minister's home (with godly *JesusFollower* parents) and been in hundreds of ministers' meetings, I have learned that there are a lot of *JesusFollowers*, holy men and women of God. There are also too many of what I have termed *"holiness preachers and teachers who aren't holy people."* "My goal in teaching spiritual formation is to show people the joy, freedom and power of becoming genuine *Holy People of God,* true *JesusFollowers*."[20]

The big question that follows that statement is, "Can we really attain this quality of relationship with God?" The resounding answer is "Yes!" Next question: "How?" Jesus told us in His *Great Invitation*: **"Look at me. I stand at the door. I knock. If you hear me call and open the door, I'll come right in and sit down to supper with you."** Revelation 3:20 (MSG) Jesus said when you open the door of your life, **"I'll come right in!"** He inhabits our inner beings, as Paul said **". . . this is the secret: Christ lives in you. This gives you assurance of sharing his glory."** Colossians 1:27 (NLT) But Jesus indicated that it goes even deeper: **"We are intimately linked in this harvest work. Anyone who accepts what you do, accepts me, the One who sent you. Anyone who accepts what I do accepts my Father, who sent me."** Matthew 10:40 (MSG)

Dennis Kinlaw says that what Jesus is describing here "is not mere *inhabitation.* It's getting close to *identity,* isn't it? Christ and the believer are

---

20 Bruce, Dr. Sam. *5 Minute± Reflections from My Wooded Prayer Trail. Florence, MS: Unpublished, in process. Come to the Waters Be Refreshed! Ministry & Music Resources, Sam & Sandie Bruce Ministries,* drsambruce"aol.com www.bruceministries.net

so closely identified that when you receive a believer, you receive Christ. If you reject a believer, you reject Christ. If you get Christ, you get the Father; and if you miss Him, you miss the Father."[21] SO! It's a bit like being *Xeroxed*, when people see a *JesusFollower* they see an image of His *likeness: His true righteousness and holiness reproduced in us*. When people see us – who we are and how we act – they should see *the likeness of Christ in us*. That's *identity*. Paul puts this concept in a nutshell picture: **"To me, to live is Christ . . ."** Philippians 1:21 (NIV) In other words, "Christ is life for me; but this also means I am to be Christ to other people."[22] In this way, God enables us to **"put on the new self, created to be like God in true righteousness and holiness"** Ephesians 4: 24 (NIV) "Holy describes what we are in our inner lives and relationships with God. Righteous describes how we live in our outer lives and relationships with other people. Putting on the new self is like God gives us a new operating system, or better, He implants a new core DNA in us that is saturated with righteousness and holiness."[23] And that, my friend is how we become genuine *Holy People of God*, true *JesusFollowers*; and He enables us to fulfill our purpose of being created to be like God – *Xeroxed* – transformed into an image of His *likeness: His true righteousness and holiness reproduced in us*. And through that relationship God can work through us to transform the lives of those we love and lead.

This *Xeroxed Transformation* is a result of *My Life Purpose Power Prayer: Empower Me, Lord, by Your Son, to Become All You Created Me to Be. Energize Me, Lord, by Your Spirit, to Accomplish All You Call Me to Do.* This is how God *Xeroxes* us in the image of Christ, which means being genu-

21   Kinlaw, Dennis F. (2001). *We Live As Christ*. Nappanee, IN: Evangel Publishing House; ISBN #1-928915-23-X. 24.

22   Kinlaw, Dennis F. (2001). *We Live As Christ*. Nappanee, IN: Evangel Publishing House; ISBN #1-928915-23-X. 24.

23   Bruce, Dr. Sam. From *5 Minute± Reflections from My Wooded Prayer Trail. Florence, MS: Unpublished, in process. Come to the Waters Be Refreshed! Ministry & Music Resources, Sam & Sandie Bruce Ministries*, drsambruce"aol.com www.bruceministries.net

ine *JesusFollowers* and not just Christians-in-name-only; people who follow Christ, act as He would act, speak as He would speak, love as He would love, and lead as He would lead.

One morning on my wooded prayer trail I discovered a wonderful illustration of God's *Xeroxed Transformation* of us in the likeness of Christ. As Elijah was getting ready for beaming up in the fiery chariot, he said to Elisha, **"What can I do for you before I'm taken from you? Ask anything." Elisha said, "Your life repeated in my life. I want to be a holy man just like you."** 2 Kings 2:9 (MSG) When I first read Elisha's request, **"Your life repeated in my life, I want to be a holy man just like you,"** it shaped *The Ultimate Prayer* for my life-purpose: *Empower me, Lord, by Your Son, to become all You created me to be. Energize me, Lord, by Your Spirit, to accomplish all You call me to do.* If God will accomplish that in my life, I will feel that I have fulfilled His awesome plan for me. This is what I have been praying on my wooded prayer trail, *"Xerox Me, Lord. Your life repeated in my life. I want to be a holy person just like You intend me to be. Empower me, Lord, by Your Son, to become all You created me to be. Energize me, Lord, by Your Spirit, to accomplish all you call me to do."* That's being *Xeroxed* by God – being the likeness of Christ, a reflection of His image in us to other people. After Lee Strobel became a *JesusFollower*, his five-year-old daughter Alison said, "Mommy, I want God to do for me what he's done for Daddy."[24] That's Christ's life repeated in a person's life – God Xeroxed Strobel, and even his five-year-old daughter recognized the transformation.

My Life Purpose Power Prayer: Xerox Me, Lord; Your Life Repeated in My Life – the image of Christ, His very presence in me reflected to others! Empower me to put on the new self by giving me a new operating system; or better, implant a new core DNA in me that is saturated with Your righteousness and holiness. Empower me, Lord, by Your Son, to become all

---

24 Lee Strobel, *The Case for Christ*

You created me to be. Energize me, Lord, by Your Spirit, to accomplish all You call me to do. Amen. [25]

Z *InChrist* God ZOOMS IN on Us[26]

"For [God] chose us in him [Christ] before the creation of the world to be holy and blameless in his sight." Ephesians 1:4 (NIV)

"You need carpel tunnel surgery on both hands . . ." That's what the neurosurgeon told Sandie. My mind flooded with memories of people who had the excruciating surgery, and weeks of pain and immobility. I thought, "After all Sandie has been through with brain tumor surgery, broken femur bone, and . . ." My mind was swirling with an array of emotions of sympathy, compassion, anxiety, disappointment, and a lot of questions. I didn't think I could bear watching her go through more pain . . .

". . . We have a new surgical procedure . . ." Dr. Thiel broke into my mounting emotional roller coaster ride, "an *Endoscopic Assisted Surgical Device*." We no longer have to cut the Transverse Carpal Ligament which is the major source of pain and lengthy immobility. We make a small incision through the skin on the wrist and insert a little tube through which we run a tiny camera with a light that zooms into the inner palm area which I can see through my electronic goggles attached to the camera. With a set of mini tools, also inserted through the little tube, I remove the pain-causing obstructions. The pain and immobility are greatly reduced, often to only one or two days." Sandie said, "Put that scope in my hand and clean out the source of pain and numbness!" My heart leaped for joy! Although I did

25 Bruce, Samuel K. *Your Life Repeated in My Life: Story Devotions for JesusFollowers. Unpublished, in process.*

26 Bruce, Samuel K. (©2012). *Reflections from My Wooded Prayer Trail: The ABC's of InChrist in Ephesians. Florence, MS: Unpublished, in process. Come to the Waters Be Refreshed! Ministry & Music Resources, Sam & Sandie Bruce Ministries,* drsambruce"aol.com.

not know what to pray for – I had no idea the *Endoscopic Assisted Surgical Device* existed – I had been praying for a better way for Sandie than the traditional type of surgery. We immediately and joyfully decided to go for it.

The surgical team took her in at 1:00 on Monday afternoon. When I took her home that evening, she was a bit wobbly and disoriented from the general anesthesia. Twenty-four hours later, she picked up her fork and ate dinner; she held a mug of water her hands. She had some pain from the surgery, but her wrists, hands and fingers were remarkably flexible; and the numbness was gone. After using her hands to eat breakfast on Wednesday, we covered her bandages with latex gloves, and she took a shower on her own. She told me that if I would get on the other side of the bed, she could make it with my help. It worked! On Thursday morning, she washed, folded and put the laundry away. She took a shower and washed her hair. Dr. Thiel and his new *Endoscopic Assisted Surgical Device* were a miraculously successful surgical team!

That device illustrates Paul's concept that God, *InChrist*, chooses us **"to be holy and blameless in his sight"** Ephesians 1:4 (NIV). I counted 39 occurrences of *InChrist*, *Through Christ*, *By Christ*, etc. in Ephesians, at least 1 for each letter in the Alphabet. The "Z" word, *zoom,* illustrates **"In his sight"**, *to zoom in, as with a microscope* – like an *Endoscopic Assisted Surgical Device* – better known as the Holy Spirit. When we are *InChrist* the Holy Spirit sees deeply within us with infinite accuracy – the good or bad, helpful or harmful, right or wrong, destructive attitudes or positive thoughts. He *zooms in on us* through His searchlight of love. Using His healing, restoring tools of the Word, prayer, worship and other spiritual disciplines He removes anything that is not **"holy and blameless in his sight"**– harmful, painful, destructive attitudes, sins, and desires – and replaces them with His healing, strength, and resources. He restores our inner beings as He created us to be – empowered by His love, joy, peace and holiness. He transforms our spirits, minds, emotions, and relationships to the "original equipment" He intended us to live as people of deep spirituality, ethics, and integrity. This is how we fulfill Apostle Paul's desire for us: **"You were taught, with regard to your former way of life, to put off your old self, which is being corrupted by its deceitful desires; to be made new in the attitude of your minds; and to put on the new self, created to be like God in true righteousness and holiness."** Ephesians 4:22-24 (NIV)

Prayer: *Lord, zoom in on me; as You see anything that's not holy and blameless in Your sight, clean it out and restore me to the person you created me to be. Implant in me your love, joy, and peace. Fill me with Your healing grace; strengthen me with the power of Your restoring Spirit. Then work through me to bring those You call me to love and lead into your presence to experience the healing and wholeness You've given me. Make me a channel of your love, joy and peace to every person I meet. Amen.*

S - *InChrist* God SEQUENCES Us[27]

"I pray that you . . . may be filled to the measure of all the fullness of God . . . attaining to the whole measure of the fullness of Christ." Ephesians 3:17-19; 4:13 (NIV)

Whatever we allow to fill your inner core – our mind, our thoughts – with, is what will be visible to others. When we are "filled to the measure of all the fullness of God . . . the fullness of Christ" people will recognize His presence in our actions; our interactions with other people; and our reactions to temptations, opportunities, and circumstances that come your way. Luke illustrated this principle as he said: "When they saw their

---

27   Bruce, Sam. (2013). *5 Minute± Reflections from My Wooded Prayer Trail, Florence, MS: Unpublished, in process. Come to the Waters Be Refreshed! Ministry & Music Resources, Sam & Sandie Bruce Ministries.* <u>drsambruce"aol.com</u>.

courage they couldn't take their eyes off them – Peter and John standing there so confident, so sure of themselves! Their fascination deepened when they realized these two were laymen with no training in Scripture or formal education. They were astonished and they took note that these men had been with Jesus." Acts 4:13 (NIV & MSG)

You know, there's just something attractive, captivating, and fascinating about a true Christ Follower. People notice something different – life-transforming – about a Christ Follower. Peter and John were recognized as JesusFollowers because, Acts says, the people around them "took note that these men had been with Jesus" in more than a casual relationship because with means to be in close association with a person; to participate in what he is and does – to transfer or sequence28 that person's qualities to other people. It's more than being physically present with a person; it's being transformed by taking on his/her characteristics. With means a particular order in which related things follow each other29 – His presence transforms who I am. The fact that Peter and John had been with Jesus made them so confident, so sure of themselves that there was no question that they were related to Him – His character was sequenced into their lives – true JesusFollowers – genuine holy people, real People of God!

Sandie and I have an Alesis Sequencer, which is a digital recorder that you can play a midi keyboard into, and it records (sequences) whatever she plays, every note, sustain pedal, dynamics, her choice of electric or grand piano, strings, trumpets, drums. When you play it back, there's no doubt that it's Sandie's recording. If you heard the live and recorded versions, you couldn't tell the difference. That is what JesusFollowers are – we live so closely to Jesus that His thoughts, attitudes, motives, desires, and actions are played back or sequenced through us to those we love and lead. This describes what John Wesley called "the heart of it all" – sanctification,

---

28 *Strong's Talking Greek & Hebrew Dictionary, WordSearch Bible Program.*
29 *Oxford University Press Dictionary, Corel WordPerfect.*

holiness which "sets us apart for the service of God."30 A person who, like those apostles, has been with Jesus in this close, intimate relationship has been sequenced into a JesusFollower – someone who thinks like Christ thinks and acts like Christ would act.

When Jesus was ready to select His apostles, through whom He would entrust the planting of His church that would grow and thrive throughout time to bring people to Him, Mark says, "Jesus went up on a mountainside and called to him those he wanted, and they came to him. He appointed twelve – designating them apostles – [get ready, here comes the spine-tingling truth!] that they might be with him and that he might send them out to preach and to have authority to drive out demons." Mark 3:13-15 (NIV) There's that word with again! They were with Him so they could participate in His plans; He could sequence into them His God-breathed Word, His unconditional love, His goals of evangelism and disciple-making, His life-transforming power and His unending resources to fulfill His plans. So, against that breath-taking backdrop Luke could say about Peter and John that when the people "saw their courage they couldn't take their eyes off them standing there so confident, so sure of themselves! They were astonished and they took note that these men had been with Jesus." Acts 4:13 (NIV & MSG) Now, that's a holy and proper self-esteem, and it comes with hangin' out with Jesus consistently; and His inner being rubs off on ours. The question is, when people meet us, has enough of His inner being rubbed off on ours that are they astonished; and do they take note that we have been with Jesus? Do they see us as sequencers, channels of His God-breathed Word, unconditional love, goals of evangelism and disciple-making, life-transforming power, and unending resources to fulfill His plans? What you're filled with is what will come out.

I'll never forget that night. A group of men who met weekly for Monday Night Football at the Trail's End Saloon, which they had built on a ranch

---

30 Harper, Steve (1983). *John Wesley's Message for Today.* Grand Rapids, MI: Zondervan Publishing House, 98.

just outside town, said, "Sam, we invited you here because there's something different about you, and we want to know what it is. You don't push us, you just live it, and we know you care about us; we want you to help us understand more about it." In the coming years, around the campfire, with plates full of hickory-fired steak and sausage, God sequenced His love and life-changing power through me to a group of men who noticed that I had been with Jesus. This is not about me; it's about Christ sequenced in and through me; I was just the vessel He chose to deliver His love and message through. What is sequenced through your life?

Lord, I want to be with You like that, living every day of my life so that people take note that I have been with Jesus. Use me as an anointed sequencer – a true JesusFollower – genuine holy person, real Person of God – to transfer your God-breathed Word, unconditional love, goals of evangelism and disciple-making, life-transforming power, and unending resources to all you bring across my path to love and lead. Thanks. Amen.

S - *InChrist* God *SYNCHRONIZES* Us with Each Other – The Harmony in Marriage Principle[31]

> "Submit to [live in sync with] one another out of reverence for Christ . . . live in harmony [live in sync with] with one another; be sympathetic, love as brothers, be compassionate and humble." 1 Peter 3:8, Ephesians 5:21 (NIV/DSP[32])

---

31 Bruce, Samuel K. (©2012). *Reflections from My Wooded Prayer Trail: The ABC's of InChrist in Ephesians.* Florence, MS: Unpublished, in process. Come to the Waters Be Refreshed! Ministry & Music Resources, Sam & Sandie Bruce Ministries, drsambruce"aol.com.

32 DSP: Dr. Sam's Paraphrase: not to change the meaning of Scripture, but to give some notes for applying the truth of the Scripture to our lives. Paraphrased words are usually enclosed in brackets.

When I was quoting through Ephesians on my Prayer Trail one morning, I had a revelation about this passage that I have never heard anyone discuss. It is in the verse just before wives, submit to your husbands (Ephesians 5:22), which is where most people usually launch into the rights and responsibilities of wives and husbands. Paul said, "Submit to [live in sync with] one another out of reverence for Christ." Ephesians 5:21 (NIV/DSP[33]) Verse 21 applies the larger scriptural context to verses 22-29; and it could be the most important verse in the whole section because it sets the principles for our marriage relationships and all other relationships, too! If husbands and wives lived in this verse, "Submit to [live in sync with] one another out of reverence for Christ," then Ephesians 5:22-29 would never be an issue. If each person is concerned about the best interests of the other person, then they are both working in the best interests of their marriage, putting each other first, loving, caring, supporting, being faithful, showing respect and preference to each other. In this kind of close relationship there not an issue of authority and submission; decisions are made through loving, mutual consent. Couple that verse with Peterson's rendition of 1 Corinthians 13:4-5 (MSG): "Love never gives up. Love cares more for others than for self. Love doesn't want what it doesn't have. Love doesn't strut, doesn't have a swelled head, Doesn't force itself on others, Isn't always "me first." Living in these verses will build unusual love and cooperation to couples and their families. This high-quality, Christ-centered relationship will lead to the fulfillment of what I call The In-Sync Harmony in Marriage Principle: "Husbands and wives, submit to [live in sync with] one another out of reverence for Christ." Ephesians 5:21 (NIV/DSP34)

---

33 DSP: Dr. Sam's Paraphrase: not to change the meaning of Scripture, but to give some notes for applying the truth of the Scripture to our lives. Paraphrased words are usually enclosed in brackets.

34 DSP: Dr. Sam's Paraphrase: not to change the meaning of Scripture, but to give some notes for applying the truth of the Scripture to our lives. Paraphrased words are usually enclosed in brackets.

"I appeal to you, dear wives and husbands, by the authority of our Lord Jesus Christ, to live in harmony with [live in sync with] each other. Let there be no divisions in your marriage. Rather, be of one mind, united in thought and purpose." 1 Corinthians 1:10 (NLT/DSP[35]) Living in sync with one another – out of reverence for Christ (which is the source of our InChrist relationship) – is what brings harmony to our marriages (and all other relationships, too!) The Big Tough Fisherman Peter, now under the anointing and image of Christ in him, agrees fully when he adds, "Finally, all of you, Marriage Partners, and everyone else, live in harmony with [live in sync with] one another; be sympathetic, love as sisters and brothers, be compassionate and humble" 1 Peter 3:8 (NIV/DSP[36]), and together you will produce a creative, productive, workable, excellent marriage and family relationship that will glorify God, honor your successful teamwork, and provide helpful, renovative, and transformative strategies for the marriage relationship you and God are building together! This quality of love-relationship is expressed in the song I hear often on KLOVE: "Your love never fails, never gives up, Never runs out on me."[37] And this is how InChrist God SYNCHRONIZES Us – and helps us live in harmony – with Each Other!

---

35 DSP: Dr. Sam's Paraphrase: not to change the meaning of Scripture, but to give some notes for applying the truth of the Scripture to our lives. Paraphrased words are usually enclosed in brackets.

36 DSP: Dr. Sam's Paraphrase: not to change the meaning of Scripture, but to give some notes for applying the truth of the Scripture to our lives. Paraphrased words are usually enclosed in brackets.

37 (Brian Johnson, Jeremy Riddle, Christa Black Gifford Bethel Music Publishing 2010 http://www.elyrics.net CCLI License No. 2542096)

Chapter 4

My Personal Quest in Spiritual Formation

Dr. Sam Says . . .

Always listen to the small voice of God.

My Personal quest in spiritual formation-personal quest in spiritual formation began in early childhood, for I was reared in a wonderful Christian home by Godly parentsgodly parents who Models of spiritualityBruce, Walter & Loismodeled the principles of spirituality both in private home life and in public ministry. The attitudes, behavior, morals, ethics, and interpersonal relationships which they exhibited in public were also demonstrated in private. They not only Talk the talk, walk the walk, live the lifetalked the talk, but they also walked the walk and lived the life. My parents were godly, Christian people, who dedicated their entire lives to Christian ministry. Bruce, WalterDad served in various ministries that included Bible college president (the same college of which I was president for 12 years), pastor, and director of foreign missions. Mom worked as a nurse to help sustain the financial income, while also devoting herself to her family and to helping in the various ministries.

The nature of their ministry determined much of my lifestyle from infancy to this day. From the time I was three years old through elementary school days, I spent many hours in college classes and chapel services, family camps and youth camps, children's services, early-morning and late-night prayer meetings. Most of our weekends and all our summers were spent traveling across the country from church to church in ministry. It was not unusual to be involved in two or three services, and one or two conferences, plus a couple of prayer meetings each day during a camp or revival meeting in a local church.

When I was about eight years old, Dad made me an official part of the evangelistic team as a vocalist in most of the services. He paid me ten cents a song. Most of the money was saved to buy school clothes when we returned home in the fall.

Although I often grew tired of all the travel and services, and even though I drifted away from consistent personal spiritual formation for many years, these experiences formed the foundation for my life and ministry today.

Become People of Prayer

After I finished seminary and had been in my first pastorate (which lasted 21 years) for several years, I was sensing a Spiritual drynessspiritual dryness and a desire for a refreshing movement of God in my life and ministry. Although the ministry of the church was going along rather well, and the church was growing slowly but steadily, it seemed that we had reached a spiritual plateau. I began praying for God to show me a clear vision of what we needed to move us to the next level of ministry. As I prayed, the impression I consistently sensed in my inner spirit was, "Become a man of prayer. Become a man of prayer."

I responded, "But Lord, I do pray—every morning and night with our daughters, at mealtime, at weddings and funerals, in church services, at grand openings for all kinds of businesses, for various community and civic functions (I was chaplain for the Chamber of Commerce), when I need a new sermon for Sunday morning, and any other time I feel the need to do so."

Still, the challenge kept flooding my mind, "Become a man of prayer."

Then I remembered the lifestyle of people like my Bruce, Walterfather, who was recognized as a Bruce, Walterman of prayerman of prayer by all who knew him well. As consistently as the sun rises, he arose every morning at five o'clock and went to his study for prayer and meditation on the Word of God. I thought of some of the biblical prayer giants like DanielDaniel, ElijahElijah, PaulPaul, PeterPeter, and the greatest model—our Lord Jesus ChristJesus Christ. When I compared my prayer life to theirs, I realized that while I prayed often, I was not a man of prayer. Against that backdrop I made a covenant with the Lord that I would become a man of prayer. I attempted to follow the example of our Lord, as Luke described His devotional practices. Within a few verses, Luke mentions three times the source of His power: **"At daybreak Jesus went out to a solitary place . . ."** (Luke442Luke 4:42). **"Jesus withdrew to lonely places and prayed . . ."** (Luke516Luke 5:16). **". . . Jesus went out into the hills to pray, and spent the night praying to God"** (Luke Luke6126:12). I began going to my study early in the morning, before most people were awake, and before the phone started ringing, to spend considerable time alone with God in prayer and the Word.

Among other issues, I Praying for the church boardprayed daily for my Church boardchurch board. Those men were wonderful Christian men, and we were great friends. We had splendid fellowship with one another. We hunted and fished together, went out for pie and coffee after the board meetings, and visited in one another's homes. However, during the board meetings something changed between us. We could spend an hour or more haggling over a ten-dollar expenditure, or about some program or ministry issue.

Feeling like a change needed to be made at the top, I began praying, "Lord, please give me a new Board." I did not care how He accomplished that request—either by putting new persons on the Board, or by making new persons out of the existing members. I prayed that prayer consistently for a year without seeing much outward change. Then one night following a time when I had been out of town for nearly a month, just before the close of our monthly Board meetingboard meeting, Chairman Holiday, JerryJerry said to me, "Sam, after the meeting is over, I need to talk to you."

After the other members had left, Jerry said, "Sam, while you were away, we had a board meeting."

I thought, "Oh, no, I've heard of meetings like that!"

Jerry continued, "We were discussing the condition of our church . . ."

I thought, "Here it comes! The next statement will be, 'and you're the problem.' So, here is my resignation."

Then came the shocker, ". . . and we realized that we have not been giving you the support you need as our pastor; but that has changed. A couple of weeks ago we began an early morning prayer meeting on Thursdays to pray for you and the church, and we invite you to join us!"

I was ecstatic! After a solid year of praying with very few visible results, God had given me a new Board. He had also given them a new pastor, for the time spent with Him alone in prayer had affected my life deeply in my inner spirit. Our board meetings took on a new tone in the months that followed, for we spent much time in prayer and Bible study together, and a little time on the business affairs of the church. We practiced this for another year without seeing many visible changes in the congregation.

Meanwhile, during that year, I sensed the Lord leading me to preach about prayer often, so often that I was sometimes concerned that the people would get tired of hearing about prayer. Several months later, people began sharing how God was answering prayers in their lives, families, jobs, and schools. Miraculous things were happening. After two years of intense prayer, the church was growing, alive, healthy, and vibrant. New people were coming weekly. People's lives were being changed. It was an exciting time. The theme of our church was becoming a reality: "Where love is thick, faults are thin; try our love!Where love is thick, faults are thin; try our love!" Visitors often commented on the love, acceptance, and warmth they sensed when they came to our services.

Become People of the Word

Sometime during this intense prayer renewal time, the Lord began challenging me to become, not just a man of prayer, but also a Man of the Wordman of the Word. After several months of procrastination, and a few weak attempts at Scripture memory, I covenanted with the Lord to become a man of the Word. I began committing entire books, and shorter passages, to memory. As I realized the power of the Word in my own life, I started leading my congregation into Scripture memory. This deepened our appreciation for the Bible, and our ability to use it effectively in ministry increased greatly. It achieved immeasurable changes in our lives, relationships, and ministries.

At some point in this process, I learned of the Spirituality and Ministry Class that was offered at Fuller Theological Seminary Spirituality and Ministry Class Fuller Theological Seminary with Eugene Peterson, EugenePeterson as the teacher. That course helped bring meaning and cohesiveness to the deep spiritual changes that had been occurring in my life and our congregation. My project for the Spirituality and Ministry Class was a series of lessons for our Christian Growth GroupsChristian Growth Groups, which I taught to the leaders on Sunday nights after the evening services. The leaders taught the lessons in their small groups throughout the week. As we began teaching the principles of spiritual formation, we often stood in awe as we watched God shaping us as people of the Word, and people of prayer. Renewal in prayerRenewal in prayer was leading us into renewal in the WordRenewal in the Word.

Become People of Worship

The process of becoming people of the Word and people of prayer led us into renewal in Worship renewalworshipRenewal in worship as we were becoming People of Worshippeople of worship. By worship renewal I mean that we began exploring new ways of worship. We were learning to worship God simply because He is worthy to be worshiped. Both our private and public worship took on new meaning and brought fresh blessings. I developed a series of messages about worship—ways of worship and why we worship God—which helped us in our quest of becoming people of worship.

Become People of God

Through the disciplines of becoming people of the Word, people of prayer, and people of worship, we were becoming —exhilaratingly, people of God. People began discovering and using their spiritual gifts to revitalize current ministries and begin new exciting ministries.

Practice What We Already Know

In attempting to address issues of such great spiritual importance, I understand Paul's statement, **"Not that I have already obtained all this, or have already been made perfect, but I press on to take hold of that for which Christ Jesus took hold of me"** (Philippians312Philippians 3:12). The more I learn about spiritual formation, the more I know I need to learn. I heard about a young Farm advisorfarm advisor who offered some new pamphlets about helpful farming techniques to an older farmer. The farmer said to the young farm advisor: "Son, don't give me any of those fancy pamphlets . . . why, I don't farm half as well as I know how to now!" (Parables, Etc., 1990) Another man said, "It concerns me that I don't know more about the Bible." His friend replied: "It's not what I don't know about the Bible that concerns me, it's what I do know and don't do that alarms me."

That is the way most of us approach spirituality, or spiritual formation. We really do not need any more lessons on how to pray, study the Bible, worship, or experience spiritual formation and growth. We just need to practice what we already know God asks of us in His Word.

In writing these lessons and teaching these principles, I do not presume to present myself as one who has all the answers to spiritual formation and Christian living. Rather, I share as a fellow struggler, a colleague in the Christian faith. Nor do I offer them as an exhaustive theological treatise in spiritual formation. My prayer is that these studies will be a source of mutual encouragement, as Proverbs423Proverbs 4:23 says: **"As iron sharpens iron, so one man sharpens another."** As a brother in the Lord, I hope to spur ahead the persons I teach in the exciting adventure of being shaped in the image of Christ. This is one facet of spiritual formation.

What I am sharing in these lessons is not theoretical or philosophical, although there is a time and place for that kind of study. I hope to share where

I have been attempting to live, and where I have been venturing to lead the people to whom God has called me to minister across the past several years.

The principles I am sharing here have been learned by studying the truths of God's Word, through the practice of prayer, and from personal experience. Many of these principles of spiritual formation were first entries in my journal which I wrote in response to my study of the **"living and enduring Word of God"** (1 Peter 1:23b) along with other books I was reading in the areas of spiritual formation and worship. Later, I put them in the form of the lesson plans to use in teaching the Christian Growth Groups mentioned earlier.

I come not as an expert or specialist in spiritual formation, but as one who is learning, sometimes painfully, sometimes joyously, the rewards God gives to those who grow and stretch themselves in the spiritual life.

What we are doing in spiritual formation is building lives and lifestyles that will last for an eternity, and that will keep us steady and online during the darkest nights of the soul. While there are many other spiritual disciplines that are important and necessary, the principal facets that I shall attempt to address are *becoming people of the Word, people of prayer, people of worship—people of God.* These, I believe, are the foundational principles in the study of spiritual formation: the forming of our inner lives and relationships with God in a way that transforms our outer lives and relationships with other persons. A myriad of other spiritual disciplines grows out of or are dependent on these four disciplines.

The Power of the Quiet Place

When I was taking the spiritual class under Eugene Peterson, I attended a retreat, with 35 other ministers who were from across the United States and from many different nations around the world, at the St. Andrews Retreat Center in the high desert above The Mojave Desert. I went for a walk on a desert trail to reminisce, reflect, and remember times in the past when I sensed God's presence in my life. I came to an oasis, a beautiful little lake in the desert, surrounded by beautiful trees and lush green grass. A fountain was springing up in the middle of the lake. Ducks and geese were swimming gracefully across the water. As I sat alone beside the water, soaking up some of the beauty of my Father's creative handiwork, I was reminded that the past year had been one of desert dwelling for me -- a time of struggle, pressure, and spiritual dryness. Although I had been in touch with God through His Word and through prayer -- and I was certain that these were what had brought me through -- I was sensing spiritual barrenness, physical tiredness, and mental and emotional weakness.

But I knew God had been faithful. Through His Word and prayer, and coming away from the busyness of life, He had already begun to refresh me at a very deep level of my inner spirit. In Christ I found an oasis in the middle of my desert-dwelling experience. Like my shady retreat there in the desert, my Lord was leading me to the shady green pastures of His presence and love. I welcomed His refreshing power, for it was good!

As I sat there, quietly praying, reading my Bible, and writing in my journal, I was reminded that we all go through those *desert dwelling times* in our relationships with God, with others, and with ourselves — spiritually, mentally, emotionally, physically, relationally, and vocationally. I realized that moments such as these are important times in our lives, for what happens next can set the tone for the next stages of our lives. As we spend quality time in the quiet places with our Lord in the Word, in prayer, and in worship, we discover that He meets us there to bring refreshment, renewal, and revival. In those times He renovates, reshapes, and transforms our inner beings and refocuses, redirects, and energizes our ministries. It is my sincere prayer and hope that this course in spiritual formation will lead us all to the *Quiet Place* of spiritual renewal and empowerment. Ralph Carmichael caught the meaning of the *Quiet Place* in a song he wrote.

A Quiet Place[38]

There is a quiet place, far from the rapid pace,
Where God can soothe my troubled mind,
Sheltered by tree and flower,
There in my quiet hour with Him,
My cares are left behind.
Whether a garden small or on a mountain tall,
New strength and courage there I find;
Then from this quiet place I go prepared to face
A new day with love for all mankind.

PRAYER RESPONSE

Lord God, my Savior, please shape my inner life and relationship with You in a way that will transform my outer life and relationships with other persons. May I learn the rewards You give to those who are becoming people of the Word, people of prayer, people of worship—people of God. Create in me a lifestyle and relationships with You and with other persons that will last for eternity—and that will keep me steady and online during the darkest nights of the soul. Empower me to **"press on to take hold of that for which You took hold of me"** *(Philippians 3:12). Equip me to practice all that You ask of me in Your Word. Help me to lead the people to whom I minister into the depths of*

---

38   Carmichael, Ralph. © 1967 Word Music.

spiritual living that is exhilarating, invigorating, refreshing, and empowering. Lead me to the Quiet Place where You refresh, renew, and reshape me in my inner being. As I emerge from that special Quiet Place, then refocus, redirect, and energize my ministries to other persons. In the name of Him who is called Mighty God, I pray. Amen.

PART 2

FORMING PEOPLE OF THE WORD

Chapter 5

The Power of the Word – the Infrastructure

The disciplines of spiritual formation – *the forming of our inner lives and relationships with God in a way that transforms our outer lives and relationships with other persons* – provide the foundation, the infrastructure, for empowering the inner person, forming vital interpersonal relationships, and energizing dynamic ministries. An infrastructure is comprised of "the substructure or underlying foundation; the basic installations and facilities on which the continuance and growth of a community [person, family or church] depends, such as roads, schools, power plants, transportation, and communication systems."[39]

The infrastructure of the inner world of a person is shaped around becoming people of the Word, people of prayer, and people of worship. These help shape us into people of God. I believe it would be safe to say that all the other spiritual disciplines such as fasting, spiritual direction, solitude, and fellowship (and all the others) can be viewed as the tools

---

39   Webster's New World Dictionary. (n. d.).

we use for incarnating, living out and practicing, the disciplines of the Word, prayer, and worship. Those disciplines provide the curriculum for our training in spiritual things, interpersonal relationships, and ministries as well as the internal power and fortitude needed to bear up under the strains of life and to stand victoriously in Christ.

The disciplines furnish us with an effective communication system between God and us, and between us and other persons. As an integral part of the infrastructure of our lives, the disciplines provide the foundation on which the inner spiritual life and the outer relational life are built. They are the avenues along which we walk, with the Word of God serving as both the infrastructure and the road map which guides us safely to our destination of becoming people of God.

The Word of God Is the Underpinning of the Spiritual Disciplines

The underpinning for all the spiritual disciplines is the Bible, the Word of God, which has proven in the test of time to be the only dependable foundation for all life. The reason for this is the fact that the Bible is not just any old book. It is the **"living and enduring Word of God"** (1 Peter 1:23). Paul expressed to Timothy the importance of the Scriptures when he wrote,

> **But as for you, continue in what you have learned and have become convinced of, because you know those from whom you learned it, and how from infancy you have known the holy Scriptures, which are able to make you wise for salvation through faith in Christ Jesus. All Scripture is God-breathed and**

is useful for teaching, rebuking, correcting and training in righteousness, so that the man of God may be thoroughly equipped for every good work. In the presence of God and of Christ Jesus, who will judge the living and the dead, and in view of his appearing and his kingdom, I give you this charge: Preach the Word; be prepared in season and out of season; correct, rebuke, and encourage—with great patience and careful instruction (2 Timothy 3:14-4:1).

The Word is **"God-breathed,"** it is **"inspired by God."** Therefore, Peter could call it the **"living and enduring Word of God"**—God breathed into the words of the Word the breath of life, just as He breathed into Adam **"the breath of life, and man became a living being"** (Genesis 2:7). Thus, the Word is the faithful guide **"for teaching, rebuking, correcting and training in righteousness, so that the man of God may be thoroughly equipped for every good work."** This is an integral part of the process of spiritual formation.

The ministry of the Word was so important that Paul mentioned it as one of the three most consequential elements in ministry. He said,

Until I come, devote yourself to the public reading of Scripture, to preaching and to teaching. Do not neglect your gift, which was given you through a prophetic message when the body of elders laid their hands on you. Be diligent in these matters; give yourself wholly to them, so that everyone may see your progress. Watch your life and doctrine closely. Persevere in them, because if you do, you will save both yourself and your hearers (1 Timothy 4:13-16).

The first thing Paul mentioned that is of deep importance in the ministry is the **"public reading of Scripture."** Preaching and teaching should flow out of Scripture to guide the process of spiritual formation in the people in the church. Paul said that Timothy (and we) should **"be diligent in these matters."** He should **"give himself wholly to them . . . persevere in them."** By doing so, he would **"save both himself and his hearers."**

Let the Word Dwell in You Richly

In Colossians 3:5-17, the Apostle Paul tells us how we can be clothed like Christ, which is another description of the process of spiritual formation. He begins by listing some of the things God wants to clear out of our lives:

> **Put to death, therefore, whatever belongs to your earthly nature: sexual immorality, impurity, lust, evil desires and greed, which is idolatry. Because of these, the wrath of God is coming. You used to walk in these ways, in the life you once lived. But now you must rid yourselves of all such things as these: anger, rage, malice, slander, and filthy language from your lips. Do not lie to each other, since you have taken off your old self with its practices and have put on the new self, which is being renewed in knowledge in the image of its Creator** (Colossians 3:5-10).

He wants us to clear out those things in order to make room for the things with which He wants to clothe our lives:

> **Therefore, as God's chosen people, holy and dearly loved, clothe yourselves with compassion, kindness, humility, gentleness and**

patience. Bear with each other and forgive whatever grievances you may have against one another. Forgive as the Lord forgave you. And over all these virtues put on love, which binds them all together in perfect unity (Colossians 3:12-14).

Then in verses 15-16, Paul tells us how to accomplish all this: by allowing the "peace of Christ" to rule in our hearts, and by permitting the "Word of Christ" to dwell in us richly. He says,

Let the peace of Christ rule in your hearts, since as members of one body you were called to peace. And be thankful. Let the word of Christ dwell in you richly as you teach and admonish one another with all wisdom, and as you sing psalms, hymns and spiritual songs with gratitude in your hearts to God (Colossians 3:15-16).

Verse sixteen gives another key to spiritual formation: **"Let the word of Christ dwell in you richly"**—the forming of our inner lives and relationships with God— **"as you teach and admonish one another with all wisdom"**—in a way that transforms our outer lives and relationships with other persons. This should be the central guiding factor as we plan programs and curriculum, teach classes, have family devotions, structure our lives, plan for growth, and participate in worship. The Word must be central in all we teach and in all we do. Pastors and teachers must be rooted in the Word; in fact, the entire Christian family, every person, needs to be immersed in the Word, to the point that it **"dwells in us richly."**

Dwell means to *be at home*. Christ needs to be at home in our hearts. He should not be a stranger or even a guest. Paul carries this thought even further when he says that the Word of Christ should dwell in us richly, that is, abundantly, without limits. Maxie Dunnam writes,

> The ministry that is given to all Christians, and for which the Holy Spirit gives us gifts, is that of sharing Christ. We are the communicators of our Lord. This communication is not directed only to those outside the Christian fellowship, but it is the dynamic relationship of persons within the church. We teach and admonish one another, presenting the things we are learning, sharing our insights, being with, holding responsible, challenging, supporting, questioning, guiding—all for the building up of the Body, that we might all be equipped for ministry within and outside the church.[40]

The Word will transform our lives if we will allow it to dwell in us richly, for it is the underpinning of our spiritual formation.

When I was a minister of music at the Shartel Church in Oklahoma City, at the beginning of a Sunday morning worship service, Pastor Atwell accidentally picked up the previous Sunday's worship folder instead of the one for the current service. After he opened the service with the invocation, he looked at the order of worship and announced the opening hymn number. I realized that he had picked up the wrong folder, and as I walked to the pulpit to lead in worship, I announced the correct hymn number. Pastor Atwell whirled around and looked at me in shock because it was different from the number he had announced. I responded, "Sorry, you have the wrong order of worship. That's last Sunday's folder." Everyone laughed, and we went on with the worship service.

As I later reflected on that rather humorous incident, I realized that there are a lot of leaders who are giving people wrong directions and mis-

---

40   Dunnam, M. (1982). *The Communicator's Commentary (Vol. 8). Waco, TX: Word Books.*

guided information, not only about hymn numbers, but also about life, morality, ethics, what is right and what is wrong, family values, social issues, and spiritual values. Therefore, we need to become people of the Word, for the Word of God provides us with the truth about all areas of life.

Paul warned us about such people in Colossians.

My purpose is that they may be encouraged in heart and united in love, so that they may have the full riches of complete understanding, in order that they may know the mystery of God, namely, Christ, in whom are hidden all the treasures of wisdom and knowledge. I tell you this so that no one may deceive you by fine-sounding arguments. Although I am absent from you in body, I am present with you in spirit and delight to see how orderly you are and how firm your faith in Christ is. So then, just as you received Christ Jesus as Lord, continue to live in him, rooted and built up in him, strengthened in the faith as you were taught, and overflowing with thankfulness. See to it that no one takes you captive through hollow and deceptive philosophy, which depends on human tradition and the basic principles of this world rather than on Christ. For in Christ all the fullness of the Deity lives in bodily form, and you have been given fullness in Christ, who is the head over every power and authority (Colossians 2:2-10).

We who are entrusted with the ministry of discipling persons in the Christian faith must guard against "fine sounding arguments" and "hollow and deceptive philosophy which depends on human tradition and the basic principles of this world rather than on Christ," and which lead people away from Christ and advocate lifestyles that are contrary to the "**living and enduring Word of God**" (1 Peter 1:23). This is the reason why the Word of God must be central in our lives and in all our ministries. The Bible must be the foundation on which our education and ministries are founded. Jesus gave the basis of this truth in Matthew 7:24-27, when He said,

> **Therefore everyone who hears these words of mine and puts them into practice is like a wise man who built his house on the rock. The rain came down, the streams rose, and the winds blew and beat against that house; yet it did not fall, because it had its foundation on the rock. But everyone who hears these words of mine and does not put them into practice is like a foolish man who built his house on sand. The rain came down, the streams rose, and the winds blew and beat against that house, and it fell with a great crash.**

The Word of God is the only infrastructure around which to configure our spiritual formation—both in the inner being and in the outer relationships and circumstances. It is the only dependable foundation on which to build a lasting ministry—a ministry that will glorify God and build the Kingdom of God. Any other foundation is like shifting **"sand"**— **"human tradition and the basic principles of this world,"** which will erode and disintegrate.

When I was studying at Fuller Seminary, one of my classes was held in a church in San Clemente, California, overlooking the Pacific Ocean. Every afternoon, as soon as class was over, I went jogging 4 or 5 miles on the beach. I was amazed to see how many large, expensive homes were built on the cliffs overhanging the beach. As I jogged along the beach, I noticed that there were no rocks underneath the homes—just shifting sand. The ocean tides and the rains were eroding the very foundation out from under many of the homes. Some had already begun to slide into the sea as the sand disintegrated beneath them.

Similarly, any life or ministry that is not solidly founded on Jesus Christ (the living, eternal Word of the Father), and the Bible (the written and "enduring Word of God") cannot stand the tests of time and eternity. It is like those beautiful and expensive homes that are built on the sandy cliffs looking out over the ocean. Since there are few, if any, solid boulders underneath, the rains and winds are eroding the very foundation from beneath the homes, and some of the homes have already fallen down the cliff. Just so, a life, a home, a church, or a nation that is not built solidly on the Rock Jesus Christ and His Word is built on sand, according to Jesus' teaching. When the winds of adversity blow and the floods of calamity flow, collapse is inevitable.

This is the central reason, among many, for why we must practice, model, and teach the principles and disciplines of spiritual formation in our homes, churches, and schools. The Word of God is the source of these principles, and it will guide us into a relationship with God that will keep us steady, dependable, and on-line throughout time and eternity. The consistent practice of these principles will shape us into persons whom God can use mightily in helping others to learn how to walk with Him. Let us determine with all our hearts to become people of the Word. As we do, we will discover that it is the solid, powerful, unshakable foundation for our lives, families, and ministries.

Chapter 6

Meditating on the Word

There are several spiritual disciplines that enable us to grow in our relationship with God. These disciplines are given to us by God "as a means of receiving His grace. The disciplines allow us to place ourselves before God so that He can transform us."[41] While the discipline itself does not produce the change, Richard Foster says it puts us in the place where the change can occur . . . [where] God's gracious work takes over our inner spirit and transforms the ingrained habit patterns of our lives. Once we have lived in the way of disciplined grace for a season, we discover internal changes. If we are willing to listen to the Heavenly Monitor, we will receive the instruction we need. Our world is hungry for genuinely changed people. Leo Tolstoy observed, 'Everybody thinks of changing humanity and nobody thinks of changing himself.' Let us be among those who believe that the inner transformation of our lives is a goal worthy of our best effort.[42]

---

41   Foster, R. J. (1978). *Celebration of Discipline: The Path to Spiritual Growth*. New York, NY: Harper & Row.

42   Foster.

The Discipline of Meditating on the Word of God

One of the powerful disciplines for changing our lives and bringing us close to God is the discipline of meditating on the Word of God. We are not discussing here the Eastern religions and their distorted forms of meditation, but Christian meditation, studying the living, eternal, life-changing Word of God as found in the Bible. Meditating on the Word of God, "boldly calls us to enter into the living presence of God for ourselves. It tells us that God is speaking in the continuous present and wants to address us."[43]

The Bible itself gives us reasons to meditate on the Word:

Do not let this Book of the Law depart from your mouth; meditate on it day and night, so that you may be careful to do everything written in it. Then you will be prosperous and successful (Joshua 1:8).

But his delight is in the law of the Lord, and on his law he meditates day and night (Psalm 1:2).

I remember the days of long ago; I meditate on all your works and consider what your hands have done (Psalm 143:5).

May the words of my mouth and the meditation of my heart be pleasing in your sight, O Lord, my Rock and my Redeemer (Psalm 19:14).

I have quoted and prayed the latter verse many times, yet as I read it in its context, I see that the preceding verses describe the only way the words of my mouth and the meditation of my heart can be acceptable in God's

---

43   Foster.

sight. God, in His Word, has given us the instruments we need to enable us to live in a way that is pleasing to Him:

> **The law of the Lord is perfect, reviving the soul. The statutes of the Lord are trustworthy, making wise the simple. The precepts of the Lord are right, giving joy to the heart. The commands of the Lord are radiant, giving light to the eyes. The fear of the Lord is pure, enduring forever. The ordinances of the Lord are sure and altogether righteous. They are more precious than gold, than much pure gold; they are sweeter than honey, than honey from the comb. By them is your servant warned; in keeping them there is great reward** (Psalm 19:7-11).

The laws, statutes, precepts, commands, and ordinances of the Lord are not just a lot of binding, stifling, dampening, negative rules and regulations. They are the means by which we are empowered and enabled to live in harmony with our Creator and His eternal plan for our lives. Yet, in human terms, at first view these can seem to imprison rather than to empower, to restrict rather than to release, to fetter rather than to free.

Looking at the meaning of these words helps to understand them in their empowering and enabling capabilities.

"The law of the Lord is perfect, reviving the soul." The basic meaning of law, in Old Testament terms (*torah*), is teaching or instruction focused on how a person should live rather than on abstract or academic subjects. This is best illustrated in passages describing older people teaching younger ones:

> **My son, do not forget my teaching, but keep my commands in your heart, for they will prolong your life many years and bring**

you prosperity (Proverbs 3:1-2). **He who scorns instruction will pay for it, but he who respects a command is rewarded. The teaching of the wise is a fountain of life, turning a man from the snares of death** (Proverbs 13:13-14).

Since it is true that following the teaching of elders lengthens the life, brings prosperity, and refreshes like a fountain, how much more will we be blessed in following the instructions of God which focus on how we should live in order to enjoy His presence and power in our lives and relationships? Rather than looking at His instructions in the Word as a set of cold, rigid rules brutally applied, we should see the warm heart and soul of the law of God as being given for our benefit. The law is God's gift, intended to show us how to live a holy and happy life in this world. A few verses of promise will illustrate this:

See, I have taught you decrees and laws as the Lord my God commanded me, so that you may follow them in the land you are entering to take possession of it. Observe them carefully, for this will show your wisdom and understanding to the nations, who will hear about all these decrees and say, "Surely this great nation is a wise and understanding people." What other nation is so great as to have their gods near them the way the Lord our God is near us whenever we pray to him? And what other nation is so great as to have such righteous decrees and laws as this body of laws I am setting before you today? (Deuteronomy 4:5-8).

For Israel, obedience to the laws of God enabled them to possess the promised land. Today, obedience to the laws of God enables us to possess the life of victory and to appropriate the promises God has given us in His Word.

Then the Lord your God will make you most prosperous . . . if you obey the Lord your God and keep his commands and decrees that are written in this Book of the Law and turn to the Lord your God with all your heart and with all your soul (Deuteronomy 30:9-10).

Be strong and very courageous. Be careful to obey all the law my servant Moses gave you; do not turn from it to the right or to the left, that you may be successful wherever you go. Do not let this Book of the Law depart from your mouth; meditate on it day and night, so that you may be careful to do everything written in it. Then you will be prosperous and successful. Have I not commanded you? Be strong and courageous. Do not be terrified; do not be discouraged, for the Lord your God will be with you wherever you go (Joshua 1:7-9).

Observe what the Lord your God requires: Walk in his ways, and keep his decrees and commands, his laws and requirements, as written in the Law of Moses, so that you may prosper in all you do and wherever you go (1 Kings 2:3).

Observing the Will of God: Key to Blessing

Observing the will of God as revealed in His laws was the key to blessing in Old Testament times. It is the same today. Although the New Testament teaches that obedience to the law is not what saves us, nor can it save us, when we trust in Jesus and His Spirit for salvation, and we follow the moral commandments of the Bible with respect, we sense the holiness of God and we experience the power of God enabling us to do what we could not do and become what we could not become on our own. Lawrence Richard says,

When we read "Do not" or "Do" in Scripture, we praise God, for we see the kind of person He intends to help us become. And then, without even trying, we simply give ourselves, reaching out to love and to share.

How marvelous that in our loving—of God and others—we suddenly realize the truth. The requirements of the law are finding expression in our lives—not because we are trying to be good, but because the love of Jesus is working to transform us from within, and the Holy Spirit is prompting us to acts of love that fulfill every demand of law.[44] (Richards, 1985, 398)

When we live in this way, the words of our mouths and the meditations of our hearts become acceptable to God. They empower our lives, and they provide a powerful witness to others of the glory and radiance of God in our lives. This lifestyle becomes not a means to salvation, but a pathway to the blessings of God in our lives, as the writer of First Kings said, **"so that you may prosper in all you do and wherever you go"** (1 Kings 2:3b).

Dietrich Bonhoeffer, in *Life Together*, writes about the importance of meditating on the Word of God:

As there are definite hours in the Christian's day for the Word, particularly the time of common worship and prayer, so the day also needs definite times of silence, silence under the Word and

---

44　Richards, L. O. (1985). *Expository Dictionary of Bible Words. Grand Rapids, MI:* Zondervan.

silence that comes out of the Word. These will be especially the times before and after hearing the Word. The Word comes not to the chatterer but to him who holds his tongue. The stillness of the temple is the sign of the holy presence of God in His Word . . . Silence is the simple stillness of the individual under the Word of God . . . Silence is nothing else but waiting for God's Word and coming from God's Word with a blessing.[45] (Bonhoeffer, 1954, 79)

The Foundation of Our Spiritual Formation

The Word of God is the foundation of our spiritual formation. This is the reason it is so important for us to spend adequate time studying and meditating on the Word. David Watson comments on the days before his operation for the cancer that ultimately took his life:

As I spent time chewing over the endless assurances and promises to be found in the Bible, so my faith in the living God grew stronger and held me safe in his hands. God's word to us, especially his word spoken by his Spirit through the Bible, is the very ingredient that feeds our faith. If we feed our souls regularly on God's word, several times each day, we should become robust spiritually just as we feed on ordinary food several times each day and become robust physically. Nothing is more important than hearing and obeying the word of God.[46] (Watson, 1984, 39)

---

45   Bonhoeffer, D. (1954). *Life Together. New York, NY: Harper & Row Publishers, Inc.*

46   Watson, D. (1984). *Fear No Evil: A Personal Struggle with Cancer. London: Hodder and Stoughton.*

The Word of God is the soil from which our prayers should grow. Planted in the soil of the Word our lives grow and flourish according to God's plan. Eugene Peterson says that the reason our lives grow stagnant and stale and our prayers are ineffective and unproductive is that they have been uprooted from the soil of the Word of God. These so-called prayers are cut-flower words, arranged in little vases for table decorations. As long as they are artificially provided for with a container of water, they give a touch of beauty. But not for long: soon they drop and are discarded. Such flowers are often used as the centerpiece for a dinner table. They are lovely in these settings. But they are never mistaken for the real business of the table, the beef and potatoes that promise full bellies and calories for a hard day's work.[47]

Prayer Is Answering Speech

We usually think of prayer—speaking to God—as the starting point in our relationship with God, to get His attention, to ask His help, to seek His blessing, to find His comfort, or to enlist His guidance. But, says Peterson,

. . . prayer is answering speech. The first word is God's word. Prayer is a human word and is never the first word; never the primary, initiating and shaping word . . . In creation God has the first word. Genesis describes the work of creation **"in the beginning"** by means of speech: God said, "Let there be light;" and there was light. The word is repeated: **"God said . . . God said . . . God said . . ."** The word that God speaks originates, initiates, shapes,

---

47 Peterson, E. H. (1987). *Working the Angles. Grand Rapids, MI: Eerdmans*

provides, orders, commands, and blesses. God's Word is the creative means by which everything comes into existence.[48]

Everything outside us, everything inside us came into existence by the Word of God. When we hear God speaking to us through His Word, our response is to answer Him. The way we respond to God is through prayer.

Prayer is the language used to respond to the most that has been said to us, with the potential for saying all that is in us. Prayer is the development of speech into maturity, language in process of being adequate to answer the One who has spoken most comprehensively to us, namely, God . . . prayer is human answering speech to the addressing speech of God.[49]

Prayer That Can Change Lives, Empower Relationships, Heal Hurts, and Move Mountains

Thus, prayer that grows out of meditating on the living, powerful, transforming, eternal Word of God is prayer that can change lives, empower relationships, heal hurts, and move mountains. However, in our meditating on the Word, our focus must not be on our problems, needs, wishes, or requests, but on God: His glory, His honor, His will, His plans, and His desires. Richard Foster said, "We must center our attention on the Word alone and leave the consequences to its action."[50] However, we can be certain that as we "leave the consequences"—of our meditating on the Word and our prayers—to God, our needs will be met, our lives will be

---

48 Peterson
49 Peterson
50 Foster.

transformed, and our relationships will be made fresh and new. The Psalm writer understood this when he wrote,

By the word of the Lord were the heavens made, their starry host by the breath of his mouth. He gathers the waters of the sea into jars; he puts the deep into storehouses. Let all the earth fear the Lord; let all the people of the world revere him. For he spoke, and it came to be; he commanded, and it stood firm (Psalm 33:6-9).

Just as the Word of God enables the heavens to stand firm, so also meditating on the Word and praying in response to the Word will enable us to stand firm. It will bring a refreshing newness to our lives. Henri Nouwen writes about taking an early morning walk in the woods with Brother Elias, when

. . . nature was still waking up. The clouds were heavy, and the paths were covered with the colored leaves pulled from the branches by the heavy rain. "The Lord is so good, so good to me," Brother Elias said repeatedly. And then he spoke about the sun and the clouds, the rain and the winds, the wheat and the weeds, the heat and the cold, all as great gifts of the Lord given to bring Elias into a closer, more intimate contact with Him. "Isn't the rain beautiful?" he said. "Why do we keep resisting rain? Why do we only want the sun when we should be willing to be soaked by the rain? The Lord wants to soak us with His grace and love. Isn't it marvelous when we can feel the Lord in so many ways and get to know Him better and better! He lets us experience His presence even now in all that surrounds us. Imagine how it must be when we can see Him face to face!"[51]

---

51 Nouwen, H. J. (1976). *The Genesee Diary: Report from a Trappist Monastery*. Garden City, NY: Image Books, Doubleday & Co.

As we meditate on the Word of God, His grace and love refresh us and give us confidence that God is in control of even the impossible-seeming situations of our lives.

Nouwen talked with his spiritual director, John Eudes, about the fatigue which kept plaguing him every time he became involved with people. Eudes said that he should accept this condition by taking the necessary extra sleep, but he also made it clear that it was a psychosomatic situation. Nouwen said,

> I put too much energy into any encounter, as if I must prove each time anew that I am worth being with. "You put your whole identity at stake—and every time you start from scratch," John Eudes suggested. "Prayer and meditation are important here because in them you can find your deepest identity, and that keeps you from putting your whole self on the line every time you work with other people." He also told me that it is a proven fact that those who meditate regularly need less sleep. They are more at one with themselves and don't use others in their identity struggle.[52]

Meditating on the Word of God Can Bring Refreshment at the Core of Our Inner Persons

We can now see that meditating on the Word of God as He addresses us in all the situations, circumstances, relationships, and needs of our lives can bring refreshment at the core of our inner persons.

When Lawrence of Arabia took the Arabian chiefs to England, they were supposedly most impressed with the faucets of running water in the hotel bathrooms. When Lawrence was ready to leave the hotel to board the

---

52 Nouwen, H. J. (1976). *The Genesee Diary: Report from a Trappist Monastery.* Garden City, NY: Image Books, Doubleday & Co. 159.

train, the chiefs were not to be found in the lobby. He went back upstairs to look for them, and he found them in the bathrooms unscrewing the faucets to take them back to their homes in the arid deserts of Arabia. They thought that if they had the faucets, they would have an unending supply of water in the desert. What those Arabian chiefs did not realize was that the value of the faucets was in their connection to the source of water.

There are many people today whose lives are like empty water faucets in a desert. They are stagnant and stale. Their prayers are ineffective and unproductive because they are not connected to the source of refreshment, the Word of God. We should not just turn on the faucet. Rather we should be certain that it is connected to God through His Word. The water of life flows from the deep subterranean springs and rivers that are found in the soil of the Word. Then prayer becomes our encounter with God in the deserts of life. His Word provides the nourishment we need to be renewed, fresh, and alive!

Three Questions We Need to Ask Ourselves

When we discover ourselves in one of those "deserts of life," and we feel dry and empty on the inside, there are three questions we need to ask ourselves. Answering these questions will set us on the way to the adventure and refreshment of the abundant life:

1. Who is on the throne of your life?
2. What is the source of power in your life?
3. Who gets the glory from your life?[53]

---

53 Ogilvie, L. (Television message, February, 1988).

When the Lord Jesus is on the throne of our lives, His Word provides us with the inner resources we need to live victoriously. This glorifies Him and He makes us glorious and radiant. Paul confirms this when he says,

With this in mind, we constantly pray for you, that our God may count you worthy of his calling, and that by his power he may fulfill every good purpose of yours and every act prompted by your faith. We pray this so that the name of our Lord Jesus may be glorified in you, and you in him, according to the grace of our God and the Lord Jesus Christ. (2 Thessalonians 1:11-12)

Meditating on the Word of God Implants the Word in Our Inner Beings

Meditating on the Word of God implants the Word in our inner beings and empowers us to be worthy of the calling of God, and to glorify God in all we do.

When Sandie and I were leading conferences at a church camp in Alaska, Fred Mamaloff,[54] an Eskimo missionary, shared with us the way the Eskimos and Indians train their young boys to become successful hunters. This training also prepares them well for spiritual disciplines when they become Christians. Their story gives us some insights into the power of meditating on the Word.

The young Eskimo boys are trained to concentrate wholeheartedly on the specific work they are doing at a particular time. They are taught to give all their attention to every detail of what they are doing—not to allow their thoughts to wander to other things, or to be distracted by noises and activities going on around them. They are to use all their senses and give all their attention to one thing only—the job before them. They are to think about it, smell it, listen to it, feel it, see it, and be totally aware of it.

---

54   Mamaloff, Fred. Eskimo Missionary shared in a conference led by Sandie Bruce. Alaska Church of God Campmeeting. 1983.

This training makes them skilled craftsmen in the job they have been given to do. However, it also serves as training for the day when they become old enough to become hunters. They realize that their very lives depend on their ability to find and prepare the food they need for their families. They must be good hunters! Their lives depend on it.

Before a hunt they go through a ceremonial cleansing. They sit in a room with hot fires to cause them to perspire and clean out the pores in their skin. Then they wash their bodies thoroughly—absolutely clean of dirt or smells of the past few hours or days. Then they go to the top of a hill in the area where the hunt will take place, and they find a place to sit. For three days they sit there and look over the land and concentrate on the animal for which they are hunting. If they are going to hunt moose, they look out over the landscape before them for three days, and they think about and look for moose. They are literally meditating on moose—concentrating on the smell of a moose, the sounds a moose makes when eating or walking in the woods, the way a moose moves, the places a moose would go to eat or drink or rest, the size of a moose in comparison to themselves, the feel of a moose to the touch, how a moose tastes and satisfies their appetite, and what a moose sounds like when communicating with other moose. For three days they saturate themselves with the thoughts of moose until it becomes a reality to them.

Our Eskimo missionary friend said, "I can literally smell a moose 10 miles away, but I can't smell a pork chop burning in the kitchen!" Once they have spent this extensive time meditating, then they move out to make their disciplined thoughts become a reality. They go out and get the moose!

Visualize our time in the Word in the light of this story. We can rush through our daily lives with the busyness that dictates our schedules and grab a few precious minutes here and there to talk with God and read His Word, and that can be somewhat beneficial—at least superficially. But consider what could happen in our lives if we would develop this capacity to meditate on the Word of God like the Eskimo hunter concentrates on the moose. The Word would become the sustaining food for our inner beings.

Think of what could happen if we would pull away from our busyness (daily for a period of time, and occasionally for an extended time) and offer ourselves to God's Spirit, asking for His cleansing blood to clear the channels of our minds and spirits from all the clutter. What if we confess our sins, give God our shortcomings and failures, and turn all our problems and strengths over to Him. What if we cleanse ourselves, not carrying into our meditation time any clutter from the past hours, days, or years. Then, as we begin to meditate reflectively on the Word of God, He begins to shape our prayers and our entire lives as we allow Him. I offer the following excerpt from my Journal as an example of meditating on the Word and praying in response.

PRAYER RESPONSE

"Give ear to my words, O Lord, consider my sighing. Listen to my cry for help, my King and my God, for to you I pray" (Psalm 5:1-2).

O my Lord,
    You know that for several months now,
        I have been sighing—
        and crying
    praying to You for
    direction,
    help,

encouragement,

stamina,

rest.

By faith,

I knew You were there for me.

I knew You were concerned about me.

I knew You were listening to me.

I knew You were preparing me.

But somehow, I didn't seem to be connecting:

    I grew tired

    and stale.

    I felt empty

    and weak.

    I was struggling

    and hurting.

Yet, all along, You were there— "JEHOVAH-SHEMMAH"

    working,

    shaping,

    refining,

    purifying,

    helping,

    strengthening.

"But I, by your great mercy, will come into your house; in reverence will I bow down toward your holy temple. Lead me, O Lord, in your righteousness because of my enemies—make straight your way before me" *(Psalm 5:7-8).*

    I have prayed—

        You have heard.

    I have asked—

You have given.

You are faithful—

I am renewed!

"But let all who take refuge in you be glad; let them ever sing for joy. Spread your protection over them, that those who love your name may rejoice in you" *(Psalm 5:11).*

Thank You, Lord, for

new joy in my spirit,

song of victory in my heart,

fresh confidence in Your faithfulness,

renewed vision for my ministry.

"Morning by morning, O Lord, you hear my voice; morning by morning I lay my requests before you and wait in expectation" *(Psalm 5:3).*

My covenant with You, my Lord:

To be faithful

in studying and memorizing Your Word,

in prayer,

in leading the people to whom I minister to become

people of prayer and people of the Word.

Enable me, Lord, to be consistent in this—

morning by morning,

day by day,

moment by moment.

"Lead me, O Lord, in your righteousness" *(Psalm 5:8a).*

Anoint me with Your Spirit

Fill me with Your love.

Endow me with Your resources.

Enable me with Your presence.

"For surely, O Lord, you bless the righteous,
You surround them with your favor as a shield" *(Psalm 5:12).*
Lord,

I need Your blessing.

I need Your help.

I need Your enabling power to be faithful in my walk with You.

I need Your protection from the enemies of my soul that would draw me away from You.

I wait before You, my Lord,

in expectant faith,

believing You for Your best for my life.

    I love you,

      my King and my God!

Lord, I want You to reign on the throne of my life. I have no power except that which You give me. I am committed to living my life in a way that glorifies You. Help me, as I meditate on Your powerful, life-changing Word to grow, develop, and mature in my relationship with You—to become the person You want me to be. Speak to me through Your Word and enable me to respond in joyful obedience and with wholehearted devotion to You. Amen.

Chapter 7

Spiritual Formation in Children

One of the most special services for me as a pastor was the dedication service for little children and their parents. The dedication service should be an early part of the spiritual formation of children, as the parents dedicate their children back to the Lord, and as they commit themselves to rearing them in an atmosphere of spiritual formation and worship.

Raising children is a challenge. By the time you learn what to do, you have finished. Bill Cosby said, "Now that I have five children, my only hope is that they are all out of the house before I die."

Shaping the lives of children, not just surviving them, is our task as parents and church leaders. How are we to do this? By instruction and example, in a context of love, reinforced by consistent discipline. Pastors, Sunday school teachers, and other Christian leaders also share an important role in helping shape the inner lives of the precious children entrusted to their ministries. The foundation for shaping their lives is found in teaching and modeling the Word of God.

Too often parents are busy giving *things* to their children when they should be giving *themselves* and the *Word* of God. It is true that children need to experience love. Then they will respond positively to the instruction and example of their parents. Parental commitments and expectations must be clearly and consistently communicated both orally and behaviorally. Children quickly detect major discrepancies between what we say and what we do.

In biblical times, the spiritual formation of children began while they were just babies – teaching them the Word of God from the beginning of their lives. It is important to begin as soon as possible. One of the tragic, naive mistakes made by many parents and churches is the postponement of instruction in the Word and discipline until the child is older. But it is better to be lovingly firm and consistent while children are young; then as they grow older and seek adult identities, parents may loosen up, gradually allowing them to make their own decisions and mistakes, developing self-discipline as they move toward mature adulthood. For, even at the age of one, two, or three, children are already beginning to form habit patterns and the way they visualize life, God, relationships, and responsibilities. One of the best ways to build healthy parent-child relationships, as well as healthy self-esteem, is to praise the accomplishments and virtues of your children. Give them helpful, consistent, positive discipline. Stand by them in love and give support and encouragement even when they fail or hurt. Above all, teach them the Word of God and pray daily for them. Eventually, God will accomplish His way in their lives. **"The living and enduring Word of God"** instructs us: **"Train up a child in the way he should go, and when he is old he will not turn from it"** (Proverbs 22:6).

This training needs to begin while they are young — the younger, the better! In our churches we must be committed to helping parents and children cope with the many problems and pressures they face in the growing-up process, beginning the experiences of spiritual formation at an early age. Family Builders Classes and other Bible studies can give guidance and encouragement to parents in child rearing; graded Sunday School and Wednesday Celebration classes should start children learning about God – His Word, His love and His plan for their lives – when they are just toddlers. Part of the consistent training and teaching of children must begin by making certain they are in these classes on a regular basis, beginning when they are infants and continuing as they grow and mature. It is important that parents set a good example by being consistent in attending worship and Bible studies, as well as reading Bible stories in the home.

The Psalm writer said,

"...I will utter things hidden from of old -- things we have heard and known, things our fathers have told us. We will not hide them from their children; we will tell the next generation the praiseworthy deeds of the Lord, his power and the wonders he has done. He decreed statutes . . . and established the law . . . which he commanded our forefathers to teach their children, so the next generation would know them, even the children yet to be born, and they in turn would tell their children. Then they would put their trust in God and would not forget his deeds, but would keep his commands" (Psalm 78:3-7).

Here is an important pattern: begin children's spiritual formation in the Word while they are young, teaching them the truths of the Word of God and His love for them. This gives them a solid foundation on which to build their lives throughout time and eternity.

I Just Love Hugs!

In our Vacation Bible School one summer, the teachers gave out play money to the children for such things as attendance, bringing their Bibles, bringing a friend, memorizing their Bible verses, and so forth. The money could be spent in the VBS store to "purchase" various toys and games.

One little boy – William – said to his teacher Janet, "If I say my Bible verse twice, can I be paid twice?"

The teacher replied, "No, I'm sorry, you can only be paid once for each verse."

William then asked, "Well, can I say it for fun?"

The teacher said, "Sure!"

So, he quoted his verse, "Love is patient, love is kind. First Corinthians 13:4a."

The teacher, deeply touched, said, "That deserves a big hug," and she leaned over and gave him one.

A few minutes later, William inquired, "If I say yesterday's memory verse, may I have another hug?"

"You sure may," she responded with a smile.

"If I give all I possess to the poor and I have not love, I have gained nothing. First Corinthians 13:3," he quoted proudly.

She gave him another hug.

Now the kid's on a roll: "If I say Tuesday's verse, can I get another hug?"

"Sure can!"

"If I speak in the tongues of men and of angels, but have not love, I am only a resounding gong or a clanging cymbal. First Corinthians 13:1."

Hug number three.

As the little guy backed away, and their eyes met, he responded, "I just love hugs!"

And is not that what kids (of all ages) need most: hugs. Physical, verbal, emotional hugs. Words and actions that say, "I really love you and care about you. You are very special to me!" That is spiritual formation at its finest!

That kind of love needs to come from parents, family members, and friends as well as from people in the church who will care enough to say, "I am willing to risk a little to reach out and touch the lives of others, to give myself, my love, my time, and my resources to help our children know the love of God our Father and His Son Jesus."

Does Christian Education Pay?

Someone may ask, "Does Christian education pay?" Consider the following true story. I do not know where I first heard this story (Unknown), but it has a powerful challenge to families and churches today.

A family in the state of New York, the Jukes, never attended Sunday school, either as children or adults. There was no Christian education at all in their family.

A study of the 1900 descendants of the Juke family revealed that they cost the State of New York nearly three million dollars due to crime, immorality, poverty, disease, depravity, suicide, and deportation. They spent a combination of 1300 years behind bars. They were known to be: 771 criminals, 250 arrested for various offenses, 60 thieves, 39 convicted murderers, and 50 women with venereal disease.

On the other hand, look at the Jonathan Edwards family. Edwards was the famous New England revival preacher who became President of Princeton University. This family attended Sunday school and worship regularly.

The 1400 descendants of the Edwards family cost the State not one cent in law and order. None spent time in jail or in the poorhouse. There were 13 college presidents, 65 university professors, 100 lawyers, one dean of a law school, 30 judges, 56 physicians, three mayors of large cities, three United States Senators, three governors, one Vice-president of the United States, 100 missionaries, 600 preachers of the gospel, 80 holders of public office, and one United States controller.

That is an excellent example of a godly heritage – evidence of principles of spiritual formation in the Word of God begun in children and continuing in adulthood – one that should be emulated in all our homes and churches.

Spiritual Formation Models and Teachers Needed

We need people who will volunteer to teach, to be teachers' helpers, to provide transportation, to supply refreshments and fun activities, to give financially — to say, "Lord, wherever and however you want to use me in ministry, I am available. I am willing to be what You want me to be and to do what You want me to do. As You enable me, I will serve in whatever capacity of ministry You give me. I am Yours to command."

It is important that we do everything we possibly can to reach our children (and youth, too!) — in their tender age, while they can be taught and shaped into the likeness of Christ. We need to give our best — as a church, as parents, and simply as obedient Christians who care deeply — to ensure that our children and youth receive the love, care, encouragement, help, guidance, and instruction they need in order to become the people God created them to be. May the Lord enable us to "teach the children" so they will not forget what God has done and what He wants to do in their lives. Spiritual formation like this that is begun early in life will build a strong foundation for the church for future generations.

Blessing for Little Children

Little child, for you Jesus Christ has come; He has fought, He has suffered. For you He entered the shadow of Gethsemane and the terror of Calvary. For you He uttered the cry "It is finished!" For you He rose from the dead and ascended into heaven. And there for you He intercedes. For you little child, even though you do not know it. But in this way the Word of the Gospel becomes true, "We love Him because he first loved us." [55]

An Extra Special Story for Kids of All Ages

George and Ann Schmidt were faithful members of the congregation I pastored in California. During their college days, Ann was stricken with polio and had to spend some time in an iron lung. Although she did have some physical limitations following her encounter with polio, she reared a lovely daughter who is today an outstanding minister of music and worship. She was able to work successfully in a highly responsible job for many years. She was involved in various ministries across the years. She was a wonderful, supportive, inspiring Christian lady who lived her life with a strong faith and confidence in the Word of God. A couple of years before she died, after I had preached a message on the Twenty-Third Psalm, Ann said to me as she gave me a hug, with tears in her eyes, "Sam, that Psalm was what got me through the iron lung!"

Ann's testimony – she had learned Psalm 23 as a child – is a good indication that the Word is a powerful foundation for our spiritual formation, and especially for our children. Apart from it, there can be no spiritual formation, and there is no effective underpinning for a fulfilling life.

---

55 Unknown author.

PRAYER RESPONSE

Lord God give us the people who will catch Your vision of children's ministry. Enable us to so shape these little ones of Yours so that when they grow into adulthood, they will not depart from You and Your Word. Give us persons who will be good examples for them to follow in learning how to walk with You. Give us people of faith and faithfulness, gifted people who will love the children and teach them the life-changing principles of Your Word. Give us dynamic Christian parents, who will build godly homes that are set solidly on the foundation of our Lord Jesus Christ and Your Word. Raise up ministers, missionaries," and other Christian workers from this generation of children who will become the leaders of the future to keep passing along the Good News to future generations. Help us to be faithful in our children's ministries and youth ministries. In the Name of our Lord Jesus, I pray. Amen.

Chapter 8

Memorizing the Word of God and Spiritual Formation

Dr. Sam Says . . .

Always listen to the small voice of God

One of the most life-transforming disciplines that I have discovered in spiritual formation is the discipline of memorizing Scripture. Although I have found very little writing about Scripture memorization, I have learned from personal experience that it is extremely helpful in shaping the inner person. The Psalm writer understood the value of memorized Scripture when he said, **"My heart is stirred by a noble theme as I recite my verses for the King; my tongue is the pen of a skillful writer"** (Psalm 45:1). This verse gives me great encouragement and confirmation in my pursuit of Scripture memorization. My heart is always stirred when I am quoting portions of the **"living and enduring Word of God"** (1 Peter 1:23b). The Word of God is filled with noble themes. Whether it is the theme of salvation by grace, atonement, reconciliation, sanctification, holy living, spiritual formation, worship, giving, creation, new creation, eternal life, forgiveness of sins, Christian living . . . it is always a magnificent feast at the table of God.

How to Memorize the Word

Often when I quote a book of the Bible, like Colossians or Ephesians, from memory in a worship service, a college class, or a conference, people will say something like, Wow! You really are gifted with a great memory. I wish I could do that. I do not have a photographic memory. All my Scripture memory is done through two avenues: discipline and hard work. It is difficult and time-consuming work that demands tenacious discipline. I believe that anyone can memorize large portions, if not entire books of the Bible, if they will commit themselves to discipline and work, and make it a high priority in their agenda. I know that there are many books and programs that can be purchased that give ideas, ways, and means of memorizing any and every kind of material. Any good bookstore will likely have some of these kinds of books. I will briefly describe here what works for me, my usual practice in memorizing Scripture.

When I am planning to memorize a book of the Bible, such as James or 1 Timothy, or a passage like the Sermon on the Mount, I begin by reading through that entire book one or two times a day for a couple of weeks. I read aloud, saying all the chapter and verse numbers and the paragraph headings. This helps me picture the location of the verses on the pages of the Bible, and to remember the various subjects covered in the passage. Next, I select the first paragraph of five to seven verses and read those aloud several times during the day.

The last thing I do before going to sleep that night is read that paragraph aloud several times. The next morning, I read through the first verse several times. Then I quote as much of that verse as possible, looking back and forth at the Bible, until I can comfortably quote it several times without looking. Then I move to the second verse and do the same thing. When I have that verse, I go back and quote verses one and two together several times. I keep moving through the verses in this way until I have the whole paragraph.

Throughout the day, when I am driving to appointments, sitting in a hospital waiting room, or a receptionist's office, I keep a copy of the passage handy as I continue to review it. That night I begin reading the next paragraph just before going to bed, and the next morning I start the process all over again. Throughout that day I quote that paragraph along with the one from the day before. I continue this process for four to six weeks until the whole book is ingrained into my memory bank. Now perhaps you understand better why I said earlier that the process of Scripture memory is not some mystical gift, or a super mind; it is simply discipline and work, and I might add, priorities. Anyone can memorize more Scripture if he or she decides to do so. It is hard work. It takes a commitment of time and effort, but it is worth it to me when I view the changes it has made in my own life and in the lives of the persons to whom I have ministered through the memorized Word.

When I am jogging, driving on trips or around town, or sitting in waiting rooms, I use the time to quote through all the passages I have memorized to keep them fresh and useful. When I am in a public place, I quote silently to avoid disturbing others, or having them think I am talking to myself. If I do not do this consistently, I will lose much of the word-for-word memory work. This practice transforms the time spent jogging, driving, and waiting. I know now how the Apostle John felt when he said,

I, John, your brother and companion in the suffering and kingdom and patient endurance that are ours in Jesus, was on the island of Patmos because of the word of God and the testimony of Jesus. On the Lord's Day I was in the Spirit (Revelation 1:9-10).

John was exiled on the Island of Patmos, away from family and friends and the comforts of home, but he said also, **"I was in the Spirit."** It did not matter where he was, or what his circumstances were, he was in an attitude of worship on the Lord's Day. While he was in that intimate relationship of worship, God pulled back the curtain of eternity so that John could get a glimpse of the grand worship service that is going on perpetually in heaven around the throne of God. Our worship and spiritual formation in this life are a foretaste of the magnificent worship in which we will be involved in eternity. John's journal entries became what we now know as The Revelation of Jesus Christ. I, too, have often been immensely blessed, sometimes painfully convicted, in the strangest of places and the most unusual circumstances, as I was silently quoting some passage of the Word. Such joys are reserved for those who are willing to discipline themselves to do the work and arrange their priorities to memorize the life-changing, situation-rearranging, marriage-mending, church-transforming Word of God.

Memorizing Scripture Renews Our Minds

As I memorize the Word – saturating my spirit, mind, soul, imagination, faith, relationships – I sense change at a deep level in my inner being. When I quote in public worship portions of the Word, which now come from God through me to my listeners, it is as though we have stepped into the Throne Room, the very presence of our Father God Himself. There we have precious communion together as Spirit meets with spirit. As the words from the Word come streaming from my mouth, my tongue becomes **"the pen of a skillful writer,"** not because of who I am, but because of Whose Word I am quoting. The writer is the Holy Spirit, who first breathed the

Word of God into the hearts of faithful men who **"spoke from God as they were carried along by the Holy Spirit"** (2 Peter 1:21).

When I read a passage out of a book, I may or may not remember what it said, and therefore it may or may not affect my thoughts and actions. However, when the Word inhabits my inner being, it is like loading it into a computer. I have a computer Bible program, *The WORDsearch*. When I do a search for a particular word or phrase, the verses in which it is found come up on the screen. As I move from verse to verse, the word or phrase is highlighted, and it flashes on-and-off to make it easy to view. Similarly, the Holy Spirit has access to all the portions of the Word that reside in my mind, and He can call up to my conscious thinking those portions that He wants me to consider. While I might ignore something, I read in a book, it is difficult to ignore a portion of Scripture when the Holy Spirit highlights it right there inside my mind. Thus, as I incorporate the Word into my inner being through memorization,[56] and then through continuous quotation, live in it and live by it, my spirit is more vigorously sensitized to hearing God's voice, realizing God's presence, being shaped according to God's perfect pattern, and appropriating God's resources for my life and for the lives of the persons to whom I minister. I have discovered that when the Word is resident in my mind, spirit, and emotions, it affects my lifestyle in much deeper and more profound ways than simply reading it from the written page.

Paul accents the importance of Scripture memory when he writes, "Therefore, I urge you, brothers, in view of God's mercy, to offer your bodies as living sacrifices, holy and pleasing to God – this is your spiritual act of worship. Do not conform any longer to the pattern of this world,

---

56 To date I have memorized the following Scripture passages: Ephesians, Philippians, Colossians, 1 Thessalonians, 2 Thessalonians, 1 Timothy, 2 Timothy, James, 1 Peter, 2 Peter, 1 John, Romans 5, the Sermon on the Mount, in Matthew 5-7, and over 200 random verses and passages throughout the Old and New Testaments.

but be transformed by the renewing of your mind. Then you will be able to test and approve what God's will is his good, pleasing and perfect will" (Romans 12:1-2).

Saturating our minds with the Word of God through Scripture memorization is the path toward renewal of our minds, and thus toward the transformation of our entire lives. Paul said to the Colossian Christians, "Let the word of Christ dwell in you richly" (Colossians 3:16). As we memorize the Scripture, allowing it to "dwell in us," it will begin to come alive in us in a fresh new way. From our interior world it will begin to shape us, mold us, motivate us, and empower us. The key is for us to let it dwell in us "richly," lavishly, so as to absolutely engulf us with its power and life, for it is "the living and enduring word of God" (1 Peter 1:23). When we allow the Word to dwell in us richly, we can pray the following prayer:

PRAYER RESPONSE

Lord, please use the Word I have planted in my heart to revolutionize my relationship with You, refresh my mind, rejuvenate my body, revive my spirit, reorder my priorities, renew my relationships with other persons, and reorganize my whole life around Your plan for me. Let Your Word dwell in me richly. Amen.

Memorizing Scripture
Reconstructs the Way We Think

Although Paul does not specifically mention Scripture memory in these verses, he mentions being **"transformed by the renewing of your mind."** Implanting significant Scripture portions in our minds through memorization is the best way to transform our minds and our thought patterns, thus reconstructing the way we think. From infancy and throughout our lives we are constantly exposed to the thought patterns of the world, and those thought patterns are radically different from the thought patterns of God and His Word. The Apostle John, speaking of the spirit of antichrist which permeates the world system of thinking, says, **"They are from the world and therefore speak from the viewpoint of the world, and the world listens to them"** (1 John 4:5). Much of our culture and thought patterns have been shaped by this viewpoint of the world. By contrast, John describes the children of God, saying, **"You, dear children, are from God and have overcome them, because the one who is in you is greater than the one who is in the world"** (1 John 4:4).

Paul said, **"So from now on we regard no one from a worldly point of view. Though we once regarded Christ in this way, we do so no longer. Therefore, if anyone is in Christ, he is a new creation; the old has gone, the new has come!"** (2 Corinthians 5:16-17). In Christ, our way of thinking is reconstructed. We no longer consider decisions, people, and desires from a worldly point of view. We are new creations; the old has gone, the new has come! Thus, we begin to think God's thoughts, to follow God's plans, to want God's desires, and to do God's will.

The Psalm writer understood this when he wrote, **"How can a young man keep his way pure? By living according to your word. I seek you with all my heart; do not let me stray from your commands. I have hidden your word in my heart that I might not sin against you"** (Psalm 119:9-11). Memorizing Scripture is an effective way to hide the Word, or to lay up the Word in our hearts, as Eugene Peterson translates this verse, **"I have laid up thy word in my heart that I might not sin against thee."** Then he comments, "The heart well-stocked with God's word is like a well-armed arsenal. Confident in the strength of its weaponry, it is fearless in the face of attacks from without or insurrection from within."[57] Peterson quotes from Edwin Hodder's *Thy Word Is Like a Garden, Lord*: "Thy Word is like an armory, where soldiers may repair, and find for life's long battle day, all needful weapons there. O may I find my armor there: Thy Word my trusty sword, I'll learn to fight with every foe the battle of the Lord."[58] Memorizing scripture reconstructs the way we think.

Memorizing Scripture Rebuilds the Way We Make Decisions

The spiritual discipline of hiding – laying up, memorizing – the Word in our hearts renews our minds and reconstructs the way we think, thus enabling us to no longer be conformed to the thinking patterns of the world system. It also rebuilds the way we make decisions. Paul said that the transformation of our minds would empower us to test and approve what God's will is – His good, pleasing and perfect will (Romans 12:2). Knowing God's will helps us make decisions based on His infinite knowledge and wisdom rather than on our finite information and intelligence. When our minds are saturated with Scripture, we can view our decisions in the light of God's pattern rather than the plans of the world system which has dominated most of our thinking in the past. Life is filled with opportunities and problems, avenues and obstacles, decisions and hesitations. According to M. Scott Peck, discipline is the basic set of tools we require to solve life's problems,[59] and I might add, to fulfill opportunities, follow the right avenues, overcome obstacles, make the right decisions, and disarm our hesitations. Scott Peck, describing discipline as *The Road Less Traveled*,

---

57 Peterson, E. H. (1979). *A Year with the Psalms. Waco, TX: Word Books.*
58 Peterson.
59 Peck, M. S. (1978). *The Road Less Traveled. New York, NY: Simon & Schuster.* 15.

declares, "Without discipline we can solve nothing. With only some discipline we can solve only some problems. With total discipline we can solve all problems."[60]

The spiritual discipline of Scripture memory arms us with a more than adequate arsenal with which to make decisions according to God's plan. After I had quoted several books and passages of Scripture, over a period of a couple of years, one of the young men in our California congregation made a remark in a testimony one evening regarding his appreciation for the discipline of Scripture memory. He said something like, well, when you have a pastor who is a walking Bible . . .! He was referring to some counsel I had given him, using memorized Scripture. This is a biblical principle: God desires to incarnate His word in our lives. Paul elucidated this concept when he wrote to the Corinthian Christians,

> **"You yourselves are our letter, written on our hearts, known and read by everybody. You show that you are a letter from Christ, the result of our ministry, written not with ink but with the Spirit of the living God, not on tablets of stone but on tablets of human hearts. Such confidence as this is ours through Christ before God. Not that we are competent in ourselves to claim anything for ourselves, but our competence comes from God"**
> (2 Corinthians 3:2-4).

Recording significant portions of Scripture on the tablets of our hearts fashions us into living letters of love, wisdom, understanding, comfort, and help in making right decisions, to assist people who are searching for answers to life's problems, hesitations, frustrations, obstacles, and questions. As letters from Christ, then, we do not rely on our competence or

---

60   Peck. 15-16.

wisdom in making decisions, but our competence comes from God! That is what the world system is lacking, and that is the reason why so many people's lives are empty, inconsistent, and unfulfilled.

When we memorize Scripture, we are engrafting the Word of the eternal, Almighty God Himself into our minds. Jesus said, **"I am the vine; you are the branches. If a man remains in me and I in him, he will bear much fruit; apart from me you can do nothing. If you remain in me and my words remain in you, ask whatever you wish, and it will be given you"** (John 15:5, 7). When branches are grafted into a vine, they bear the fruit of the vine, and when we plant the Word in our hearts, our lives will bear the fruit of God's righteousness, holiness, wisdom, and knowledge. James said, **"Therefore, get rid of all moral filth and the evil that is so prevalent and humbly accept the word planted in you, which can save you"** (James 1:21).

The spiritual discipline of hiding – laying up, memorizing – the Word in our hearts renews our minds and reconstructs the way we think, thus enabling us to no longer be conformed to the thinking patterns of the world system. It rebuilds the way we make decisions, and it redirects our emotions.

Memorizing Scripture Redirects Our Emotions

God created us as emotional beings. However, when we simply follow our human emotions rather than our Scripture-saturated hearts, we leave ourselves open to feelings of discouragement, frustration, anger, impossibility, depression, indecision, and defeat. Sometimes our emotions come in the form of irritations, disappointments, and heartaches. Saturating our minds with Scripture can affect our responses to these and all other emotions. The Holy Scriptures gives us God's perspective on such feelings. That is why we need to always take them with us, day and night. As we memorize them, they take up around-the-clock residence within us, and in so doing the Scriptures present us with God's outlook on feelings and the circumstances and people that affect them. The Psalm writer must have understood this when he said of the person who is truly blessed, **"His delight is in the law of the Lord, and on his law he meditates day and night. He is like a tree planted by streams of water, which yields its fruit in season and whose leaf does not wither. Whatever he does prospers"** (Psalm 1:2-3). The Psalm writer's personal experience is expressed in these words: **"Oh, how I love your law! I meditate on it all day long"** (Psalm 119:97). The difficult, sometimes long nights of the soul can be faced in this way: **"My eyes stay open through the watches of the night, that I may meditate on your promises"** (Psalm 119:48).

I heard about a family that was facing persecution for their Christian faith, and who hid their Bible in a pie, to avoid having the Bible stolen and their being thrown in jail for having it. I have read many stories of people having their Bibles confiscated and destroyed when communism and other godless religions were in control. Such incidents are tragic because when such persons turn out the lights at night, or when we are away from our Bibles, the Word of God is, in a sense, taken away from us. However, when we hide the Word in our hearts through memorization, we can meditate on it day and night, even during the long watches of the dark nights of the soul. Then we can understand the Psalm writer's joy as he said,

"Then I thought, to this I will appeal: the years of the right hand of the Most High. I will remember the deeds of the Lord; yes, I will remember your miracles of long ago. I will meditate

on all your works and consider all your mighty deeds. Your ways, O God, are holy. What god is so great as our God? You are the God who performs miracles; you display your power among the peoples. With your mighty arm you redeemed your people" (Psalm 77:10-15).

Remembering the mighty deeds, works, miracles, and power of the Lord displayed on behalf of His people in the past gives us the confidence to know that He will act on our behalf in the present as well as in the future. Realizing this provides us with the certainty that enables us to redirect our emotions from fear to assurance, from insecurity to trust, from doubt to faith, from inadequacy to superabundance, from inferiority to healthy self-esteem.

As I was thinking of the power of the Word to redirect our emotions, I remembered the night my daughter Janette was having a personal struggle. She began praying for God to give her some guidance and direction. She asked Him to give her a verse of Scripture as a promise for that situation. Remembering that Sandie and I have said many times that when you are troubled, read the Psalms as a source of encouragement and guidance, she turned to them. As she began reading, she found this verse: **"And in righteousness I will see your face; when I awake, I will be satisfied with seeing your likeness"** (Psalm 17:15). Those words spoke comfort and encouragement to her spirit, and she prayed, "God, help me to be able to go to sleep tonight, and in the morning, I will awaken and be satisfied with your likeness. God heard and answered her prayer. She went to sleep in confidence that God was in control of the situation that was troubling her."[61] The next morning, she awakened with a sense of peace and satisfaction. Memorizing Scripture renews our minds, reconstructs the way we think, rebuilds the way we make decisions, redirects our emotions, and readjusts our desires.

---

61   Bruce-Bock, Janette. Her Journal. 1985.

PRAYER RESPONSE

Thank You, Lord, for helping us to demonstrate the importance of Your Word to our children. Help them always depend on the truth and instruction of Your Word and Your presence in their lives. Enable them to continue to build their lives on the foundation of your living and enduring Word. Amen.

Memorizing Scripture Readjusts Our Desires

Memorizing Scripture can readjust our desires because it fills our minds with God's Word which helps us face and conquer temptations to sin and to be less than our best, as God created us to be. Our Lord Jesus Christ is the prime example of this concept. When He went on a forty day and night spiritual retreat in the desert, and Satan came tempting Him to pull Him away from His mission, He responded to each temptation with a quotation from Scripture. He repeatedly responded to Satan, **"It is written . . . it is written . . ."** (Matthew 4:1-11). There is no temptation, emotion, desire, decision, relationship, habit, reaction, attitude, activity, or involvement known to humankind that does not have a stated principle in Scripture to give directions for how to respond and behave according to God's plan.

The writer of the Psalms was said to be a man after God's own heart. When we read through the Psalms, we discover that the writer was a man of many emotions and feelings. Time after time, he opens those emotions and feelings up to the close scrutiny of God Almighty, and as he does, he discovers God's resources to face and conquer them. Paul says we should **"offer our bodies"** as well as our emotions, spirits, and desires **"as living sacrifices, holy and pleasing to God."** This is our spiritual act of worship.

Speaking of Jesus Christ, Paul said, **"God placed all things under his feet and appointed him to be head over everything for the church, which is his body, the fullness of him who fills everything in every way"** (Ephesians 1:19-23). Paul is describing Kingdom authority here. When we are in Christ, we are partakers of His divine rule and authority. This means that we do not have to yield to temptation, to Satan's intimidating attacks, to selfish indulgence, to negative attitudes, or to failure to be all God created us to be. In Christ, and especially as we live in His Word and by His Word which resides within us as we memorize it, we can appropriate God's victorious authority over every circumstance, obstacle, relationship, or situation, including Satan's attempts to discourage or distract us. Christ is the head over everything for the church, which includes us, for in Christ we are part of His Church. His limitless resources are available to give us His mastery over everything that Satan might throw at us. When Christ fills us with His fullness, He begins to cleanse and purify us from those things that keep us from being the persons He created us to be. He shapes us into vessels He can use to accomplish His purposes in the world in which we live.

For this reason, we need to **"keep asking that the God of our Lord Jesus Christ, the glorious Father may give [us] the Spirit of wisdom and revelation, so that [we] may know him better"** (Ephesians 1:17). Leslie Brandt paraphrased that verse: **"May the Spirit of God break through the numbness of our small thinking and reveal to us something of who we are and what we have become through Christ."**[62]

Realizing **who we are and what we have become through Christ** encourages us to keep growing in our relationship with Him, to be faithful in following His plan for our lives. This also challenges us to abandon those attitudes, motives, activities, temptations, and relationships which

---

62 Brandt, L. F. (1976). *Epistles/Now. St. Louis, MO: Concordia.*

build barriers between us and Him. God's **incomparably great power** and **fullness** are accomplishing this in our lives. In fact, Peter said:

> His divine power has given us everything we need for life and godliness through our knowledge of him who called us by his own glory and goodness. Through these He has given us his very great and precious promises, so that through them we may participate in the divine nature and escape the corruption in the world caused by evil desires (2 Peter 1:3-4).

In this way God is nurturing our spiritual formation which, in my definition, **"forming our inner lives and relationships with Him in a way that transforms our outer lives and relationships with other persons."** As we immerse ourselves in His Word through Scripture memorization, He is renewing our minds, reconstructing the way we think, rebuilding the way we make decisions, redirecting our emotions, and readjusting our desires. He is also replenishing our inner beings.

Memorizing Scripture Replenishes Our Inner Beings

Jesus illustrated this principle in a story He told in the twelfth chapter of Matthew:

> When an evil spirit comes out of a man, it goes through arid places seeking rest and does not find it. Then it says, I will return to the house I left. When it arrives, it finds the house unoccupied, swept clean and put in order. Then it goes and

takes with it seven other spirits more wicked than itself, and they go in and live there. And the final condition of that man is worse than the first. That is how it will be with this wicked generation (Matthew 12:43-45).

We need to take charge of what we allow to come into our minds. The man Jesus talked about cleaned the house and put things in order but left it unoccupied. There was no one there to keep out the wicked spirits. Unless we fill our minds, which have been cleansed in our salvation experience, with the sharp and powerful Word of God, we will have little or no defense against the thought patterns of the world system which are always pressing in against us. On the other hand, when our minds are drenched in the Word of God, the memorized Scripture edges out those renegade ideas, impure thoughts, negative feelings, unholy desires, ungodly morals, unhealthy actions, wrong motives, and misaligned priorities.

Paul tells us to **"take the helmet of salvation and the sword of the Spirit, which is the word of God"** (Ephesians 6:17). The writer of Hebrews says, **"The word of God is living and active. Sharper than any double-edged sword, it penetrates even to dividing soul and spirit, joints and marrow; it judges the thoughts and attitudes of the heart"** (Hebrews 4:12). When those negative, binding, unwholesome spirits see that sharp sword at work in our lives, guarding our spirits, emotions, minds, hearts, and relationships, they decide to go and find an easier place to inhabit. The Word drives them out and keeps them out! This allows us, as the U. S. Army slogan says, to *be all that we can be* in the army of the King of kings and Lord of lords.

As we immerse ourselves in His Word through Scripture memorization, God is renewing our minds by replenishing our inner beings. This is the best way to avoid the possibility of a spiritual collapse.

PRAYER RESPONSE

O Lord communicate to me, and through me, Your Words of Life, so that I may hear and be changed at a very deep level in my inner being; so that I may be sculptured by Your competent and creative hand. As I immerse myself in Your Word through Scripture memorization, renew my mind by reconstructing the way I think, rebuilding the way I make decisions, redirecting my emotions, readjusting my desires, and replenishing my inner being. Then communicate through me Your eternal Words of Life to the people You entrust to my care, teaching, and ministry. May I be faithful to the Word planted in [me] which can save [me]. [63] *Enable me to plant it in the hearts of others in a powerful, life-transforming way that will renew and refresh them, as well as give them abundant and eternal life. Shape me into a person of the Word. Thank You, my Lord, for Your Word. Amen.*

---

63   James 1:21

PART 3

FORMING
PEOPLE OF PRAYER

Chapter 9

Prayer: Releasing the Power of the Word

Dr. Sam Says . . .

While the Word of God is the foundation for our spiritual formation, prayer is the key to releasing the power of the Word to transform our lives and to focus on our requests and the needs of others. The Word of God is the soil from which our prayers should grow. Planted in the soil of the Word our lives grow and flourish according to God's plan. We usually think of prayer—speaking to God—as the starting point in our relationship with God to get His attention, to ask His help, to seek His blessing, to find His comfort, or to enlist His guidance. But, says Peterson, "prayer is answering speech. The first word is God's word. Prayer is a human word and is never the first word, never the primary, initiating and shaping word"[64] (Peterson, 1987, 33-34).

---

64   Peterson, E. H. (1987). *Working the Angles. Grand Rapids, MI: Eerdmans.*

Combining Prayer with Reading the Word

This is the reason it is so important to combine prayer with the reading of the Bible. As we study the Holy Scriptures, we discover how people of faith have prayed in the past and how God answered their prayers. This shows us how God wants to relate to us and answer our prayers as well. When we read the Bible, we discover many patterns for our prayers. More importantly, when we pray based on the Word of God, we discover the God of the Bible Himself—listening, understanding, caring, responding, helping, encouraging, giving answers—communicating with us through His **"living and enduring Word"** (1 Peter 1:23b). When we pray because of the Word of God and the promises He gives us in the Word, we can come boldly before the throne of grace, giving expression to our needs "before God in the power of the Spirit and with the confident expectation that God will surely hear and act on requests."[65]

The worries, fears, and anxieties of our lives, and the lives of others, can be settled in prayer. Luther once said that prayer gives to the Christian the "power to bear his troubles and to overcome them."[66] Richard Foster highlights the importance of prayer in the life of the Christian: "It is the Discipline of prayer itself that brings us into the deepest and highest work of the human spirit. Real prayer is life-creating and life-changing." [67] (Foster, 1978, 30).

It is important to realize that we need balance in our study of the Word and prayer. Otherwise, we will end up just drifting through life, tossed back and forth by the waves of trouble and the winds of turmoil.

---

65 Bloesch, D. G. (1980). *The Struggle of Prayer.* New York, NY: Harper & Row Publishers, Inc. 43.
66 Bloesch. 43.
67 Foster, R. J. (1978). *Celebration of Discipline: The Path to Spiritual Growth.* New York, NY: Harper & Row. 30.

Suppose I want to try sailing in a boat. I rent a boat and a rudder and launch out into the lake. I position the rudder so that it will head me in the precise direction I want to go. I am apparently in control, but I am going nowhere. So, I paddle back to the dock and explain to the boat owner that I want better action than this and would like to trade the rudder in for a sail. Back on the lake, my greatest hopes are immediately realized. My sail catches the wind and suddenly I am racing across the water—right into the rocks on the other shore! To navigate successfully, I cannot choose between a rudder and a sail. I must have both.[68]

Similarly, as we live the Christian life, developing our inner beings, we need both the Word and prayer. The Word is the rudder that gives us the direction we need to live as God teaches us. Prayer is the sail that catches the wind of the Spirit, Who then carries us to the destination of our spiritual formation. Thus, while the Word of God is the foundation for our spiritual formation, prayer is the key to releasing the power of the Word to transform our lives and to focus on our requests and the needs of others.

PRAYER RESPONSE

Lord, I want You to reign on the throne of my life. I have no power except that which You give me. I am committed to living my life in a way that glorifies You. Help me, as I meditate on Your powerful, life-changing Word to grow, develop, and mature in my relationship with You—to become the person You want me to be. Speak to me through Your Word, as the rudder which gives guidance and keeps me moving in Your direction, according to Your will and plan for my life. Enable me to keep the sail of prayer hoisted high to catch the wind of the Spirit, as You propel me into your presence and into precious

---

68 *Ministry Magazine. (1984, March). p. 10.*

fellowship with You. May I respond in prayer, in joyful obedience, and with wholehearted devotion to You. Amen.

Shutting Out the Jazz of the World

Jacques Ellul confesses, "The man of our times does not know how to pray; but much more than that, he has neither the desire nor the need to do so. He does not find the deep source of prayer within himself. I am acquainted with this man. I know him well. It is myself."[69] This is tragically true of the majority of our society today. Many ministers and other Christian leaders, when they are genuinely truthful, would agree that they do not know how to pray anything more than a rather general, harmless, ineffective, superficial prayer. Most of the time, as Ellul said, "they neither have the desire nor sense the need to do more. They do not find the deep source of prayer within themselves."[70] Therefore, concerted prayer for them is difficult and something to be avoided.

On the other hand, there are others with whom I have conversed who say they would like to participate in a more meaningful and consistent practice of prayer, but they do not know how. They excuse themselves, saying that they do not have time; they are too busy; their schedules are too rushed; they have too much pressure in their lives to take time out for prayer. By the time they get to the end of the day, they are so fatigued and frazzled, frantic and frenzied, drained and devoured, devitalized and dissipated, that they just cannot pray. Life is so rambunctious and rowdy, cluttered and chaotic, disruptive and disorganized, that they cannot find the silent space in which to shape an intimate, prayerful relationship with God, so they often need a tranquilizer to get them through the night.

---

69   Ellul, J. (1979). *Prayer and Modern Man. New York, NY: Seabury Press. Vi.*
70   Ellul, J. (1979). *Prayer and Modern Man. New York, NY: Seabury Press.*

Ellul cuts right to the core of the problem and its solution when he says that we know all these justifications so well.[71] They rest upon a mistaken point of view! Is not prayer precisely of itself peace, silence, and strength since it is a way of being with God? If we agree that prayer is indeed a sharing, which God wills to have with man, a sharing of His will, of His power, of His love, through the medium of human speech, how can we fail to see that the sole prior condition is that decision on the part of God? All the favorable psychological and sociological conditions are secondary and may even be lacking. If prayer is a gift from God, then it is this gift which fulfills all the necessary psychological and sociological conditions.[72] (Ellul, 1979, 68).

In the practice of prayer, we discover the ability to pray and the conditions for prayer. I have often discovered, in times when I did not feel like praying and on occasions when words did not come easily, that as I began to pray and persisted in prayer, all the necessary conditions for prayer began to surface. John Wesley challenged Mr. Trembath, "O begin! Fix some part of every day for private exercises. You may acquire the taste which you have not: What is tedious at first will afterwards be pleasant. Whether you like it or not, read and pray daily. It is for your life; there is no other way; else you will be a trifler all your days, and a pretty superficial Preacher."[73] When we begin to pray, we discover that the time for prayer is there; the energy for prayer permeates our spirits, minds, emotions, and bodies.

The words for prayer flow from God's heart to ours, for Paul promised, **"In the same way, the Spirit helps us in our weakness. We do not know what we ought to pray for, but the Spirit himself intercedes for us with groans that words cannot express. And he who searches our**

---

71   Ellul. 68
72   Ellul. 68
73   Wesley, J. (1986). *Wesley's Notes upon the New Testament.* Peabody, MA: Hendrickson
     Publishers, Inc. 254.

hearts knows the mind of the Spirit, because the Spirit intercedes for the saints in accordance with God's will" (Romans 8:26-28).

Paul validates this promise, adding, *"Do not be anxious about anything, but in everything, by prayer and petition, with thanksgiving, present your requests to God. And the peace of God, which transcends all understanding, will guard your hearts and your minds in Christ Jesus"* (Philippians 4:6-7).

When the **"God of peace"** (Philippians 4:9) is with us then the **"peace of God will rule in our hearts"** (Colossians 3:15). The peace of God will guard our hearts and minds from the noise and distractions of the world.

I heard about a man who was flipping through the radio channels one Christmas Eve, trying to find some beautiful Christmas music. On station after station, he heard raucous jazz at its worst. Suddenly, he heard the resounding praise of a choir and orchestra in a magnificent performance of the *Hallelujah Chorus* from Handel's *Messiah*. He said, "And I held that out against all the jazz of the world!"[74] When we determine to come into the intimate presence of the God of peace in prayer, then the peace of God stifles all the jazz of the world outside. Jacques Ellul confirms this, saying, "Prayer creates its own required time. It is the prayer which restores my energies, takes away my fatigue, and which to the very end makes tranquilizers useless, for it eases every tension, every conflict."[75]

Such effective prayer must have its roots firmly implanted in the Word of God. Bonhoeffer said:

"The Scripture meditation leads to prayer. The most promising method of prayer is to allow oneself to be guided by the word of the Scriptures, to pray on the basis of a word of Scripture. In this way we shall not become the victims of our own emptiness. Prayer

---

74   Unknown Source.
75   Ellul, J. (1979). *Prayer and Modern Man.* New York, NY: Seabury Press. 69.

means nothing else but the readiness and willingness to receive and appropriate the Word, and what is more, to accept it in one's personal situation, particular tasks, decisions, sins, and temptations. What can never enter the corporate prayer of the fellowship may here be silently made known to God. According to a word of Scripture we pray for the clarification of our day, for preservation from sin, for growth in sanctification, for faithfulness and strength in our work. And we may be certain that our prayer will be heard because it is a response to God's Word and promise. Because God's Word has found its fulfillment in Jesus Christ, all prayers that we pray conforming to this Word are certainly heard and answered in Jesus Christ."[76] (Bonhoeffer, 1954, 84-5)

This gives us great encouragement to discipline ourselves to regularly take the time to meditate on the Word and pray. Ellul continues,

Prayer, however fervent, spontaneous and new, is never other than a sequel, a consequence, a response, to the word of invitation first made known in Scripture. It is discerned as word through faith and is received as the Word of God by the action of God alone. It is futile to believe in an authentication on our own, or in a transformation of Scripture into word by means of a method. If it is not God who is speaking, then there is nothing.[77] (Ellul, 1979, 123)

When we pray based on the Word, we can be confident that God and we will commune in fellowship and partnership in life and in ministry.

---

76 Bonhoeffer, D. (1954). *Life Together. New York, NY: Harper & Row Publishers, Inc. 84-85.*
77 Ellul, J. (1979). *Prayer and Modern Man. New York, NY: Seabury Press. 123.*

PRAYER RESPONSE

Lord of peace, please help me to commit my whole self to Your will and purposes for my life. Remind me to guard against the distractions which hinder my QuietTimes with You. Inspire me to keep the focus that will aid me to determine to abide in the intimate presence of the God of peace in prayer, in order that the peace of God may stifle all the jazz of the world outside. May I enjoy constantly that quiet inner space where You reside in the temple of my life, and there in that private world may I be always overtaken by Your fullness in the sufficiency of the Word, so that it is impossible for me to miss anything that You want for me. Grant me Your peace, solitude, and quietness to drown out the noise and distractions, clutter and chaos, panic and frenzy, fatigue and frustrations. Amen.

Reaching a Quota, or Shaping a Relationship

Von Balthasar cautions that…

Prayer must never be seen as carrying out a program, fulfilling a quota. As soon as God's word strikes me, I must leave everything and follow it. As soon as my wings have developed and I am off the ground, I am to be governed by the laws of the air, of the Spirit. When I am overtaken by God's fullness in the fullness of the word, it is impossible for me to "miss" anything.[78] (Von Balthasar, 1955, 133)

The disciplines of the Word and prayer should never be regarded as a program or a regimen to be carried out just for the sake of appearing pious. When I was a sophomore in high school, I won a Sunday school Bible reading contest at our church. I picked out all the shortest Psalms I could

---

78 Von Balthasar, H. U. (1955). *Prayer. New York, NY: Ignatius Press. 133.*

find, and then I speed-read them over and over, scanning them as rapidly as I could, so I could honestly accumulate more chapters than anyone else in the church. It worked - I won the contest! However, I am not sure that much of it really connected with my inner being, because my focus was on winning the contest, not hearing the Word and living in intimate relationship with the God of the Bible.

When we focus on the Word to learn from it and to be touched by it, rather to fulfill a quota, complete a program, or to appear pious, we can be certain that the Word will speak to us at the level of our needs.

PRAYER RESPONSE

O God, my Father, keep me from ever viewing the study of the Word and prayer as simply carrying out a program, or fulfilling a quota. When Your Word connects with my inner spirit, help me to leave everything and follow it. When my wings have developed and I am off the ground, enable me to be governed by the laws of the wind of Your Spirit. When I am overtaken by Your fullness in the sufficiency of Your Word, may it be impossible for me to miss anything that You have planned for my life. May I practice the disciplines of the Word and prayer, never as a program or a regimen to be carried out just for the sake of appearing pious, but rather as the high privilege of living in intimate relationship with You, the God of the Bible. In the name of Him who is the Living Word, my Lord Jesus Christ, I pray. Amen.

Unity of Spirit, Mind, Emotions, and Body

To guard against the distractions which hinder our *Quiet Times* with God in the Word and in prayer, writes Balthasar, we find that we must

. . . get ourselves together in order to want to pray, as one speaks of a horse gathering his forces when he is about to put out a great effort to jump over a crucial hurdle. We must take in hand all the scattered parts of the self, all those energies applied to this or that task, all the attentions and affections, all the strengths and despairs, all the understandings and humiliations. If this totality is not brought together, then we cannot pray.[79] (Von Balthasar, 1955)

When I was a minister of music in Oklahoma City, I learned a lesson about the importance of the unity of spirit, mind, and emotions to effective prayer. One of my best friends was Gene, a firefighter by profession, an ex-marine, and an expert in karate. He taught me the principles of breaking a board with my bare hand. The board was laid between two bricks that we stood on end about fourteen inches apart. One of the main principles was concentrating, not on the board, but on reaching the air space under the board before pulling my punch back. In order to make certain the board broke, my hand had to reach that spot beneath the board. The other main principle was that every fiber of my mind and every muscle in my body had to work together to break the board. If the board did not break when I hit it the first time, it could break my hand. After Gene's expert tutoring, and my practicing, preparing for this fearless feat, I set up the board on the bricks. Then I addressed the board, took several deep breaths, holding the last one for a powerful burst of energy. At the appropriate moment, every muscle tensed and pulled together, I let out a shout of triumph, threw a mighty punch, and the board splintered into pieces before my very eyes. I was stunned. It worked!

Admittedly, my breaking that small board did not make me a karate expert by any stretch of the imagination. However, it reminded that just as

---

79　Von Balthasar, H. U. (1955). *Prayer. New York, NY: Ignatius Press.*

there had to be a unity of spirit, mind, emotions, and body for me to break that board with my bare hand, so there must be a unity of spirit, mind, will, emotions, and body for us to pray effectively. We must cultivate a desire for an intimate relationship with God through His Word and prayer. Then we need to acquire the determination to be consistent. When the body is tired, the emotions are fickle, and the mind is cluttered, the inner spirit must take charge and say, "Let's pull together, for this relationship with God is the most important relationship in life and eternity!"

Every time we venture to pray, says Ellul, "it is a victory over temptation, over the giving up of the struggle with the self, over the divided heart."[80] The pressures of our society lead to disunity of the inner being, splintering the personality, dividing the mind, disconnecting the emotions, and dampening the will. The disciplines of listening to the Word of God and answering in prayer lead to uniting the whole individual around the person, presence, power, and purposes of God. Such unity comes when we determine, by an act of the will, to go against the tide of the natural tendencies within us, and to allow God to empower us to take control of all the scattered parts of ourselves, and to apply all our energies to seeking, finding, and following Him. Amid busy calendars, iPhones, cluttered schedules, and hectic lifestyles; and in spite of the noise, disarray, and chaos around us, we must determine to create the silent space in which to shape an intimate, prayerful relationship with God through His Word and prayer.

PRAYER RESPONSE

My Creator God, Lord of my life, as I fellowship with You, help me to guard against the distractions which hinder my Quiet Times with You in the

---

80 Ellul, J. (1979). *Prayer and Modern Man. New York, NY: Seabury Press. 143.*

Word and in prayer. When my body is tired, my emotions are fickle, and my mind is cluttered, empower my inner spirit to take charge and pull myself together, because my relationship with You, my Lord, is the most important relationship in life and in eternity! Every time I venture to pray, give me victory over temptation, over the struggle with the self, over the divided heart. The pressures of the society around me try to cause a disunity of my inner being, a splintering of my personality, a dividing of my mind, a disconnecting of my emotions, and a dampening of my will. Through the disciplines of listening to Your Word and answering in prayer, please lead me to a reunification of my whole being around the person, presence, power, and purposes of You, my God. Provide this unity as I determine, by an act of my will, to go against the tide of the natural tendencies within me. Help me to allow You to empower me to take control of all the scattered parts of myself and to apply all my energies to seeking, finding, and following You. During the busyness, the cluttered schedules, the hectic lifestyles, the noise, clutter, and chaos, implant in me not only the desire and the will, but also the competence to create the silent space in which to shape an intimate, prayerful relationship with You. In the name of Him who can bring order out of scatteredness, I pray. Amen.

The Importance of the Timeout

In the final seconds of one memorable football game, the Dallas Cowboys were behind by four points, several yards from the goal line, fourth down, and one timeout remaining. They needed a touchdown, for a three-point field goal would not be enough to tie, much less win the game. This was nothing new, for the Cowboys have been in that position many times. Roger Staubach called timeout and ran to the sideline to confer with Coach Tom Landry. After the timeout, Staubach and the offensive team went back on the field to face the opposing defensive line. After Staubach gave the count, as the offensive line pushed the defenders back and the receivers ran past the goal line, he fired an accurate pass into the hands of a receiver who caught the football and won the game.

The victory is not so important now, but the principle is important: the timeout is vital, not only in those tense moments toward the end, but all through the game. Whether you are ahead or behind, it is important periodically to take a timeout, to stop the action, and consult with the coach. Listen to his counsel; be refreshed with a drink of water or Gatorade; regroup your thoughts, your energy; and refresh the game plan.

This is even more true in life than it is in a ball game. We need to take time out to be with God, to listen to His Word, to pray, and to encourage one another. The very fact that we are so busy, so desperately driven by responsibilities, worries, or demands, makes this timeout more important. Those moments with the Lord God, Who is so much wiser than we are, can give us the guidance we need, the delightful reassurance that He is with us. In that setting we are renewed with a refreshing, revitalizing drink from His powerful, life-transforming Word. Then it is time to get off the sidelines, to get back in circulation, and to do the work God has called us to do together.

Prayer is like a timeout that unleashes the power of the Word to transform our lives, to regroup our thoughts, to reveal God's game plan, to replenish our energies, and to move ahead in confidence and victory as we follow the guidance of our Lord.

PRAYER RESPONSE

Lord God, thank You for being the unifier of my life around Your Word and prayer. Thank You for the supreme privilege of living in close, intimate relationship with You. Again, amid the busyness, the cluttered schedules, the hectic lifestyles, the noise, clutter, and chaos, please empower me to create the silent space in which to shape an intimate, prayerful relationship with You through Your Word and prayer. Enable me to take the appropriate timeouts, which are of paramount importance in my relationship with You. Remind me of the necessity of the timeouts to listen to Your directions, to be refreshed in Your presence, and to receive a renewed vision of who You want me to be and what You want me to do. Then take me back into my world as a transformed person whom You can use to touch the lives of others with Your love and unifying power. In the name of the Prince of Peace I pray. Amen.

Chapter 10

Biblical Lessons about Prayer

I am convinced that we could spend a whole year, a whole lifetime studying prayer, and we would never learn all there is to know about praying. However, there are some important lessons we can learn about prayer as we study the Word of God, and as we consistently practice praying. These lessons were begun as entries in *My Journal* and edited for this setting.

The More We Practice, the Better We Get

"Have nothing to do with godless myths and old wives' tales; rather, train yourself to be godly. For physical training is of some value, but godliness has value for all things, holding promise for both the present life and the life to come" (1 Timothy 4:7-8).

Prayer, in many ways, is like any other discipline in which we might participate. The more we practice, the better we get. In jogging, for instance, there are times when the practice seems like hard work and drudgery, yet when the practice is consistent and determined, a person begins to get in shape, to feel better, and even to enjoy jogging. When I first started jogging, I was out of breath by the time I got out of my driveway and struggled to jog a block or two. After a few months of consistent practice, I stretched it to a couple of miles; and after a couple years, I could go six or seven miles, depending on my consistency and available time for running. In fact, one Fourth of July morning, I ran in a benefit jogathon. I ran in the two-mile contest. I even won a second-place red ribbon in my age bracket. The other fellow got the first-place blue ribbon. In addition to the red ribbon, they gave me a T-shirt commemorating the event, but they did not invite me to participate in the twenty-six-mile marathon. However, it was an accomplishment for me to just complete the two miles, which I ran faster than I ever had before. It indicated to me that my practice and discipline were beginning to pay off, for I could not have completed that race a year earlier.

An effective prayer life, in fact the whole process of spiritual formation, is like a race. The key is a determined, disciplined, consistent practice of prayer. Just as those who run in the twenty-six-mile marathons must make running a major priority in their lives, those who wish to live in the power of a godly life must consistently pursue the spiritual disciplines, and prayer is one of the most important disciplines. In his first letter to Timothy Paul said, **"Have nothing to do with godless myths and old wives' tales; rather, train yourself to be godly. For physical training is of some value, but godliness has value for all things, holding promise for both the present life and the life to come"** (1 Timothy 4:7-8). Certainly, physical training is valuable. It strengthens the body and gives a person more energy. It often enables a person to do a better job in his or her vocation. How much more important is training ourselves to be godly! This is the process of spiritual formation, forming the inner life and relationship with God. While physical training is important for this life, training in godliness is important both in this present life and in the life to come—in eternity. As physical strength depends on a strict regimen of proper diet and exercise, so our spiritual vitality and endurance depend on a rigorous system of spiritual discipline.

Beginning the Day with Prayer

In the life and teaching of our Lord Jesus, we see some principles for developing the kind of determined, disciplined, consistent practice of prayer that makes it effective in a person's life. The Scriptural record says, **"Jesus returned . . . in the power of the Spirit"** (Luke 4:14), and then Luke begins to give an exciting account of the wonders He performed. Within a few verses, Luke tells us three times the source of His power: **"At daybreak Jesus went out to a solitary place . . ."** (Luke 4:42). **"Jesus withdrew to lonely places and prayed . . ."** (Luke 5:16). **". . . Jesus went out into the hills to pray, and spent the night praying to God"** (Luke 6:12). Amid a heavy, hectic, demanding schedule, Jesus made time to pray. It was His source of power from God, for His own life and for the people to whom He ministered.

If Jesus placed such a premium on the value and power of prayer—Jesus, who is God's only unique Son, who is God Himself—can we mere followers of His do any less? What is our source of power for living victoriously by faith? Is it our fabulous talents, amazing gifts, or great abilities? No, our source of power for victorious living and for touching other persons is our relationship with our God through prayer.

Jesus, after having prayed all night, went out and called His twelve disciples the next morning: **"One of those days Jesus went out to a** mountainside to pray, and spent the night praying to God. When morning came, he called his disciples to him and chose twelve of them, whom he also designated apostles" (Luke 6:12-13). He made major decisions only after, and based on, a concentrated prayer time. Then He poured His life into those apostles for three years. At the end of the three years, Jesus went to the Garden of Gethsemane alone and prayed for them again—and they went out and turned the world upside down, and people's lives right-side-up! Jesus also prayed for us that night: "My prayer is not for them alone. I pray also for those who will believe in me through their message" (John 17:20). We were in His heart that night in the Garden, in the shadow of the Cross, because we have believed in Him through the message of the disciples handed down through generations of believers! From our Lord's example we learn the extreme importance of praying intensely over important decisions, events, and persons. It is the source of power for life, ministry, and people.

PRAYER RESPONSE

Father, help me to learn to follow my Lord's model in prayer and to see the definite, specific results of such prayer. Amid a heavy, hectic, hurried, demanding schedule, enable me to make time to pray. This is my only source of power from You, my God, for my own life and for the people to whom You lead me to minister. May I acquire by regularly coming into Your presence the practice, consistency, discipline, and determination to develop a prayer pattern that is effective, life-changing, relationship-mending, and enjoyable. Keep me in a rigorous system of training in godliness that will intensify my spiritual vitality and expand my spiritual endurance. Amen.

Very Early in the Morning

In Mark 1:29-45, we are again given the secret of Jesus' relationship with God and His power to change the lives of people. Mark says, **"Very early in the morning, while it was still dark, Jesus got up, left the house and went off to a solitary place, where he prayed"** (Mark 1:35). That morning in the life of Jesus came after what must have been an extremely hectic day. He had been teaching in the synagogue with such authority that the people were **"amazed"** (Mark 1:22, 27). When his teaching was interrupted by a man with an "evil (or unclean) spirit," Jesus again amazed the people by commanding the evil spirit to leave the man, and He restored him to wholeness. Leaving the synagogue, Jesus visited the home of Simon and Andrew, where He cured Simon's mother-in-law of a high fever. After sunset, all the people in the surrounding area who were physically, emotionally, and spiritually sick were brought to Him, and with **"the whole town gathered at the door, He healed many and drove the demons out of many people."**

How could Jesus keep up this rigorous schedule? After that full, hectic, demanding, emotion-packed day, Mark says about Jesus, **"Very early in the morning, while it was still dark, Jesus got up, left the house and went off to a solitary place, where he prayed"** (Mark 1:35). It doesn't make sense does it? Jesus knew this day would be at least as full and hectic as the day before. He knew that many demands would be made upon Him. He knew that the crowds of people would be pressing in on Him with such force that He could no longer **"enter a town openly"** (Mark 1:45). He knew that wherever He went, people would be calling His name, reaching out to touch Him, begging for His help. He knew that the Scribes and Pharisees would be there criticizing Him, questioning His teaching, doubting His motives, stirring up trouble, trying to confuse and distract Him, and attempting to humiliate Him. He knew that even His own disciples would often misunderstand Him and attempt to get Him to do things their way instead of His. Do you ever have a day like this? Of course, we all do.

Therefore, facing such a demanding schedule and so many clamoring people, how could Jesus eke out time for solitude and prayer? Shouldn't He get another hour of rest in order to gain the energy for such a rigorous day? No, He knew there was no way He could accomplish all the things he had to get done unless he did make time to pray!

It is true that most of us live with such heavy, demanding schedules that we feel we can never accomplish all we need to do on a day-to-day basis. Can we learn a lesson from our Lord Jesus? Like Him, we stand in the need of consistent daily prayer. Even if it means arising earlier, it will enable us to accomplish His plans throughout the day with surprising skill, energy, and efficiency. This is true, because in the discipline of prayer, we are seeking His agenda, strength, stamina, priorities, and resources. This enables us to live our physical lives in His strength and to accomplish His plans with supernatural stamina, as we live by faith in our Lord Jesus Christ. Speaking of the necessity of being faithful and consistent in prayer, Andrew Murray writes:

I want to secure absolutely the presence of Christ for the entire day, to do nothing that can interfere with it. I feel that my success for the day will depend upon the clearness and the strength of the faith that seeks and finds and holds Him in the inner chamber. Above everything else, it is this fixed determination to secure Christ's presence that will overcome the temptation to be unfaithful or superficial in the keeping of our pledge. It is this determination which will make the morning watch [prayer time] itself a mighty means of grace in strengthening character, and enabling us to say "No" to every call for self-indulgence. It is this determination which will enable us, when we enter the inner chamber and shut the door, to be there with our whole heart, ready at once for our communication with Christ. And it is this determination that, from the morning watch on, will become the keynote of our daily life.[81]

An anonymous poet wrote the following:
I rose one morning early,
And rushed into the fray.
With so much to accomplish,
I had no time to pray.
Troubles tumbled 'round me,
And heavy was each task.
But where was God to help me?
God said, "You didn't ask."
I tried to see the bright side,
But things turned grey and bleak.
I asked God for the reason.
He said, "You didn't seek."[82]

Prayer is not a method of keeping God informed about our life situation. He already knows everything there is to know about it. Prayer is not a method of telling God what we, in our finite wisdom, think we need. He already knows everything there is to know about our needs. Prayer, at its root, is a willingness to let God be God. **"Be still and know that I am God,"** the Lord said to an ancient Psalm writer (Psalm 46:10). Prayer, at

---

81 Murray, Andrew (1980). *The Inner Life. Grand Rapids, MI: Zondervan. 1.*
82 Unknown Source.

its root, is listening for the voice of God in our inner beings. "Ask not what God can do for you. Ask what you can do for God. Ask not what God can give to you. Ask what you can give to God"[83] (Murray, 1980).

A great scientist, a man rooted in prayer, which is to say, he was rooted in God, once said, "I can take my telescope and look millions and millions of miles into space. But I can lay it aside and go into my room, shut the door, get down on my knees and see more of heaven and get closer to God than I can assisted by all the telescopes and material things on earth" (Unknown). The following story beautifully illustrates the importance of prayer in a person's life:

Once upon a time, a stately tree realized that its strength was beginning to wane. When the wind was strong, the once proud tree shook ominously and made suspicious creaking sounds. With great effort, the tree grew some fine new branches and began to feel secure once more. But when the next gale came, it felt some of its roots snapping and had it not been for the support of a friendly neighbor tree, it would have fallen to the ground. When the tree recovered from the shock, it turned to the one who had saved it and asked, "How is it that you were able not only to stand your ground, but to help me also?" The other tree replied, "When you were busy growing new branches, I was busy strengthening my roots."[84] (Unknown)

This story illustrates a powerful truth. In our spiritual formation, if we wish to experience continued growth, our life in Christ must be constantly nourished and strengthened at its roots. We do this through prayer. At the root level of our Christian living, we need to be still before God and

83   Murray, Andrew (1980). *The Inner Life. Grand Rapids, MI: Zondervan.*
84   Unknown Source.

know that He is in control. We must become still and listen for His voice, through His Word, in our inner beings. The best time for such life-changing prayer, in the example of our Lord, is **"early in the morning . . . in a solitary place"** (Mark 1:35). There in that lonely place, Jesus prayed to know the will of His Father. In seclusion, Jesus prayed before going out to face the demands of a hectic, rigorous schedule. In solitude, Jesus found the strength, stamina, and stability to complete the will of His Father for that day. There we, too, can discover the strength, stamina, and ability to complete the will of our Father for the day. Beginning the day in this way will set the tone for the awesome day God has planned for us.

Listening for His Voice

When God arranged for Elijah's spiritual formation retreat in the cave on the mountain, God told him, **"Go, stand on the mountain at attention before God. God will pass by."** Elijah heard **"a hurricane wind,"** **"an earthquake,"** **"a fire,"** but God was not to be heard in any of them. Then, as he listened, he heard **"a gentle and quiet whisper. When Elijah heard the quiet voice, he muffled his face with his great cloak, went to the mouth of the cave, and stood there. A quiet voice asked, "So Elijah, now tell me, what are you doing here?"** (1 Kings 19:11-13 MSG)

Elijah discovered that God was not to be found in the external noises, but when he listened carefully, he heard the **gentle and quiet whisper**, and it was the voice of God. It is often difficult for us, too, to hear God's voice during the storms, fires, and shaking that the world, people, and circumstances throw at us. That is why we need to spend quiet, significant time with our Lord in prayer, listening for His voice and directions in the middle of the chaos that often engulfs us.

Dr. Harold Leestma (former co-pastor with Dr. Robert Schuller at the Crystal Cathedral, and one of my teachers in D.Min. studies at California Graduate School of Theology) told a story that powerfully illustrates this concept. Leestma's son, a soldier in the Vietnam War, was studying to be a radio technician specialist in order to listen to and interpret radio communications of the enemy forces. In preparation for his assignment, he had to learn Mandarin Chinese. In the class sessions the instructor spoke to the trainees through earphones, simulating the voices of enemy soldiers. After they began learning the language, as they were listening over the earphones, the instructor would inject all sorts of piercing noises, music, and other voices trying to drown out the sound of his own voice. The purpose of the exercise was to train the technicians to crowd out all the other noises, sounds, music, and voices and to listen explicitly to the instructor.[85]

This is how it is in the world in which we live, as we attempt to live the Christian life and walk closely with God. Many noises, voices, and distractions call us away from the voice of God, but we must train ourselves to listen to that still, small voice of the Spirit of God that comes to us within the inner recesses of our minds and hearts.

This takes spending quality time alone with the Master, learning to recognize the sound of His voice amid all the clamor and clatter of other voices and noises. Such a relationship is cultivated in the solitary place. It is as the Lord told Isaiah, **"This is what the Sovereign Lord, the Holy One of Israel, says: In repentance and rest is your salvation, in quietness and trust is your strength . . .** (Isaiah 30:15 NIV). When we are praying, it is important that we spend some quiet time listening for the **still, small voice** of God as He directs our hearts in prayer.

---

85   Leestma, Harold. Evangelism and Church Growth Course. California Graduate School of Theology. Instructor in Dr. Sam's DMin. Course.

Keeping Our Minds on the Main Goal

My son-in-law used to train dogs for obedience, protection, police work and drug detection. He has told me that a Seeing Eye dog trainer trains the dog so that when other dogs and cats come around him, he completely ignores them. Of course, the natural tendency is to go and play with the other dog or chase the cat. But if the Seeing Eye dog is to be effective in leading his master, he cannot take his mind off his job for even a moment.

So it is with us. Often, we have a job to do, but attitudes of our hearts and minds, distractions, and other things crowd in upon us and threaten to side-track us. We must train and discipline ourselves to keep our minds on our main goal—that of pleasing our Master. In the words of the Apostle Paul, **"One thing I do: forgetting what is behind and straining toward what is ahead, I press on toward the goal to win the prize for which God has called me heavenward in Christ Jesus"** (Philippians 3:14b-15). The beginning of this kind of training is in the discipline of going regularly to the quiet place for fellowship, communion, and training with the Master of our lives in prayer and the Word. Following is a reflective meditation to help us keep our minds on the main goal of listening to the voice of our Lord so that we can follow His directions explicitly.

Reflective Meditation on Prayer

In Luke's Gospel, Jesus talked about the consequences of being too busy to spend adequate time with the Master. It is easy to give excuses, but in the end, failure to spend quality time with Him shortchanges us in the formation of our inner beings, thereby shortchanging our outer lives. Here are the words of our Lord:

> Jesus replied: "A certain man was preparing a great banquet and invited many guests. At the time of the banquet he sent his servant to tell those who had been invited,' Come, for everything is now ready.' But they all alike began to make excuses. The first said, 'I have just bought a field, and I must go and see it. Please excuse me.' Another said, 'I have just bought five yoke of oxen, and I'm on my way to try them out. Please excuse me.' Still another said, 'I just got married, so I can't come.' The servant came back and reported this to his master. Then the owner of the house became angry and ordered his servant, 'Go out quickly into the streets and alleys of the town and bring in the poor, the crippled, the blind and the lame.' 'Sir,' the servant said, 'what you ordered has been done, but there is still room.' Then the master told his servant, 'Go out to the roads and country lanes and make them come in, so that my house will be full. I tell you, not one of those men who were invited will get a taste of my banquet'" (Luke 14:16-24).

The following entry from *My Journal* is based on Luke 14:16-24 (above); Luke 4:14, 42; 5:16; 6:12; and Mark 1:29-45. It is an example of the kind of commitment needed to make time for the disciplines of spiritual formation—time spent alone with God in prayer and in His Word. Please use this for your own personal reflection, as well as a model for praying out of the Scriptures.

Alone Before God

Busyness—misplaced priorities
 rob me of my greatest
 power,
 joy,
 blessing,
 inner strength.
Yet this does not leave room for
 laziness,
 sluggishness,
 procrastination.
It means I must pause to
 listen,
 reflect,
 open myself to
 His promptings,
 His way,
 His will.
I develop a receptive attitude of mind,
 letting myself go,
 hearing my deepest longings,
 sharing them with God,
 realizing what life is about,
 penetrating reality—
 making a space for God in my life
 through prayer,
 by His word,
 with quiet contemplation.

There I discover
  an awareness of what holds the world together—
  my true identity,
  my mission,
  my relationship with God.
Just as Jesus needed to listen to God,
  so do I!
  I need to come away
    from people,
    from my work,
    and the hectic places where I am needed
  to be
    refreshed,
      replenished,
      rejuvenated,
  and to be emptied of all that
    distracts,
    distorts,
    disrupts,
So that I can be
  full,
  fulfilled,
  at the depth of my inner being.

As the artist of my soul,

    under the guidance of the Master Artist,

    I need to develop

        a deep insight into reality,

        a capacity to see beneath the surface

          of nature and people,

        an awareness that uncovers a spiritual vitality in

          my world—myself—

            and points toward God.

The source of this is in my becoming

    a truly contemplative

    and prayerful person,

    developing in my inner world:

        a capacity for seeing deeply into reality,

        an ability to pay attention to what is beneath the surface,

        a willingness to concentrate long enough to catch a vision.

Jesus,

    in His aloneness before His Father,

    found His source of power.

    There, I also must find mine!

Amen.

Chapter 11

The Power of Intercessory Prayer

Dr. Sam Says . . .

While it is true that all kinds of true prayer are important, one of the most powerful, effective, and needed forms of prayer is the prayer of intercession. Intercession, basically, is prayer offered to God in behalf of another person. Intercessors, for a time, ignore their own personal needs and focus their concern, prayer, and faith on another person.

To intercede, says Dick Eastman, is to be a mediator between God and another person, "praying that this person will come to know about God and His salvation."[86] As Edward Bauman explains, "When we pray for others, we do not stand with outstretched hands hoping to receive something for ourselves. We stand at God's side, working together with Him, in the task of redeeming others."[87] While it is true that our prayer does not save another person or change his life, "somehow it serves to prepare his heart for the moment word reaches him of Christ's love."[88] E. M. Bounds writes, "Prayer must be broad in its scope—it must

---

86 Eastman, D. (1978). *The Hour That Changes the World: A Practical Plan for Personal Prayer. Grand Rapids, MI: Baker Book House.*
87 Bloesch, D. G. (1980). *The Struggle of Prayer. New York, NY: Harper & Row Publishers, Inc.*
88 Eastman.

plead for others. Intercession for others is the hallmark of all true prayer
. . . Prayer is the soul of a man stirred up to plead with God for men"[89]
(Eastman, 1978).

Intercession Leads Persons into the Healing Presence of God

Donald Bloesch says that the essence of true prayer is a "heartfelt supplication," bringing before God a person's deepest needs and requests "in the confident expectation that God will hear and answer."[90] The Hebrew and Greek words used for prayer in the Bible reflect this meaning of "supplication," which is making a request of God, or a petition to God. Intercessory prayer is making a request or a petition to God on behalf of another person. There are many examples of intercessory prayer throughout the Bible. It was common for the prophets and kings to intercede for their people before God.[91] Paul urged the Ephesians to "pray in the Spirit on all occasions with all kinds of prayers and requests. With this in mind, be alert and always keep on praying for all the saints. Pray also for me, that whenever I open my mouth, words may be given me so that I will fearlessly make known the mystery of the gospel, for which I am an ambassador in chains. Pray that I may declare it fearlessly, as I should" (Ephesians 6:18-20).

Paul told Timothy, "I urge, then, first of all, that requests, prayers, intercession and thanksgiving be made for everyone—for kings and all those in authority, that we may live peaceful and quiet lives in all godliness

---

89   Eastman.
90   Bloesch.
91   See Exodus 32:11-14; 1 Samuel 12:7ff; 2 Kings 19:14-19; 1 Chronicles 21:16, 17; Lamentations 5; Daniel 9:16.

and holiness. This is good, and pleases God our Savior, who wants all men to be saved and to come to a knowledge of the truth" (1 Timothy 2:1-2).

The very clear instruction in both passages is that we are to pray for one another. As Christian leaders, both ministers and lay ministers, we are often brought into relationships with people who are hurting, wounded, broken, searching for answers. Such persons are imprisoned emotionally and spiritually by internal fears, doubts, sins, failures, and worries. They are sometimes captives to bad habits, broken or strained relationships. They are in desperate need of help beyond their own resources and abilities— and beyond ours as well. The usual answer we give is, "I will pray for you." Sometimes I get the feeling that when people say, "I will pray for you," it means in reality very little more than saying, "I wish you good luck in this," or "I really feel sorry for you, and I offer you my concern." Then we go on our way feeling like we have done all we could do. When we tell someone, "I will pray for you," we should respect this extremely important promise. It means that we enter a covenant with them to lift them before the throne of God who is capable of helping them in the midst of their need and hurt. If we go on our way, and forget or neglect to truly pray for them, we have broken our pledge to them. We leave them vulnerable to further attacks.

On the other hand, when we enter intercessory prayer for them, we bring God into the covenant relationship, and we lead them into the healing presence of God,[92] where both they and we can be touched by Him in the center of our beings. When we are in Christ, our bodies, our inner beings, become temples of the living God. Our hearts become dwelling places of God, and they are transformed into hearts large enough to embrace the needs of other people as well as our own. Then we can carry in our hearts "all human pain and sorrow, all conflicts and agonies, all torture and war, all hunger, loneliness, and misery, not because of some great

---

92   Nouwen, H. J. (1981). *The Way of the Heart. New York, NY: Seabury Press.*

psychological or emotional capacity, but because God's heart has become one with ours."[93]

When we engage in intercessory prayer for others we begin to understand and to enter into the intimate connection between prayer and ministry. The ministry of leading people with their struggles, hurts, failures, sins, and needs to the throne of God is one of the disciplines of prayer and of ministry. Nouwen writes, "As long as ministry only means that we worry a lot about people and their problems; as long as it means an endless number of activities which we can hardly coordinate, we are still very much dependent on our own narrow and anxious heart. But when our worries are led to the heart of God and there become prayer, then ministry and prayer become two manifestations of the same all-embracing love of God."[94] Bloesch wrote,

The power of prayer is nowhere more clearly manifest than in the intercessions of the faithful. Through the prayers of the church, people are healed, lives are transformed, and nations are changed. Hannah Hurnard, a Quaker mystic, has called intercessors "God's transmitters," since through their prayers God acts and speaks. Prayer, she insists, releases the power of God, which is likened to electricity. In a similar manner, Hallesby describes prayer as "the conduit through which power from heaven is brought to earth." Admittedly such views suggest on the surface a semi-magical outlook; nonetheless, it is recognized that God acts only in His freedom, though it is held that He freely binds Himself to the prayers of His people.[95]

---

93 Nouwen.
94 Nouwen, H. J. (1981). *The Way of the Heart*. New York, NY: Seabury Press.
95 Bloesch, D. G. (1980). *The Struggle of Prayer*. New York, NY: Harper & Row Publishers, Inc.

Intercession Revitalizes the Life of the Intercessor

Bloesch points out the fact that intercessory prayer not only powerfully aids persons for whom we pray, but...

> it also revitalizes the spiritual life of the intercessor. William Law discovered that when we intercede for others "all little, ill-natured passions die away" and our heart "will grow great and generous." The missionary Bible translator Henry Martyn observed that in times of dryness and nagging depression he had often found inward renewal in the act of praying for the conversion or sanctification of others.[96]

Corrie Ten Boom talked of being gripped by fear during a scary car ride through the California mountains. She was able to regain her internal confidence as she began praying for friends in school years ago, persons with whom she had traveled, and her companions in a German concentration camp.[97] Her intercessory prayers for others helped put her own fears into perspective.

When I was a child, my mom or dad would ask me to walk down to the corner store to buy a few groceries. When they gave me the grocery list and the money to pay for the groceries, they usually would then say, "And here is a nickel for you to buy a candy bar or a Dr. Pepper!" It is the same way when we go before the Lord in intercessory prayer. I personally have never gone on an errand to God's Throne on behalf of someone else without receiving a blessing or benefit for my own life. Even though the primary purpose in going before God was to intercede for another person,

---

96   Bloesch.
97   Ten Boom, C. (1977). *Amazing Love. New York, NY: Harcourt Brace Jovanovich.*

just being in His presence in prayer often results in personal blessings and help for the intercessor.

Intercession Is a Covenant Relationship

I am learning that our most important work is that of prayer—intercessory prayer. The needs of the people to whom we minister, our family's needs, our own needs—are all too great for us to handle in our own strength. Our resources of time, energy, wisdom, money, advice, and ability are so limited that they cannot even begin to fill all those needs. But our God is more than able, and His resources are more than adequate. Therefore, it is necessary that our best time, energy, and efforts be given to intercessory prayer. This is the most effective work we can do, for it is the work that will make a life-changing difference to those we love and to those God wants to love through us.

Don Postema presents a dynamic summary of the power of intercessory prayer:

Prayer helps us get in touch with God and with ourselves, and makes us aware of others. We find others before God in their need, just as we are there before God in our need. "Intercessory prayer" becomes bringing people to God or joining people before God. We suffer with God in Christ for the salvation of the world, for freedom for the oppressed, for the cessation of war, for the healing of sickness, for the comfort of the anxious and sorrowing. In prayer, we gradually identify with the people for whom we pray as we bring them to the care of God. We hear people there! The act of praying for someone commits us to working in other ways for that person or situation. [Karl Barth said,] "To clasp the hands in prayer is the beginning of an uprising against the disorder of the world." Prayer is one way we are actively engaged in changing the world.[98]

This helps us understand better that when we say to someone, "I will pray for you," we are entering into an intercessory prayer covenant with them. Intercessory prayer is more than a good luck wish, an expression of personal concern. It means that we vow to lift them before the throne of God who can help them during their need and hurt. We are clasping hands together with them and with God to assault the disorder of the world that is invading their lives. Thus, we become the conduit through whom God can send His healing, restoring power.

How Does a Person Pray Intercessory Prayers?

The obvious question is "How does a person pray intercessory prayers?" The general consensus of evangelical Christianity is that we should pray for people by name, mentioning specific needs, and asking for definite solutions. I find, just as I have heard others suggest, that it is good to keep a private, written prayer list to remind me daily of the persons that God has placed on my heart to remember in prayer. I have a space to record the answers when I learn of them. Across the years of my ministry, I have witnessed several persons for whom I had prayed (sometimes for many years) come to know the Lord.

---

98 Postema, D. (1983). *Space for God: The Study and Practice of Prayer and Spirituality.* Grand Rapids, MI: *Board of Publications of the Christian Reformed Church. 158.*

PRAYER RESPONSE

Lord God enable me to be the intercessory prayer warrior that You have called me to be. It's tough work. The demands and time-pressures will try to choke out my prayer time, especially when it's meaningful and effective in bringing about spiritual change in my life and in the lives of those for whom I pray. Since You have called me to this intercessory prayer ministry, I will need Your strength to enable me to be consistent. Help me to always realize that my responsibility is to be faithful in the ministry of prayer. The answers to those prayers are Your responsibility. Lord, please make my prayers fruitful and productive according to Your pattern and resources. May I see the results of being a person absolutely dedicated to You. Let me pray and live under Your anointing presence and power. Thank You for calling me to be involved in the lives of people around me. Help me to see them through Your eyes. Enable me to keep them and their needs before Your throne of mercy until I see those needs met out of Your limitless resources. Sensitize my heart to feel what others feel so I can enter with them into the realm of life-changing, situation-rearranging, relationship-mending intercessory prayer for them. Help me to know the specific prayers that I should pray for them. Fill me with Your compassion for them. Make me effective as an intercessory prayer warrior. In the name of my Lord Jesus Christ, and in reliance on the presence of Your Holy Spirit, I pray to You, my Father. Amen.

Chapter 12

Real Life Stories of Intercessory Prayers Answered

Following are several stories of people's lives that have been touched and changed as a result of intercessory prayer. They are all true stories that I have witnessed firsthand

From Agnostic to Creationist

They called him Grandpa Rogers. I first met him at Thanksgiving dinner in the Newcomb's' home overlooking Millerton Lake in the Sierra Mountains above Madera, California. Fred Rogers was probably seventy-seven years old when I met him. Fred was a brilliant and exceptionally successful lawyer and land developer for many years. He also was an avowed agnostic. A staunch advocate of evolution, he had neither desire nor time for God, and he most certainly did not believe in creation. However, through his relationship with the Newcomb family (members of the church I pastored and close friends of my family), Fred became a friend of mine. He took me duck hunting and fishing. We had some wonderful times together. We talked about law, politics, farming, hunting, fishing, psychology, current events, and education. However, when I would begin moving the conversation toward God, or Christ, or Christianity, he would quickly move it in a different direction. So, for fifteen or so years, the Newcomb family and I prayed for him.

One day Eleanor Newcomb called to tell me that "Grandpa" had cancer, and the doctor's prognosis was that he would not live much longer. She asked me to go with her to see him at the home of his son Russ. When we walked into his room, Eleanor said, with intensity and urgency, "Grandpa, I brought Pastor Sam to see you. He is going to tell you how to ask Jesus into your life so you can go to heaven, and we can come to be with you for all eternity. You need to listen carefully to what he has to say."

Fred broke into her sentence when she said, "He is going to tell you how to ask Jesus into your life," patted her on the shoulder, and said with a smile, "My dear, I already have!"

Eleanor didn't hear what he said, because she was so intent on his listening to what I was going to tell him about Jesus, and she repeated, "Pastor Sam is going to tell you how to ask Jesus into your life so you can go to heaven, and we can come to be with you for all eternity. You just have to listen carefully to what he has to say, because heaven will not be complete for us if you're not there!"

Again, he patted her on the shoulder, and said with a smile, "My dear, I already have!"

I said, "Eleanor, listen to what he's saying. He has already invited Jesus into his life!"

I talked to him for a while, explaining the plan of salvation, and giving him some scriptural assurances to make certain he understood. He did. Over the next few days, we visited and prayed with him several times. Soon the doctors told Russ that he should take Fred to a convalescent home where he could receive better care during his last days. Knowing that he would not be able to attend church again, I suggested that we have a baptism and communion service in his room. He gladly agreed.

After the service, Grandpa told his daughter Pat, "Honey, through the years, you have been a Creationist and I have been an evolutionist; you have been a believer and I have been an agnostic. You have been a Christian; I have been a sinner. I have now joined the ranks of Christianity! I, too, am a Creationist and a believer."

We had a great time of rejoicing together as the tears flowed down our cheeks in thanksgiving and joy. A few days later, I officiated at his funeral service, which was a beautiful tribute to a special man.

This story is a testimony of the awesome power of intercessory prayer. The Newcomb's had prayed for Grandpa Rogers for twenty or more years, and I had prayed for him for perhaps fifteen years. We just never gave up on him. He was ninety-two years old when he was born as a babe in Christ.

As long as a person draws breath, there is still hope. Intercessory prayer keeps persons we love before the throne of God, whose purpose is to draw them to Himself in love, forgiveness, and reconciliation. The true spirit of intercession keeps us praying for those who are dear to us until . . . that is, until we see our prayers in their behalf answered.

"I Want to Be Baptized into the Christian Religion!"

Fred Rogers' son Russ was a man who had a deep respect and reverence for life. I first met him in 1971. He took me hunting and fishing in the Sierra Mountains of central California. He even came to church a few times. We had a great friendship, but he was not really interested in the things of the Lord—he said he was an agnostic, like his father Fred. Within two years he and his family experienced an enormous amount of tragedy. His son, David, dived in the lake, landed on a submerged sand bar, broke his neck, and became a paraplegic, confined to a wheelchair. His other son, Rick, was killed in a motorcycle accident. I officiated at his funeral, a memorial service at their home overlooking Lake Millerton. His other three teenage children got into drugs and a lot of other things that were not good for them. Then Russ went off the deep end, got involved with drugs, divorced his wife, and just wandered around for a while. I lost contact with him for several years.

I ran into him one day when I was fishing Granite Creek, high up in the Sierras. It was like "old home week." He was on his honeymoon. He had just married Lois, a beautiful lady, who, I later learned, was a committed Christian. However, Russ was still not really interested in Christianity at that time. I did not see him again for several months, until his dad became ill with cancer. We were drawn together several times across the next few months around "Grandpa Rogers" as he prepared for his home going. Russ attended the communion and baptism service we had for Fred.

Sometime later, Russ was stricken with cancer. As soon as I learned of it, I began visiting with him regularly. We renewed the friendship that had begun eighteen years earlier. A few days before Christmas, I was visiting Russ and Lois at their home. As I started to leave, he disappeared into another room for a brief time, and then came in carrying a leather western hat just like the ones he and Lois had. He put it on my head, and it fit perfectly, just as if I had gone into the store and tried it on. I will always cherish that leather hat from a dear friend, for it carries many precious memories.

Russ was deeply impressed when he witnessed his father accept Christ into his life at the age of 92, and he saw the peace that Christ brought into

"Grandpa's" life. Fred had taught his family to be agnostics all their lives, but now Russ and I talked many times about Christ and God and eternity, and the abundant life God offers us. For most of his life he believed in a "great Power in the universe" and had a certain reverence for that Power, but he did not believe in a personal God as revealed in Jesus Christ. Then, on the day before Thanksgiving, in the Veterans Hospital, I shared with Russ about how to invite Jesus into his life and receive eternal life and peace with God. We talked for a long time about who Jesus is—the Son of God, God Himself who promises not only eternal life after death, but also abundant life and peace now in this life—even in the middle of heartache and suffering. He told me that he was not ready to make that commitment yet that day, but as I walked out of his room, I knew that it would not be long before he became a Christian. My phone rang early the next morning. Russ and Lois were on the other end of the line, and Russ said, "Happy Thanksgiving, Sam. After our talk yesterday, I invited Jesus into my life last night, and I want to be baptized into the Christian religion. And the sooner, the better! How about Sunday evening in the church baptistery?" I was thrilled! A bit stunned! Overwhelmed with wonder! That good news set me up for one of my finest Thanksgiving days. The Bible says that there is rejoicing in Heaven every time a person invites Jesus Christ into his or her life. On the following Sunday evening, I baptized Russ and Lois together in our baptistery at the church, in the presence of our whole church family.

Russ became a tower of strength to those of us who were with him during the months that followed his acceptance of Christ, right down to his coronation day when he stepped out of this life into eternity to be with God, and to be reunited with Grandpa Fred and many other friends and family members who had gone ahead of him. His relationship with God became the strength that carried him through his suffering with a confidence and peace I find rare among men. As I watched him grow in his faith during his last few months, I was reminded of the words of the Apostle Paul, which I used in his memorial service:

Therefore, we do not lose heart. Though outwardly we are wasting away, yet inwardly we are being renewed day by day. For our light and momentary troubles are achieving for us an eternal glory that far outweighs them all. So we fix our eyes not on what is seen, but on what is unseen. For what is seen is temporary, but what is unseen is eternal. (2 Corinthians 4:16-18)

When Russell Rogers accepted Christ into his heart on that Thanksgiving Day, it was the fruit of many years of intercessory prayer, not only by me, but by Lois, the Newcomb family, and our congregation.

Later in the evening following Russ' memorial service, one of his close friends asked Lois how Russ found the peace that I had shared in the service. She explained to the friend the plan of salvation, and he accepted Christ into his life. He went home a new person! That was simply another result of our intercessory prayers on behalf of Russ.

Salvation to the Third Generation!

About three months before Russ Rogers' death, I visited with Russ, Lois, and Russ' son Robert. Robert had accepted Christ two weeks before this time. It was refreshing to talk with him and Russ about who Jesus is and the paradox of submitting our lives to His control and leadership. The fear of submission to someone else after being control of one's life is tough to handle. We talked about Jesus' statement that the only way to really find life is to lose one's life. The results of such a commitment are awesome.

It was encouraging to hear Russ share his commitment to Christ. Even though he was losing the battle against cancer, his faith and trust were growing.

During our conversation, when Russ was sharing his concerns about the pain, and feeling like the cancer was taking over his body, Robert reached out and placed his hand on his dad's hand. Russ said, "Robert, that big hand on mine feels great." It was a demonstration of love and compassion from a son to a father. It was inspiring to see a son and father who had come to Christ out of a tumultuous past now expressing deep love and appreciation for one another, after many years of strained interpersonal relationships—a demonstration of the reconciling power of the love of Christ. It was another graphic portrayal of the potency of intercessory prayer.

I was privileged to witness that day a live manifestation of Paul's thrilling comments to Timothy, **"I have been reminded of your sincere faith, which first lived in your grandmother Lois and in your mother Eunice and, I am persuaded, now lives in you also"** (2 Timothy 1:5). The biblical pattern is that the Good News should be handed down from generation to generation. First, there was Grandpa Rogers, then his son Russ, and now his grandson Robert. The message is: "Do not give up when you are praying for someone and the answers are not immediate. God always hears our prayers, and He is always at work with the answers. We simply wait for His timing and resources."

We Just Need to Get Together and Pray

When I was visiting in Madera in the spring of 1993, one Saturday evening I attended Kyle's wedding. After the ceremony, his mother, Ada, called me aside to tell me a story she thought might be a blessing to me. She was right!

Soon after Troy and Ada began attending our church in Madera, they learned that Kyle had gotten in some trouble with the U.S. Army in Germany. Ada requested prayer for Kyle many times. We prayed for him repeatedly in our worship services and in our Friday morning men's Bible study. She and Troy went to Germany to try to help Kyle through the crisis. One evening—during a time of extreme turmoil and agitation—after Ada had fallen asleep, she said that my face appeared in a dream. In the dream I said to her, "Ada, remember, I've told you that we just need to get together and pray about these things. Pray together."

She awakened from her sleep, woke Troy and said, "Pastor Sam said we just have to get together and pray about these things."

So, they prayed together for Kyle.

Then they woke Kyle, and the three of them stood in a circle holding hands and prayed for guidance. God answered their prayers. Soon things began working out in ways they could not have imagined. In a few months, Kyle was back in Madera. At some time during the ordeal, he invited Jesus into his life. When he returned to Madera, he began attending church and our men's Friday morning Bible study. Now he is married to a lovely Christian lady.

I am thankful for the power of prayer. God answers the prayers of His people. He is able to "do immeasurably more than all we ask or imagine, according to his power that is at work within us, to him be glory in the church and in Christ Jesus throughout all generations, forever and ever! Amen" (Ephesians 4:20-21). Now, that is a reason for rejoicing! I am also thankful for the special relationships our Lord gives to us—relationships of trust for one another. It is the kind of trust that enables us to listen to each other, pray for one another, intercede for others, and then to rest in the knowledge that our Lord is working in their behalf and ours as well. Intercessory prayer can melt the hardest heart, remove the toughest obstacle, cleanse the worst motives, clear the guiltiest conscience, and mend the most severely broken relationships, both with God and with other persons. Prayer can accomplish what we know humanly to be impossible.

God Healed Her Negative, Bitter, Critical Attitudes

"In God we make our boast all day long, and we will praise Your name forever" (Psalm 44:8). God is still in the prayer-answering, life-changing business! One Tuesday, at the beginning of my early Morning Prayer time, I wrote a list of prayer requests, leaving space to record their answers. One of those requests was for Geri,[99] who had lived a life of personal turmoil and frustration. She always had a very critical attitude, looking for the worst in almost every situation. She complained to the parents of children she taught in Sunday school about things she did not like in the church. Several of those parents expressed concern about her negative, critical attitudes. Geri found it difficult to talk constructively about changing her attitudes. She said some things that severely hurt our hand bell choir director, Penny,[100] and Geri did not want to deal with her own harsh attitudes in a positive way.

Those of us who knew about Geri's situation began praying for her. I wrote on my Prayer Request List Geri's need for healing of her negative, bitter, critical attitudes. I prayed that she would experience release from these feelings and would be able to make amends with Penny. My wife Sandie had tried to talk to Geri in a helpful way, but Geri had "turned her off."

---

99 Not her real name.
100 Not her real name.

Two weeks later, in answer to our prayers, Geri called both Sandie and Wanda, our office manager, to tell them that she regretted the way she had handled the situation with Penny. She felt that she had committed sin in the way she had acted. She had already called Penny to apologize and ask for her forgiveness.

When Geri brought a plate of Christmas goodies into my study two days later, I could sense a spirit of release in her. I was confident that God had begun His healing work in her inner being. He had, for she continued to grow spiritually and relationally. I prayed that she would allow Him to continue and complete the work, for she was one of our most capable and gifted children's teachers. If she could be released from those negative, complaining, critical attitudes, she could be used mightily by God to teach children about His love, forgiveness, and acceptance.

This is another example of the power of intercessory prayer in the healing of inner wounds and broken or strained interpersonal relationships.

Be Still and Know

He was chairman of the board. For many years he was one of my most dependable men, and one of our strongest supporters, financially and in many other ways. Harold[101] was a self-sufficient, self-made farmer, who was exceptionally successful. When our college and career group began growing, several young adults (some of whom were dating each other) started playing on our softball team, attending church and Bible studies. One of the couples was racially mixed: he was black, she was white. They were extremely popular in the young adult group. Harold's wife Sarah[102] told the couple that they should not come to our church anymore, because they were not

---

101 Not his real name.
102 Not her real name.

a good influence on the other young people. The chairman of the Board of Christian Education wrote her a very cordial, yet firm and plain letter stating that she had no authority to tell someone they should not attend our church. He sent me a copy of the letter.

The day Harold and Sarah received the letter, Harold called me to ask if I had read the letter. I responded that I had. Harold said, "Then I know that you will set that young man straight."

I said, "No, for he was completely correct in what he said. Sarah did not have the authority to tell that couple, or anyone else not to come to the church."

After a long silence, he said, "You have not heard the last of this."

Soon Harold withdrew all his financial support from the church. He told me that my ministry in that church would end, and that the payments he had been making on my car would immediately stop. I tried to reason with him. I prayed day and night and in-between for him, seemingly without any positive results. After several months of agony, without any bitterness in my heart whatsoever, I accepted the call of another church to come as pastor. We sold our house, began packing, and made plans to move. I continued to pray that Harold and Sarah would come to personal peace and would be reconciled with me.

One night in a board meeting, I told the members that I felt I had made a mistake in resigning, and that I wanted to remain at that church. Harold quickly responded that it would not work, and he concluded the meeting. No one else made any comments.

Late on Saturday night, just two weeks before we were to move, the vice-chairman of the board called, asking if Sandie and I would meet him and the other board members at a business location. When we arrived, we discovered that all the board members and their wives (except Harold and Sarah), and several past members and their wives were there.

Naomi[103] asked, "Sam, we want to know why you are leaving."

I answered resolutely, "Because I feel it is the Lord's will." It seemed like a good answer.

Several said, "No, we're not buying that, for we do not have peace about your leaving. If God were leading in this, we believe we should have the same release that you have, and we do not."

Then someone asked, "Is the problem with Harold?"

I said, "Yes. I resigned because he gave me the distinct impression that if I remained, the church would split, because a lot of people were upset about the way I had handled the incident regarding his wife's letter."

The group made various comments that let me know that Harold and Sarah were the only persons in the church who wanted me to leave. They assured me that if I did leave, the church would have a major split, because Harold already had the next pastor picked out and was running roughshod over everyone else. The vice-chairman said the board members wanted to call a business meeting of the church to vote to ask me to stay. They were going to have the meeting at the close of the service the next morning. I told them that according to the by-laws they would need to announce such a meeting a week in advance. They agreed that the vice-chairman would announce it the next morning. The meeting would be the following Sunday. As Harold walked out the door of the church, he looked at me with fire in his eyes, and said, "You're of the devil!" Then he stomped out with Sarah following close behind. My heart ached for this man and woman, with whom I had shared many wonderful times of fellowship, both at church and in their home. I prayed incessantly for them during the coming week.

Sandie and I felt that we should leave town for a few days, just to go to some quiet spot where we could pray, reflect, and seek God's perspective on

---

103 Not her real name.

the situation. We left after the morning service to go to a little town on the northern coast of California to visit her sister. I wanted to spend some time on the lonely beach in prayer, seeking the mind of Christ.

Early the next morning all our daughters and we were riding through the beautiful coastal mountains of California, viewing some of God's marvelous handiwork. We stopped at a beautiful little roadside park. Before we stopped, we were driving along with the windows rolled up. The eight-track tape deck was playing some of our favorite music. The heater was blowing with an irritating little squeak in the fan. We were all talking and having a great time together.

As we pulled into the roadside park and stopped, I turned off the tape player, switched off the heater with its irritating little squeak, turned the engine off, and opened the windows. Then Sandie said, "Listen!" When got absolutely quiet, we began to hear the rustle of a gentle breeze through the evergreen treetops, the gurgling of a refreshing stream down the mountainside, and the joyous songs of the birds flying overhead. As we listened, we became aware of a peaceful, quiet, calm sense of worship, thankfulness, confidence, and the presence of God cascading over our spirits, emotions, and minds. Then those words flooded my heart with new assurance: "Be still and know that I am God" (Psalm 46:10). Another translation says, "Cease striving, relax and let go, and know that I am God." I knew then that God had spoken to me, and that He was already working in my behalf, and that He would go back with me into the situation with which I was struggling. He would supply the answers and the resources needed to bring victory and restoration. He did, for I was able to go back home and witness God's miracle-working power as He solved the problem, I was facing in a way I could never have dreamed possible. We had a relaxing week at Ft. Bragg. I spent many hours walking the beach, praying and asking God to protect me from any bitterness toward Harold and Sarah and to bring healing, restoration, and reconciliation to them.

The next Sunday, when the vote was taken, there were three negative votes and one hundred and twenty-one positive votes asking me to stay as pastor. We stayed at that church for another fifteen years and enjoyed a fruitful ministry. Toward the end of the business meeting, Harold and Sarah walked out of the church. Soon they were attending another church. Every time they came into my thoughts, and every time I saw them after that I prayed for their healing and restoration, yet I always got a cold reception from them whenever we met anywhere. For three years I continued praying for them.

One Sunday afternoon, we were at our district campground up in the Sierra Mountains. The occasion was a picnic and fellowship for all the churches in our district. I was standing and eating alone under an apple tree when I saw Harold coming my way. I was concerned that he was coming for a confrontation, so I breathed a silent prayer for him as he approached. As he stepped into the shade of the tree, he looked me in the eyes, as his eyes filled with tears, and said, "Pastor, I am so sorry for the way things happened between us. I apologize and ask your forgiveness."

I was overwhelmed with joy and relief, as I quickly offered my forgiveness and restoration of friendship. This incident was a beautiful expression of the reconciling love of our Lord Jesus Christ.

Although Harold and Sarah had already affiliated with another congregation, when Harold had a heart attack a few years later, at the pastor's request, I went to see him in the hospital. We had a wonderful visit and prayer time together. Late that night Sarah telephoned to tell me that the doctor had called asking the family to come quickly to the hospital. She asked if I could meet them there. When we arrived, the doctor said that Harold had just gone to sleep and slipped out into eternity. I was extremely grateful for that reconciliation time a few years before. Sarah asked if I would officiate at the funeral, and I told her that I would be honored to do so. I am confident that the intercessory prayers were the reason Harold died with a clear conscience, and our friendship was restored.

Interceding for Physical Healing

Sandie got out of bed one morning at about 5:00 o'clock. When I got up shortly thereafter, she came in the room and asked me to pray for her. She said that before she arose, she felt like one whole side of her was going to explode. I put my arm around her and began praying for her healing. As I prayed, I became very weak physically; I began feeling faint and nauseous. After I finished praying, and Sandie went out into the family room, I had to just lean on the bathroom sink counter for a few minutes to regain my strength. About the time my strength began to return, Sandie came back into the room to tell me that she was feeling much better. Soon she was back to normal again. Although I did not understand my own weakness and nausea, I praised the Lord for His healing power for Sandie! We were confident that it came as a direct answer to intercessory prayer.

The day before this incident, Bonnie came to my office to tell me about an experience she had on the previous Thursday. She and Billie were observing a day of fasting and prayer on behalf of our Visitation Pastor Gene (open heart surgery) and Mickie (chemotherapy). Late in the afternoon she walked over to Billie's home to pray and visit for a few minutes. On the way back home, Bonnie became very weak and sick. She began hemorrhaging. As she continued to pray and went for a bike ride with Jerol that evening, the weakness and sickness left, except for the hemorrhaging, which lasted for a couple of days.

However, Gene Johnson came through the surgery beautifully. His recovery came much more quickly than the doctors had expected.

Although the chemotherapy made Mickie somewhat nauseous, she was not violently sick as she had been in previous treatments—each successive treatment normally gets harder than previous ones, but we praised God for his intervention this time. Our prayer was, "Lord, thank You for continuing to speak to us from Your Word about Your healing power. Amen."

"Coincidence?" someone might ask. Perhaps, but there are just too many incidents in which, as Archbishop William Temple once noted, the coincidences occurred much more frequently when we prayed.[104]

When He Prayed for His Friends

The power of intercessory prayer is dramatically illustrated in the life of Job.

"Then Job replied: 'Even today my complaint is bitter; his hand is heavy in spite of my groaning. If only I knew where to find him; if only I could go to his dwelling! I would state my case before him and fill my mouth with arguments. I would find out what he would answer me, and consider what he would say. Would he oppose me with great power? No, he would not press charges against me. There an upright man could present his case before him, and I would be delivered forever from my judge. But if I go to the east, he is not there; if I go to the west, I do not find him. When he is at work in the north, I do not see him; when he turns to the south, I catch no glimpse of him. But he knows the way that I take; when he has tested me, I will come forth as gold. My feet have closely followed his steps; I

104 Foster, R. J. (1978). *Celebration of Discipline: The Path to Spiritual Growth.* New York, NY: Harper & Row.

have kept to his way without turning aside. I have not departed from the commands of his lips; I have treasured the words of his mouth more than my daily bread" (Job 23:1-12).

Job lost his cattle, his family, and his health. However, during his pain, difficulty, struggle, and the apparent silence of God, Job kept his faith in God. He never gave up, even though his wife encouraged him to curse God and die! Job said in verse 12, *"I have not departed from the commands of his lips; I have treasured the words of his mouth more than my daily bread"* (Job 23:12). Job's focus—while he was aware of the pain, suffering, hurt, and loss—was on the God Who would eventually bring him through to victory over his struggles. He said, *"I have kept to his way without turning aside."* His faithful vision of God led him to confession and repentance, for he said, *"My ears had heard of you but now my eyes have seen you. Therefore I despise myself and repent in dust and ashes"* (Job 42:5-6).

Many people have heard of God, and even claim to know Him, but they have never really *seen* Him in an intimate, personal, life-changing relationship. Job's continued faithfulness to God in prayer led him to such a relationship and vision. His vision of God led him to intercessory prayer for his friends. Then, because he maintained his focus on God and on helping others, he was led out of his difficulties—released, renewed, refreshed—more than ever before. The biblical record says of Job, **"After Job had prayed for his friends, the Lord made him prosperous again and gave him twice as much as he had before"** (Job 42:10). His faithfulness to God, and his intercessory prayers for his friends, placed him in a position where God could touch, heal, and prosper him as never before.

So, when we feel like quitting, we can look to the God who is there and who is not silent. Keep our praying on target, and our faithfulness in order. Stay before His throne of grace and mercy in unwavering intercessory prayer. In the process, although the main purpose of intercessory prayer is to help other persons, God will give us victory in the situations we face in our own lives.

I submit that in every situation and decision that we face, particularly in those difficult times when we just cannot seem to find the answer or the resources, we need to simply let go and let God have His way. Stop trying and start trusting—in God. That trust is cultivated in the solitary place, alone with God, listening for His voice and directions. We should do everything we can to make amends, and then continue in intercessory prayer until, in God's timing, He provides the resolution, reconciliation, and restoration.

My Covenant Responsibility for You

This entry from my Journal describes the kind of covenant responsibility we have to each other in the Body of Christ for intercessory prayer and for caring for one another. It is based on 1 Samuel 12:23-24, which says, **"As for me, far be it from me that I should sin against the Lord by failing to pray for you. And I will teach you the way that is good and right. But be sure to fear the Lord and serve him faithfully with all your heart; consider what great things he has done for you."**

In these verses, I see four responsibilities that we have to one another regarding intercessory prayer, and our ministry to one another which grows out of such prayer.

A Responsibility to Pray for You

Samuel said, **"As for me, far be it from me that I should sin against the Lord by failing to pray for you"** (1 Samuel 12:23a).

It is a privilege for me to go the Throne of God in intercessory prayer on your behalf. I want God's best for you, and if I want it for you, I must ask, in faith, believing that God wants to give you His best. There is no greater privilege or responsibility that we Christians have than intercessory prayer. Yet, God never fails—every time I go to Him on your behalf, He always sends me away with some blessing for myself, as well as meeting your needs.

A Responsibility to Teach You

Samuel said, **"And I will teach you the way that is good and right"** (1 Samuel 12:23b).

The Word is my source for teaching you God's truths. In that Word, God has given us everything we need for living life in the way He wants us to live— **"the way that is good and right."** Yet, it is more than just teaching you abstract ideas and vague concepts. The best way I can teach you is by the example of my life of faith, trust, and dependence on God. As I let Him lead me, I become equipped to lead you.

A Responsibility to Admonish You

As one who loves you, and who is interested in your growth and maturity in the Lord, I am called by God to challenge you to live a life of reverence and respect, an attitude of worship, glorifying God in all you do. If I see you headed in a direction that could be dangerous or harmful to you, I need to warn you, counsel you to change your direction, and pray for God's help and direction. Samuel said, **"Be sure to fear the Lord and serve him faithfully"** (1 Samuel 12:24a). I should encourage you to be faithful to Him, for in your faithfulness lies God's opportunity to give you His greatest blessings. His promises to His chosen, faithful ones are unending.

A Responsibility to Remind You

During those times when you feel discouraged or inadequate, I am called to remind you of how God has blessed you in the past. Samuel said, **"Consider what great things He has done for you"** (1 Samuel 12:24b). Such reminders will enable you to realize that, just as he has blessed you in the past, He has all the resources needed to bless you in the present and future.

I am thankful that God has given these words of instruction and encouragement. They show how we can minister to one another through intercessory prayer.

PRAYER RESPONSE

My precious Lord, this kind of prayer is not easy. It is difficult to follow through with a commitment to pray for others, for I often face more difficulties and setbacks of my own than I can handle. Yet it is true that when I enter deeply into the needs, hurts and concerns of others, I begin to find my own needs, hurts, and concerns being met, healed, and fulfilled. For when I bring other persons before Your throne, I, too, am escorted into Your healing presence where I can be touched at the very core of my being.

Since Your heart, Lord, is "large enough to embrace the entire universe," certainly there is room there for me and for those You have entrusted to my care.

This being true, my Lord, then enable me to open my heart to Your great heart of love and compassion. Help me to develop more and more into an intercessory prayer warrior, placing before Your throne of mercy the people You have given me to love and lead. Make me effective in this, for this is the most important work I can do. Help me to **"pray in the Spirit on all occasions, with all kinds of prayers and requests. [And] with this in mind [help me to] always keep on praying for all the saints."**[105] Empower me Lord, so that "whenever I open my mouth, words may be given me so that I will fearlessly make known the gospel for which I am an ambassador."[106] Enable me to "proclaim it clearly as I should."[107] May I always "wrestle in prayer" for those for whom You have given me responsibility that they "may stand firm in all the will of God, mature and fully assured."[108] And whatever I do, help me to work at it with all my heart, as working for the Lord, not for men, since I know that I will receive an inheritance from the Lord as a reward. It is the Lord Christ I am serving![109] May I never forget this.

In the name of the One who is my Strength, my Help, my Shield, and my Source—my Lord Jesus Christ, I pray. Amen.

---

105 Ephesians 5:18.
106 Ephesians 6:19.
107 Colossians 4:4.
108 Colossians 4:12.
109 Colossians 3:23-24.

PART 4

FORMING PEOPLE
OF WORSHIP

Chapter 13

Worship Is at the Heart of Spiritual Formation

Across the past several years, as I have attempted to study and practice spiritual formation in my own life and ministry, I have become convinced that worship is at the heart of spiritual formation, both individually and corporately. Becoming *People of the Word*, *People of Prayer*, and *People of Worship* forms a triad of spiritual disciplines that shapes us into *People of God*. William Nichols wrote: "Worship is the only supreme and indispensable activity of the Christian Church. It alone will endure . . . into heaven when all other activities of the church have passed away."[110]

We Exist to Worship God

Ralph P. Martin declares the importance of worship in the church, saying,

---

110 Nichols, W. (1958). *Jacob's Ladder: The Meaning of Worship.* Louisville, KY: Knox Press.

Worship is more than just a facet of church life. It underlines and informs our understanding of all we believe and cherish concerning God and His design for the church and the world. The focus of that design is Christ in whom authentic worship finds its model and through whom our worship takes on meaning. All we believe and proclaim is affected by how we see the ministry and mission of the church and its agenda in the divine scheme.[111]

As Christian people we exist to worship God. Unless worship is given top priority in our lives, we have no basis for an enduring life of meaning and purpose. We were created, and have been called by God, to "offer the Father the sacrifices of praise and thanksgiving, and to celebrate the mighty acts of God in creation, redemption, and the final triumph of His kingdom in this world and beyond."[112] All our ministry, activities, and work should be results of our relationship with God in worship.

True worship sets a person, a family, a church, a college, or a nation in a right relationship with God. Such an alliance with God positions everything else in proper perspective: goals, motives, service, ministries, activities, interpersonal relationships, priorities, decisions. When an individual determines to become a person of the Word, a person of prayer, a person of worship, then he or she is shaped into a person of God. Worship gathers up all the other spiritual disciplines to give them cohesiveness, symmetry, and balance.

---

111 Martin, R. P. (1982). *The Worship of God: Some Theological, Pastoral and Practical Reflections. Grand Rapids, MI: William E. Eerdmans. 209.*
112 Margin.

Worship Is the Celebration of God

The reason this is true is that in worship our focus is first on God rather than on our needs or on our relationships with other persons. Worship places God at the center of our spiritual formation. Genuine spiritual formation is the result of our relationship with God through His Word and prayer. Ralph Martin defines worship as "the dramatic celebration of God in His supreme worth in such a manner that His worthiness becomes the norm and inspiration of human living."[113] This definition places God at the center of worship and makes certain that our motive in worship is not obscured or compromised.

The clear reminder of the 1975 Hartford appeal was: "We worship God because God is to be worshiped."[114] (Martin, 1982) Maintaining this focus will enable us to give our highest expression of worship, thus providing us with ample reasons for service: we serve God because of Who He is and what He has done and is doing in Christ. Therefore, in worship we discover the key to our spiritual formation. Robert Webber affirms: "The focus of worship is not human experience, not a lecture, not entertainment, but Jesus Christ—His life, death and resurrection."[115] (Webber, 1982. 11)

John Richard Neuhaus gives an appropriate warning: "The activity called worship is not true worship if it can be done legitimately in any other context . . . Worship, if done in response to anything other than the mystery of God in Christ, is idolatry."[116] (Neuhaus, 1979, 105) Keeping God central in worship will deliver us from a self-centered approach to worship.

It is true that in worship our spirits are lifted, we receive help to cope with the problems life throws at us, we gain perspective on how to

---

113 Martin, R. P. (1982). *The Worship of God: Some Theological, Pastoral and Practical Reflections. Grand Rapids, MI: William E. Eerdmans. 4.*
114 Martin.
115 Webber, R. E. (1982). *Worship Is a Verb. Dallas, TX: Word Pub. 11.*
116 Neuhaus, J. R. (1979). *Freedom for Ministry. New York, NY: Harper & Row. 105.*

strengthen broken or strained relationships with other persons, and we are given resources with which to make decisions. However, these experiences should not be the aim of worship, but rather by-products of the original purpose of worship, which is focus on God. "An encounter with [God] may be painful and [involve] a call to sacrifice, commitment, and self-denial." [117] (Martin, 1982, 5)

Such an encounter with God may result in the call, not "Smile, God loves you," but rather, "Repent, weep, tremble," because God loves you. His "love expressed in Christ's cross, suffering, and victory is no cheap idea or weak sentiment. It can only be celebrated with reverence and wonder; it will almost certainly [involve] a searching decision to share its agony and conflict." [118] (Martin, 1982)

Worship Is a Relationship Between Us and God

Whatever else it may mean, Eleanor Kreider says, "worship is a relationship, something that goes on between persons, between us and God . . .. Worship is what we call our side of the relationship . . .. Worship is our total personal response, individually and together as God's people to our God." [119] God initiates the relationship, drawing us to Himself in love through His Son Jesus Christ, by the Holy Spirit. Worship is not just an act, a ritual, a habit, a pastime. It is a living, vital relationship between God and us. The Creator God invites us into an intimate, personal relationship of fellowship. We worship Him because He is worthy of our highest adoration, worship, fellowship, and service.

---

117 Martin. 5.
118 Martin.
119 *Kreider, E. (1990). Enter His Gates. Scottdale, PA: Herald Press. 21.*

William Temple defined worship saying, "To worship is to quicken the conscience by the holiness of God, to feed the mind with the truth of God, to purge the imagination by the beauty of God, to open the heart to the love of God, to devote the will to the purpose of God."[120] This is a good summary of the first facet of spiritual formation, *the forming of our inner lives and relationships with God.* The second facet, *in a way that transforms our outer lives and relationships with other persons,* becomes the *result* of our worship of God and not the *goal.* This enables us to keep our motives, aspirations, activities, priorities, and service in proper perspective. Richard Foster says worship is

> our responding to the overtures of love from the heart of the Father. If the Lord is to be Lord, worship must have priority in our lives. The first commandment of Jesus is **"Love the Lord your God with all your heart, and with all your soul, and with all your mind, and with all your strength"** (Mark 12:30). The divine priority is worship first, service second. Our lives are to be punctuated with praise, thanksgiving and adoration. Service flows out of worship. Service as a substitute for worship is idolatry. Activity may become the enemy of adoration.[121]

Ralph Martin concludes, "If the celebration of God's worthiness is meant to lift us into the light of His presence, that elevation will provide a place from which we see our lives in a fresh light. The vision of God, Calvin noted, leads to a heightened appreciation of who we are: 'in Thy light we see light.'"[122]

---

120 *Foster, R. J. (1978). Celebration of Discipline: The Path to Spiritual Growth. New York, NY: Harper & Row.* 21.

121 Foster. 140.

122 Martin, R. P. (1982). *The Worship of God: Some Theological, Pastoral and Practical Reflections. Grand Rapids, MI: William E. Eerdmans.* 6.

Therefore, our worship is directed to God, Whose response is to bless, direct, help, strengthen, and enlighten us as we worship. Martin describes this as "the dialogue shape of Christian worship," in which worship is the "two-beat rhythm of revelation and response. God speaks, we answer. God acts, we accept and give. God gives, we receive,"[123] (Martin, 1982) and we give to others. Worship then, implies a human response in terms of giving to God. This is pictured in the biblical setting of man's sacrifice, making an offering to God. The sacrificial offering is given, not to gain something for oneself, not to make one worthy to receive blessings, but as a joyous, thankful response to the giving God Who makes His love known in Christ.

When viewed in this way, corporate worship is seen not as a preliminary to the message of the minister, but rather as the central focus of the service. The songs, prayers, emotions, giving of offerings, Scripture readings, fellowship, emphasis on social or political issues, teaching of the Word, should all be in response to our worship of the God Who is worthy of our worship, praise and adoration. Private worship is not just a personal, emotional, self-seeking ritual, but rather a vital relationship with the living creator God Himself, through His Son Jesus Christ. In such an indispensable alliance God and we join in partnership in our spiritual formation.

Worship Is Participation in What Christ Has Done for Us

The real Leader in worship is Jesus Christ, through what He has done and continues to do, by the Holy Spirit (Hebrews 9:8, 14) as the Mediator of the new covenant between God the Father and His people. He is the One who came from God as the incarnate Son of God, Son of man. In His vicarious temptations, sufferings, death, burial, resurrection,

---

123 Martin.

ascension, and High Priesthood He leads us to God in worship. Because Christ **"entered the Most Holy Place once for all by His own blood, having obtained eternal redemption"** (Hebrews 9:12), **"He entered heaven itself, now to appear for us in God's presence"** (Hebrews 9:24). Since **"He has appeared once for all at the end of the ages to do away with sin by the sacrifice of Himself,"** He is now **"the Mediator of a new covenant, that those who are called may receive the promised eternal inheritance—now that he has died as a ransom to set them free from the sins committed under the first covenant"** (Hebrews 9:15).

Marianne Micks beautifully summarizes Christ's leadership in our worship of God:

We worship in the name of Jesus Christ because God united Himself to human beings in that one person. Human beings are irrevocably united with God, bonded to Him, through the person of Christ. We bear His name, and He bears ours. He wears our nature and invites us to come into communion with His [nature]. Christian worship occurs because of that awesome connection between humanity and deity—effected in the event of Jesus the Christ, through His life and His death and His resurrection. So, we worship in the power of His Spirit. We worship in His name. And we worship in thanksgiving for His great gift of new relationship.[124]

This Jesus Christ, Mediator of a new covenant, **"who through the eternal Spirit offered himself unblemished to God, [to] cleanse our consciences from acts that lead to death, so that we may serve the living God"** (Hebrews 9:14) is the one true High Priest—the one True Worshiper **"who serves in the sanctuary, the true tabernacle set up by the Lord,**

---

124 Micks, M. H. (1982). *The Joy of Worship. Philadelphia, PA: Westminster Press. 37.*

not by man" (Hebrews 8:2). Christ is the Worship Leader in the holy places—the heavenly sanctuary, where He **"sat down at the right hand of the throne of the Majesty in heaven"** (Hebrews 8:1). This heavenly sanctuary is the **"true tabernacle set up by the Lord, not by man."**

So, Jesus comes to be the Priest of creation, to do what we cannot do by ourselves: glorify the Father in a life of perfect submission, as described in Hebrews:

> **During the days of Jesus' life on earth, he offered up prayers and petitions with loud cries and tears to the one who could save him from death, and he was heard because of his reverent submission. Although he was a son, he learned obedience from what he suffered and, once made perfect, he became the source of eternal salvation for all who obey him and was designated by God to be high priest in the order of Melchizedek** (Hebrews 5:7-10).

As the true Leader of Worship, then, Christ leads us to participate, by the Holy Spirit, in **"His reverent submission to the Father."** He assumes our rights, consecrates our humanity, dies our death, suffers for and with us, rises to be the Leader, in order that He might take us in communion with Himself, back to the Father, **"that at the name of Jesus every knee should bow, in heaven and on earth and under the earth, and every tongue confess that Jesus Christ is Lord, to the glory of God the Father"** (Philippians 2:10-11).

In worship, then, Christ the Worship Leader *"leads us in triumphal procession"* to the Throne of God, the Sanctuary, the Most Holy Place where we participate in His forgiveness, cleansing, salvation, reconciliation, and sanctification. He enables us to say with great joy and exuberance,

"Thanks be to God, who always leads us in triumphal procession in Christ and through us spreads everywhere the fragrance of the knowledge of him" (2 Corinthians 2:14).

Then, just as He came into the world as the One True Mediator to reconcile us to God (*forming our inner lives and relationships with God*) He leads us back into the world to be reconciled to others (*in a way that transforms our outer lives and relationships with other persons*). This relationship with God in worship enables us to **"spread everywhere the fragrance of the knowledge of Him"** (2 Corinthians 2:14). Paul describes Christ as the One who stands beside God and stands there as our ally and friend. The identification comes during a passage of ringing rhetoric, beginning, **"If God is for us, who is against us?"** The passage ends with the passionate assertion that nothing can ever **"separate us from the love of God in Christ Jesus our Lord"** (Romans 8:31-39). In this context Christ Jesus is described as the One who died, who was raised, who is at the right hand of God, and who indeed intercedes for us.[125]

The heart of worship is that Jesus lives to intercede forever for us (Hebrews 7:25). Micks says that in the person of the risen Lord we have a friend in the courts of heaven.[126] Unlike the Jewish high priests, who had to be replaced whenever they died, Jesus holds his priesthood permanently. **"Therefore he is able to save completely those who come [draw near] to God through him, because he always lives to intercede for them. Such a high priest meets our need—one who is holy, blameless, pure, set apart from sinners, exalted above the heavens"** (Hebrews 7:25).

Drawing near to God, in the language of the Hebrews, means worshiping. The glory of the Gospel is not just that Jesus is the only True Worshiper, but He calls us to unite with Him (*forming our inner lives*) that we too, by life in the Spirit, might carry His joy in our hearts, on our lips,

---

125 Micks, M. H. (1982). *The Joy of Worship. Philadelphia, PA: Westminster Press. 36.*
126 Micks, M. H. (1982). *The Joy of Worship. Philadelphia, PA: Westminster Press. 34.*

and in our hands into the world (forming our outer relationships) in which we live. Since Christ has opened for us **"a new and living way to God,"** we can **"draw near to God with a sincere heart in full assurance of faith"** (Hebrews 10:20, 22).

The title "Christ," or "Messiah," means "the anointed one." In Old Testament times priests, kings, and prophets were anointed with holy oil when they were inaugurated in their new leadership roles. The holy oil was called "unction," a word that comes from the Latin word for anointing. Since Christ is head of the church, this anointing is poured out on its members. We ourselves are not worthy to storm the throne of God, but since Christ wears the anointing of the High Priest—Christ, our Brother, Son of God, Son of man— "allied with God . . . He admits us into this most honorable alliance. In Him we can offer ourselves and our all to God, and freely enter the heavenly sanctuary."[127] We are invited, not only to come to the throne of God, but to **"approach the throne of grace with confidence** [boldly, KJV], **so that we may receive mercy and find grace to help us in our time of need"** (Hebrews 4:16).

By life in the Spirit in worship, Christ's prayers become our prayers that we might be His Body in worship and participate in His intercessions for, and ministry to, other persons. This is the center of true Christian worship. Calvin described Christ as "the great Choirmaster who tunes our hearts to sing His praise!"[128] (Torrance, 1989, 1993, 6)

---

127 Micks. 32-36.
128 Torrance, J. B. (1989, 1993). Theology and Ministry of Worship Class Notes, Fuller Theological Seminary, Samuel K. Bruce. Pasadena, CA. 6.

Failure to Worship God is "Edging God Out"

We have said that *worship is at the heart of spiritual formation.* Since this is true, it follows that refusal to worship God as the center of our lives (which grows from an egocentric, self-centered posture toward life) will hinder, and even destroy, our spiritual formation. Al Shine, a friend of mine, a dynamic Christian high school science teacher, and member of my Men's Bible Study Group, gave me an acrostic for the word *ego,* which graphically describes the results of refusing to worship God as the center of our lives. He said that **EGO** is *Edging God Out.*[129] This is true, for when the self is at the center of a life, there is no room for God. When God is "edged out" of a person's life, there is no place for worship, thus our spiritual formation is checkmated. The ego-centered lifestyle is the path to absolute defeat, utter frustration, total disappointment, complete havoc in a person's life.

Jesus pointedly illustrates this in Luke 11:24-26, as He describes an evil spirit coming out of a man, wandering around seeking rest, not finding it, and returning to the house he left. When he returned, he found the house swept clean and put in order. Then the evil spirit **"goes and takes seven other spirits more wicked than itself, and they go in and live there. And the final condition of that man is worse than the first."**

When we, through confession, repentance, and belief in Christ receive salvation, our lives are **"swept clean and put in order."** But unless we, through worship, place God central in our lives, we are vulnerable to the influence and domination of **"other spirits"** which can lead to the spirit of idolatry. When anything or person, other than the creator God, the God of the Bible, becomes central in a person's life and affections, it becomes an idol.

---

129 Shine, Al. Dr. Sam Bruce's Men's Group, Fourth Street Church of God, Madera, CA.

In Old Testament times, Israel was constantly bombarded by idolatry. There were various portable centers set up in the hills, under the trees, for the purpose of idol worship. People wandered from one to another of these seeking God, or gods, attempting to find satisfaction, peace and joy. But the true God of the Bible was not to be found in these. The Prophet Jeremiah called the people to return to their center, as He pleaded, **"'Return, faithless people; I will cure you of backsliding.' They answered, 'Yes, we will come to you, for you are the Lord our God. Surely the idolatrous commotion on the hills and mountains is a deception; surely in the Lord our God is the salvation of Israel'"** (Jeremiah 3:21-23). Another translation says, **"The hills are a delusion."** Anything or any personality that replaces God as the center is a delusion. Satan and the world system offer a myriad of substitute loyalties that lead only to deception and end in futility and frustration. Eugene Peterson comments:

> People who do not worship live in a vast shopping mall where they go from shop to shop, expending enormous sums of energy and making endless trips to meet first this need and then that appetite, this whim and that fancy. Life lurches from one partial satisfaction to another, interrupted by ditches of disappointment. Motion is fueled by the successive illusions that purchasing this wardrobe, driving that car, eating this meal, drinking that beverage will center life and give it coherence.[130]

By contrast, Jeremiah saw that **"A glorious throne, exalted from the beginning, is the place of our sanctuary"** (Jeremiah 17:12). Centuries later, John saw this same throne in his vision, as recorded in the Revelation. Peterson continues:

---

130 Peterson, E. H. (1988). *Reversed Thunder: The Revelation of John & The Praying Imagination. New York, NY: Harper & Row. 60.*

The throne of God—the fact of the throne and the fact of God enthroned—is the revelation of the Bible. The throne is the supreme revelation of Scripture. In early Bible history the throne is unnamed but is ever present. All the pictures of the early times are pictures of men setting their lives into relationship with the throne of God and thus finding peace, or rebelling against the government of God and thus perishing. In the failure of the chosen people to recognize the abiding fact of the throne of God lay the establishment of the monarch in Israel, that wholly evil thing. (Peterson, 1988, 60) "'They have not rejected you,' said God to Samuel, 'They have rejected me,'" and out of that rejection began all their trouble.[131] (G. Campbell Morgan, quoted in Peterson, 1988, 61)

Failure to worship God as the Center— *"Edging God Out"*—is the reason many people constantly search for peace, yet never find it; long for satisfaction, yet never realize it; seek happiness, yet never experience it. But when Christians worship with the realization that they are in the presence of the living God who rules and reigns, speaks and reveals, creates and redeems, orders and blesses, they begin to find peace, realize satisfaction, and experience happiness. "Edging God Out" is the greatest hindrance to our spiritual formation, the forming of our inner lives and relationships with God in a way that transforms our outer lives and relationships with other persons. On the other hand, giving God His well-deserved place as the center of our lives is the path to spiritual formation.

---

131 Morgan, G. Campbell. Quoted in Peterson, E. H. (1988). *Reversed Thunder: The Revelation of John & The Praying Imagination. New York, NY: Harper & Row. 61.*

Jesus Christ Holds All Things Together

Paul gives the reason for this teaching in Colossians 1:16-17, **"For by him all things were created: things in heaven and on earth, visible and invisible, whether thrones or powers or rulers or authorities; all things were created by him and for him. He is before all things, and in him all things hold together."** Placing Jesus Christ in the center of our lives is the source of our spiritual formation because **"in him all things hold together."**

A guide took a group of people through an atomic laboratory and explained that all matter was composed of rapidly moving electric particles. The tourists studied models of molecules and were amazed to learn that matter is made up primarily of space. During the question period, one visitor asked, "If this is the way matter works, what holds it all together?" For that, the guide had no answer.

We Christians have the answer: Jesus Christ! Since He is the Creator of all things, and He is before all things, He can hold all things together (Colossians 1:16-17). This is another affirmation that Jesus Christ is God. Only God exists before all creation, and only God can make creation hold together. His Son Jesus Christ is the one Person who can hold our lives together! He is the author of our spiritual formation, and we have the privilege of deciding to follow Him in the disciplines that lead to spiritual formation in our lives—particularly the disciplines of becoming *people of the Word, people of prayer, people of worship* which shape us into *people of God*.

Here is a simple illustration of how God holds all things together. It is possible for a human mechanic to leave the machine he has constructed to work without his personal supervision, because, when he leaves it, God's laws are in operation—centrifugal force, gravity, combustion, electricity, etc. Because God's laws are in control, the materials of which the machine is made retain their solidity, the steel stays solid, and the gasoline burns to give power. Gravity holds it down on the floor. Centrifugal force keeps it from flying out the window.

But God cannot leave the universe that He has constructed to itself—not even the smallest part of it, in all its immensity and intricacy of movement—for if God leaves, there is no second force to take care of the universe He has constructed. God cannot withdraw His supervision from even a single atom of matter for even a moment, for if He did, everything would fall apart. Every moment, all over the world, the act of creation must be continued. The existence of the world witnesses to the continuing creative influence of God. Active, consistent, constant power must flood the universe, or its harmonious working will stop, and its very existence will be terminated.

The signs of an all-pervading supernatural energy meet us wherever we turn. Every leaf waves in it, every plant in all its organic processes lives in it; it rolls around the clouds or they would not move; it fires the sunbeams, or they would not shine; and there is not a wave that restlessly rises and sinks, nor a whisper of the wind that blows where it wishes, that does not speak of the immediate intervention of God.[132]

What happens when people break the law of God that holds the atoms together? In November 1952, a small hydrogen bomb was dropped on Eniwetok, a small South Pacific Island. The island burned for six hours. Soon it disappeared completely. Such power can vaporize all concrete and steel within a ten-mile radius, covering 314.6 square miles. When atoms are split in this way, everything around them begins to fall apart. Similarly,

---

132 Tan, P. L. (1984). *Encyclopedia of 7000 Illustrations. Rockville, MD: Assurance Publishers. 448.*

when men and women try to live their lives without God and His Son Jesus Christ in control, everything in and around their lives begins to fall apart—emotions, logic, families . . . life! A person cannot break or ignore God's laws without tragic results.[133]

Jesus Christ, the Son of God, is the one Person who can hold our lives together. He is the one Person who can give meaning and cohesiveness to life. Jesus Christ must be at the center of life, just as the sun is at the center of the universe to hold it together and give it light, warmth and life. We must never lose sight of him! As we see families falling apart around us, people giving way to the pressures of society, lives caving in because of destructive habits, and morals being discarded in exchange for self-indulgence—we need a Center! A wheel without a center will collapse. A universe without a center would fall apart. A life without Jesus Christ at the center will disintegrate. But with Jesus Christ at the center, our lives can have meaning, cohesiveness, joy, peace, contentment, happiness, and satisfaction. Jesus Christ can provide us with all we ever need for a fulfilling life, for He is the one Person who can hold life together.

Spiritual formation through worship keeps Christ at the center of our lives and relationships, and He is the One who holds us and our relationships together. Truly, worship is the heart of spiritual formation.

---

133 See 2 Peter 3:8-18. Note especially verses 11, 14, 17-18.

Chapter 14

An Invitation

In my introductory remarks to this book, I described the stages of renewal in the Word, renewal in prayer, and renewal in worship through which God led me and the congregation which I pastored. During my early morning worship time, I was praying about worship in my own spiritual formation and the worship times we spent together as a congregation. As I continued to pray, quote and study Scripture, the following thoughts began to flood my mind, and I wrote them in my *Journal.* I share them here as a charge to the churches and persons with whom I am privileged to minister.

When King Solomon finished building the temple and the priests and people were gathered for the dedication ceremony,

The trumpeters and singers joined in unison, as with one voice, to give praise and thanks to the Lord. Accompanied by trumpets, cymbals and other instruments, they raised their voices in praise to the Lord and sang, "He is good; his love endures forever." Then the temple of the Lord was filled with a cloud,

and the priests could not perform their service because of the cloud, for the glory of the Lord filled the temple of God (2 Chronicles 5:13-14).

King Solomon and the people entered that dedication service with the right focus, the correct purpose, and the proper motives. They **"joined in unison, as with one voice, to give praise and thanks to the Lord."** They came together to worship God. When God's people join in this way, united in a spirit of worship and love, lifting their hearts and voices in praise to God—in response to God's invitation to worship Him and to be touched by His life-transforming power—God's presence and power fill the place where they are gathered in worship. This is true in both individual and corporate worship.

The above passage of Scripture inspired Steven L. Fry to write a beautiful song that invites the Lord God to be present in the worship service just as He was in the dedication service of Solomon and his people:

Oh the glory of Your presence,
We Your temple give You reverence.
So arise to Your rest and be blessed by our praise
As we glory in your embrace
As Your presence now fills this place.[134]

Worship Ushers Us into the Presence of the Creator God

It is an awesome event when people truly worship the Lord in this way. There is spontaneity, freedom, a sense of joy, peace, victory, transparency, and oneness that comes from the throne of God Himself, as the presence

---

134 Fry, S. L. (1983). *Oh the Glory of Your Presence. Chatsworth, CA: Birdwing Music/Cherry Lane Music.*

and glory of the Lord fills the place of worship. In such a setting, where hearts are set free to truly worship God, prayers can go up before Him unhampered, needs are met, lives are changed, spirits are rekindled, hearts are renewed, emotions are encouraged, relationships are mended. Evelyn Underhill affirms this, "Christian worship is always directed towards the sanctification of life. All worship has a creative aim, for it is a movement of the creature in the direction of Reality; and here the creative aim is that total transfiguration of the created order in which the incarnation of the Logos [the Word] finds its goal."[135]

Worship ushers us into the presence of the Creator God, whose purpose is to transform us by the **"renewing of our minds"** (Romans 12:1-2), spirits, emotions, and relationships. Worship like this sets the climate for the removal of negative viewpoints, divisive attitudes, dissenting opinions, critical comments, and complaining spirits. It brings spiritual renewal into the lives of worshipers. Such things happen when people determine to worship the Lord in a spirit of love, unity and oneness of purpose.

An Invitation from His Majesty about Worship

Across several months I prayed consistently to our Heavenly Father, asking Him to send a fresh breeze of revival into my own life, into the church, and across our nation. As I studied and memorized the Word of God, saturating my heart, mind, spirit, and emotions with the **"living and enduring Word of God"** (1 Peter 1:23) I sensed deep changes taking place within my inner being. I realized that the path to spiritual refreshment is to be found along the avenues of worship—worship that is alive with adoration and thankfulness to God who is worthy of our highest praise.

---

135 Underhill, E. (1989). *Worship. New York, NY: Crossroad Pub. Co. 77.*

As a result of studying the Word, reading many books on worship, practicing and leading worship in various settings, I have felt compelled to teach people in churches, camps, conferences, and Christian colleges some of the biblical principles of worship, to enable us to glorify God, to be drawn into an intimate relationship with Him. In such a relationship with Him, God can shape us into the people He created us to be. It is through worship that God can clear our minds, open our hearts, free our spirits, cleanse our souls, and re-sensitize our consciences, so that when we study His Word we may understand and respond with unhampered submission, uninhibited obedience, and unhindered faithfulness. I am seeking to be obedient to what I sense the Lord saying to me through His Word and through my prayer times.

During a quiet, early morning time of worship, prayer, and meditation on the Word, the following words flooded my mind, and I accepted them as invitation from the Lord in sort of a summarization of all I had been reading, studying, thinking and praying about worship.

Worship Me. Lead My people in worship. Teach them how to worship Me, for the path of worship is the path of renewal, refreshment, and revival. It is the source of new life, needs being met, a fresh vision for the future, a sense of unity and oneness, and the pattern I have for your lives individually and together as a church family. I want to do something fresh and new in your midst. I want to release people from the dull, drab monotony of their daily lives. I want to break the chains of fear, anxiety, tension, and frustration that bind them. I want to give them My joy, My peace, My hope, My freedom, My release, My healing, My resources, My help, My blessing—and worship opens the doors to the throne room of Heaven where I your Father sit, reigning in majesty, glory, and power. I want to pour out My Spirit on you and the persons to whom you minister, in anointing power. I want to do some **"new things"** (Isaiah 42:9, 43:19) in your midst. As you worship Me, you are opening the doors of your lives to receive My blessings that I have prepared for you from before the creation of the universe.

My children let the praise flow, let the worship flow, let the prayer flow, let the healing flow. Let the joy, the songs, the Word, and the giving flow from your hearts upward before My throne. Let the music of heaven begin to shape your lives. As you do, I will strengthen you, I will uphold you, I will direct you in the way you should go. If you pay attention to My commands and worship Me, your peace will be like a river, your righteousness will be like the waves of the sea. Your joy will be full. Your homes will be strong and happy. Your marriages will be secure. Your needs will be met. Your lives will be blessed. The ransomed of the Lord will be released from the things that bind them. They will come into My presence with singing, filled with joy and everlasting gladness; sorrow and mourning will disappear. For I am the Lord, your God; and you are My people.

As your worship and praise ascend to My throne, I will open the windows of heaven and return them to you in the form of blessings so great you will not have room enough to take them all in! Try it! Let me prove it to you as you open the doors of your hearts in praise and worship before My throne of grace, mercy, and more-than-abundant resources."[136]

---

136 Bruce, Dr. Sam. (2013). 5 Minute± Reflections from My Wooded Prayer Trail, Florence, MS: Unpublished, in process. ©Come to the Waters Be Refreshed! Ministry & Music Resources, Sam & Sandie Bruce Ministries. Used by permission. drsambruce@aol.com www.bruceministries.net

How Do We Begin to Worship the Lord in This Way?

The question, then, is "How do we begin to worship the Lord in this way, in obedience and submission so that we can honor and glorify Him and experience His presence, joy, and blessings in our lives, our worship services, and our homes?"

Worship the Lord with Gladness.

When we come either to a time of personal worship or into a worship service, we should come foremost to *worship, honor, and glorify* the Lord God Almighty and his Son, the Lord Jesus Christ who leads us through the Holy Spirit before the throne of God into an intimate and personal relationship with the Creator Himself.

Come with An Expectant Attitude

We should come with an *expectant attitude*—believing that God is up to something great, awesome, and life-changing. We need to *prepare our hearts* before we come to the sanctuary, by spending time in prayer, in personal worship, and in the Word—asking for God to anoint that service, and to free us to worship Him.

Enter the Sanctuary in An Attitude of Thanksgiving and Praise

We should enter the sanctuary in an *attitude of thanksgiving and praise*, as we remember how faithful He is to the promises in His Word. Then, when we begin to sing, read the Scripture, pray, give our tithes and offerings, greet other persons in fellowship, or proclaim the Word, we do so with *great exuberance, joyfulness, and undivided attention.*

The Bible teaches that when God is truly honored by persons gathered in His name, true worship will happen. This kind of worship connects. It connects God and His love, grace, and resources with us and all our needs. That is why, when we enter our times of worship, we should approach them with our whole hearts, believing that something good is really going to happen as we focus on the presence and resources of Almighty God. The psalm writer said, in Psalms 9:1-2, **"I will praise you, O Lord, with all my heart; I will tell of all your wonders. I will be glad and rejoice in you; I will sing praise to your name, O Most High."**

Enter Worship with Our Whole Hearts

When we enter worship with our whole hearts, in the name of our Lord Jesus Christ—seeking to honor and glorify Him in all we do—and then ask the Holy Spirit to breathe into us His life-giving power, the worship comes alive, our spirits come alive, our emotions come alive, our relationships come alive. We open ourselves up to God's powerful blessing, and His love comes radiating through us. It is in this attitude, then, that we sing songs of worship and praise, read or recite words from the Word, and let them flow from our hearts to the throne of God in praise. Then He sends the praise back to us in the form of blessings in our lives and relationships.

How Can We More Fully Enter God's Presence In This Way?

How can we more fully enter God's presence in this way, so we can experience His provisions for our lives?

The Word teaches that when Solomon was crowned king of Israel, he **"established himself firmly over his kingdom, for the Lord his God was with him and made him exceedingly great"** (2 Chronicles 1:1). That night God appeared to him and said, **"Ask for whatever you want me to give you"** (2 Chronicles 1:7). Anything Solomon desired; he could ask for. We need to realize that in the preceding verse Solomon had offered a thousand burnt offerings to the Lord. Solomon worshiped the Lord unreservedly. He lavishly poured out worship and praise to God. The result was that God blessed him immensely.

Worship God Unreservedly

We, too, need to worship God unreservedly—lavishly adoring, praising, honoring, and glorifying Him. He responds with His presence and abundant provisions for the needs of our lives and relationships. Then, just as Solomon and his people discovered in the temple on the day of dedication, the glory of the Lord will fill our lives, our homes, our worship experiences, and even our nation, as we worship God according to His clear directions in His Word.

After attending church with his father one Sunday morning, before getting into bed that evening a little boy knelt at his bedside and prayed, "Dear God, we had a good time at church today, but I wish You had been there."[137] We may be certain that God will be there when we come in the name of Jesus, under the anointing of the Holy Spirit, for the glory of God the Father, and we open our hearts, spirits, minds, lives, emotions, and relationships in worship. God shows up in majesty and power when His people freely and enthusiastically worship Him through praying, reading and studying the Word, singing, giving, and fellowshipping with one another.

Michael Green illustrates this by writing:

Suppose your next-door neighbor bought an expensive big-screen color TV set, and after it was delivered, he came over to your house to brag about his new toy. While he's bragging, he notices his favorite motion picture coming in on your little black-and-white K-Mart TV, and he exclaims: "Oh, no! They have my favorite movie on and all you have is that crummy little black-and-white thing. I'm going home to watch it on my big color set." So, he runs home and turns on his expensive set, only to find out that he can't get the channel he wanted. Why? Well, he didn't give you time to tell him that you had just subscribed to cable television. He may have the better equipment, but you're "cable ready" for the best shows.

In this same way, the natural man [or woman], the non-Christian, or the nominal Christian may have a far superior head on his shoulders and a lot of book learning, but until he gets online with the Holy Spirit by com-

---

137 Green, M. P. (1989). *Illustrations for Biblical Preaching. Grand Rapids, MI: Baker Book House.* 425.

ing to Christ by faith, he can never receive what even the most ignorant believer receives all the time.[138]

Worship God as the Central Focus

True, free, spontaneous, sincere, alive, enthusiastic worship puts us online; it connects us with the living God who can transform our lives, lift our spirits, encourage our emotions, clear our minds, fill our hearts, and energize our bodies. When we worship God as the central focus and the main priority, we open the door for Him to revive, renew, and refresh not only our lives, homes, and churches, but our nation as well.

A Prayer for Entering into Worship

Lord God, as we enter worship, please send the light of Your love to warm us, to shine through the darkness of the world so we can see You clearly. Clean the cobwebs out of our minds; clear the obstructions from our hearts. Cleanse our spirits, Lord, from any negative, bad, or unwholesome thoughts or attitudes that would hinder the flow of Your resources or quench the working of Your Spirit.

Give us receptive spirits, open hearts, clear minds, strong voices, healthy bodies. By Your Spirit, draw us together in an attitude of worship. Fill us with praise. Free our voices to sing in adoration and joy in Your presence.

---

138 Green, M. P. (1989). *Illustrations for Biblical Preaching. Grand Rapids, MI: Baker Book House.*

Break the bonds of discouragement and dissatisfaction. Enable us to experience Your forgiveness. Mend the broken or strained relationships. Carefully guide us in the paths of righteousness. May Your name be honored, and may our lives be strengthened as we enter this time of worship.

As we leave, may we go rejoicing because we have met together once again to worship Him who was born in a manger, adored by angels, wise men and shepherds; and who died, was buried, rose triumphantly, ascended to Heaven, and promised He would return for us! Glory to God in the highest Heaven, and on earth peace, goodwill to all people.

In the name of our Lord and Savior, whom we worship, we pray. Amen.

Chapter 15

Worship Shapes Interpersonal Relationships

Dr. Sam Says . . .

In spiritual formation, God and we are working in partnership, *forming our inner lives and relationships with God in a way that transforms our outer lives and relationships with other persons.* When spiritual formation results from our worship of God, it not only changes us inwardly, it also changes the way we relate to other people. As we meet God in worship, and He begins to shape our lives and relationships with Him, we gain an understanding of who we are in Christ, as Peter describes so elegantly:

You are a chosen people, a royal priesthood, a holy nation, a people belonging to God, that you may declare the praises of him who called you out of darkness into his wonderful light. Once you were not a people, but now you are the people of God; once you had not received mercy, but now you have received mercy (1 Peter 2:9-10).

As we live in the presence of God in worship and in intimate fellowship and communion with Him, we discover that through this relationship He fashions us as chosen, royal, holy people belonging to God. This is forming the inner life and relationship with God, and He then enables us to live in relationship with other persons as Peter challenges us in the next verses:

Dear friends, I urge you, as aliens and strangers in the world, to abstain from sinful desires, which war against your soul. Live such good lives among the pagans that, though they accuse you of doing wrong, they may see your good deeds and glorify God on the day he visits us (1 Peter 2:11-12).

When we realize what we are in Christ, we are given a new outlook on ourselves. We look into the heart of the Father and into the heart of Christ—we see ourselves accepted, loved, ransomed, healed, restored, and forgiven. If we look at one another, and judge one another for what we see in each other, our fellowship is broken. But when we learn to accept each other for what we are in Christ, we find a basis for *koinonia*— fellowship, acceptance, participation.[139] Our age is preoccupied with the search for self-esteem, self-fulfillment, self-realization, self-respect. When we make these the central quest of our lives, they remain elusive, unattainable. Yet as we recover the heart of worship, we recover the basis for true self-esteem. Christ has made the once-and-for-all offering that we could never make. In worship we see ourselves as Christ sees us. We are in an individualistic culture that is so preoccupied with "me," we desperately need to recover a preoccupation with a focus on God, what He has done and is doing in

---

139 Torrance, J. B. (1989, 1993). Theology and Ministry of Worship Class Notes, Fuller Theological Seminary, Samuel K. Bruce. Pasadena, CA. 6.

Christ, and to be empowered by the Holy Spirit to be led into true worship, and into a vision of who we can become "in Christ."[140]

You Are . . . But You Shall Be

In worship we are empowered to become all God created us to be and to accomplish all God calls us to do. There is a beautiful illustration of this concept in John's account of Simon's introduction to Jesus. Andrew, Simon's younger brother, had been introduced to Jesus by John the Baptist. Thrilled with his discovery of the Messiah, Andrew hurried home to Simon with the good news: **"We have found the Messiah (that is, the Christ)"** (John 1:41). So, Andrew, seizing the opportunity, excitedly led his brother Simon to Jesus and in the words of a poet, the miracle happened: "I looked at him, He looked at me, and we were one forever."[141]

Next, John 1:42 says, **"Jesus looked intently at Peter for a moment and then said, 'You are Simon, John's son—but you shall be called Peter, the rock!'"** These words describe the true source of genuine self-esteem: looking at ourselves and other people through the eyes of Jesus. Jesus knows us with infinite and amazing accuracy. He knows our hearts, and He says, **"You are . . . ."** You are what you are; you are who you are and what you have done . . . . If this were all, what tragic hopelessness would defeat us! In the same breath, and separated only by the briefest pause, Jesus quickly adds, **"You shall be . . . ."** Simon, the self-sufficient man became Peter, the solid rock of Pentecost. We, too, share gladly with Christ as He fashions our future. Remember, He not only said, **"You are . . . ,"** but also **"You shall be . . . ."** As we maintain our focus on Christ in

---

140 Torrance, J. B. (1989, 1993). Theology and Ministry of Worship Class Notes, Fuller Theological Seminary, Samuel K. Bruce. Pasadena, CA. 6.
141 Unknown Source.

worship, rather than on ourselves or on other persons, we are led into hope rather than despair, fellowship rather than competition, acceptance rather than criticism, love rather than judgmental attitudes toward other persons.

Western theology has been dominated by an emphasis on the nature and being of the individual, characterized by the *centrality of me, myself and I*. What we need is an emphasis on the nature and being of Christ, and then we will see the true worth and value of individuals in relationship with Him. When our focus in worship is on Christ, rather than on our own needs, wants, whims, and desires, the amazing result is the transformation of our lives and the meeting of our needs in ways that baffle our minds. Then we are set free to relate to others with the love and acceptance of Christ.

In that context of love and acceptance, we are enabled to deal in a Christlike manner with various interpersonal relationships and with other issues such as how to handle the question of strained family relationships, differences of opinions in churches, racial discrimination, relational clashes at work or school, and other interpersonal relationships. We can consider these issues in light of these questions: What is your understanding about Who Christ is and What He has done in regard to reconciliation and love? Answering this question will lead to others: How can you not share communion with a person of a different culture or race? How can you not treat all men and women as equals in Christ? The Old Testament Law, with its condemnations and exhortations, will never convert anyone. But realizing Who Christ is and What He has done will renovate these and all other interpersonal relationships. Spiritual formation in the context of worship will transform all our relationships with other persons.

The major task in theology today regarding understanding the problems of marriage, sexuality, and various relationships is to begin with the "Who?" question. That is, Whom do we worship? Who is the person we are trying to please in our relationships? Beginning with the "How?" question puts the imperatives before the indicatives; law before grace; works before faith; and it subordinates the Bible, as the source for meeting the needs of humanity, to human methods of meeting those needs. How do we answer the problems and meet the needs? Beginning with Who Christ is and what He has done in reconciling grace elevates the Bible as the reliable guidebook for all interpersonal relationships. Then we can view our needs and relationships in the light of the Word, and we become a part of the worshiping Body of Christ in the world. Worshiping together gives us the common ground on which to build strong, Christ-centered relationships. In that setting we are given all the resources we need for reconciliation and healing of broken, hurting, or strained relationships. James Torrance said we should ask, "Are we embodying reconciliation, unconditional acceptance, and the love of God in Christ?" If so, then we can and should act accordingly.[142]

Reconciliation Releases Worship

Jesus indicated that a prerequisite for worship is reconciliation, or right relationships among persons. His very clear instruction is, **"Therefore, if you are offering your gift at the altar and there remember that your brother has something against you, leave your gift there in front of the altar. First go and be reconciled to your brother; then come and offer your gift"** (Matthew 5:23-24). It is true, says Graham Kendrick, "Right relationships release worship."[143] I once heard a minister ask the ques-

---

142 Torrance, J. B. (1989, 1993). Theology and Ministry of Worship Class Notes, Fuller Theological Seminary, Samuel K. Bruce. Pasadena, CA.
143 Kendrick, G. (1984). *Learning to Worship as a Way of Life. Minneapolis, MN: Bethany House Pub.*

tion, "Did you ever try to pray right after you had an argument with your wife?" It is difficult, is it not? Jesus' prescription for all strained, fractured, and broken relationships is reconciliation through Jesus Christ. Worship sets the stage for the reconciling, healing grace of God to work in us and through us. Each of us, says Graham Kendrick,

> . . . shares a responsibility to make the move towards reconcili-
> ation in order that the body should be whole in every part. It is
> the same principle that resulted in Jesus, the only perfectly inno-
> cent man to have ever lived, making the first move towards guilty
> men [and women, and boys and girls], and even going as far as
> to take responsibility for our sins by dying on the cross. We must
> also remind ourselves that He did not come condemning, but with
> humility[144] and deep love for all people! Christ modeled the kind of
> love that will give, even to the point of death, in order that people
> might be reconciled to God and to one another.

I have observed with heart-breaking lament an overwhelming number of fractures in families, strife-plagued marriages, racial divisions, break-downs in communication, strained interpersonal relationships, and rifts in churches. I have often wondered if the reason that worship never gets off the ground, or is perceived as boring, uneventful, meaningless, and it seems to lack joy, freedom, and delight is that "too many people are bringing their gifts of praise, or money, or service, to the altar while making no effort to be reconciled with their fellow worshipers."[145] The altars in our churches represent the altar on which the innocent blood of the Lamb of God, our Lord Jesus Christ, was shed for our reconciliation to God and to other

---

144 Kendrick, G. (1984). *Learning to Worship as a Way of Life.* Minneapolis, MN: Bethany House Pub.
145 Kendrick.

persons. When people come to worship or to share in Holy Communion, week after week, year after year, refusing to be reconciled to one another, barriers which hinder the flow of worship are erected. Such barriers make it increasingly difficult to worship God. Reconciliation through Christ breaks the barriers, heals the rifts, mends the fractures, releases persons to worship God freely, and empowers people to be transformed through what Paul describes as **"spiritual worship"** (Romans 12:1).

I heard Tom Skinner (former *Black Panther Gang* leader) speak at a Rotary Club luncheon about Mission Mississippi, a Christian reconciliation movement (of which I serve on the Board of Directors), aimed at breaking down the walls of racial strife and disharmony. Skinner related a story about an elderly white man who, several years ago, noticed a young African American man on a street corner who exhibited intense anger and frustration. The elderly white gentleman sensed his hurt and pain. He walked over to the young man and said, "I sense that you are very angry. I feel certain, from noticing the color of your skin, that you have experienced a lot of pain and persecution from white people during your lifetime. While I personally had nothing to do with that, I want to express to you how sorry I am that this has happened to you. I want to apologize to you for what people of my race may have done to you and your people and ask your forgiveness. I want to release you from your anger and frustration." The young black man walked away, and the older gentleman never saw him again.

During the Los Angeles riots following the Rodney King trial verdicts, a television reporter noticed one black man who was working constantly to stop the fights between the blacks and whites. Several times he was seen pulling attackers off people and asking them to stop the fighting and looting. The reporter could not resist asking the man why he, a black man, was working so diligently to protect the white people.

The African American man responded, "Several years ago I met an elderly white gentleman who apologized to me for all the white people had done to my people, and he set me free from my anger!" He wanted to pass that reconciliation along to others.

Is this not what our Lord Jesus Christ has done for us? He took on Himself our brokenness, anger, disappointment, sin, enmity, and strife. Then He takes us to God the Father in reconciling grace and mercy, enabling us to participate with Him by faith in reconciliation with the Father, and in turn, with other persons. It is no wonder Peter's words reverberate throughout the centuries:

> **Peter, an apostle of Jesus Christ, To God's elect, strangers in the world, scattered throughout Pontus, Galatia, Cappadocia, Asia and Bithynia, who have been chosen according to the foreknowledge of God the Father, through the sanctifying work of the Spirit, for obedience to Jesus Christ and sprinkling by his blood: Grace and peace be yours in abundance. Praise be to the God and Father of our Lord Jesus Christ! In his great mercy he has given us new birth into a living hope through the resurrection of Jesus Christ from the dead, and into an inheritance that can never perish, spoil or fade—kept in heaven for you, who through faith are shielded by God's power until the coming of the salvation that is ready to be revealed in the last time. In this you greatly rejoice, though now for a little while you may have had to suffer grief in all kinds of trials** (1 Peter 1:1-6).

These introductory words of Peter in his first letter confidently proclaim that we have great reasons to praise God, for through Christ's resurrection He has brought us into a personal, loving relationship with the

Father. He has brought us from every race, nation, and gender, to make us one in Christ.

Paul also describes the results of our being reconciled to the Father:

> **Remember that you . . . Gentiles . . . were separate from Christ, excluded from citizenship in Israel and foreigners to the covenants of the promise, without hope and without God in the world. But now in Christ Jesus you who once were far away have been brought near through the blood of Christ. For he himself is our peace, who has made the two one and has destroyed the barrier, the dividing wall of hostility, by abolishing in his flesh the law with its commandments and regulations. His purpose was to create in himself one new man out of the two, thus making peace, and in this one body to reconcile both of them to God through the cross, by which he put to death their hostility. He came and preached peace to you who were far away and peace to those who were near. For through him we both have access to the Father by one Spirit** (Ephesians 2:12-18).

Through Christ's gift of reconciliation, we are set free from our anger and hostility toward God and toward ourselves, and in this way, we are released to be reconciled to our brothers and sisters, husbands and wives, and persons of different backgrounds and cultures. **"The barrier . . . the dividing wall of hostility"** between us and other people has been dismantled and removed by our Lord Jesus Christ! What we could not do on our own, even though attempting to obey the law with its commandments and regulations, Christ did for us as the One True Sacrifice for our sins and our separation from God and other people. The One who **"is our peace"** is the One who gives us peace with one another. He makes us one in Himself, bringing us together through the cross, putting to death our hostility, enmity, hatred, jealousy, inferiority, mistrust, insecurity, and animosity.

In Worship "Gracism" Trumps Racism and Opens the Path to Healing

In this reconciliation backdrop, I am privileged to serve on the Board of Directors for *Mission Mississippi*, a racial reconciliation movement that is making wonderful progress in addressing the racial division in a state that has had a tragic history in broken racial relations. In the Capitol City Jackson, we sponsor the Governor's Prayer Luncheon and Mayors' Prayer Luncheon (mayors from across the state). We have established several *Mission Mississippi Chapters* across the state. We come together in these and other venues to study the Word of God, pray together, worship our Lord, establish friendship relations across racial lines, and dialogue on ways to draw us together in peace through our mutual relationship with our Lord Jesus Christ. These are our *Days of Dialogue*, and our round tables look like salt and pepper as we gather across racial lines. Our vision-slogan is *"Changing Mississippi One Relationship at a Time!"*[146] Our mission-slogan is "Gracism: "the act of extending grace that we have experienced from Jesus to promote living reconciled."[147] My personal moving forward description of this is: "Gracism trumps racism and opens the path to healing."[148] And it's true, as my WisdomSketch describes: "To trump something means to disable it, stop it, squelch it, cause it to cease, put it out of business.

---

146 Mission Mississippi Vision-Slogan, Jackson MS and across the state. www.missionmississippi.org 601-353-6477

147 Mission Mississippi Mission-Slogan, Jackson MS and across the state. www.missionmississippi.org 601-353-6477

148 Bruce, Sam. A *WisdomSketch of Dr. Sam from Dr. Sam's GreenHouse Dictionary of Spiritual Formation Words*. ©*Come to the Waters Be Refreshed! Ministry & Music Resources*, Sam & Sandie Bruce Ministries. drsambruce@aol.com www.bruceministries.net

Or better yet, to trump something means to transform it into something good! SO! Gracism trumps racism into love, peace, healing, harmony, caring deeply about one another and to make our state and nation godly and great through the reconciling power of Jesus!"[149]

As I was in my Word and Prayer Journaling time with my Lord, lifting up the brokenness and division in our state and nation, I was praying for a "Win-Win Solution", better yet, a "God-Win Solution". "Lord, make us one! Draw us together in reconciliation and peace!" And even as I prayed those words, I heard, in my mind, thunderous reverberations of "No! Impossible! It can never happen that way! Somebody has to win; somebody has to lose! We are too broken and divided to be fixed!" But then, in my heart, I heard a gentle and still, small voice whisper, "Be still . . . and know . . . that I am God . . . before seeking a solution . . . seek My Heart . . . My Will . . . My Plan . . . My love . . . My grace . . . Walk this path with me until you hear My Heart . . ." And I realized, "Isn't this what our Lord prayed for in the hours just before His crucifixion – that we might be one? SO! You know it must be important to Him. And if He prayed for unity in the Body of Christ, then it must be possible in and through Him. SO! The path toward a 'God-Win-Solution' must lead through coming together in heart-unity, seeking His Heart . . . His Will . . . His Plan . . . until . . . we hear His Heart . . . Lord, help us to walk the path of 'Gracism-Unity' until . . . we hear Your Heart . . . and help us to walk together with You and each other." And I wondered, "What if . . . we tried that together . . .?

Here's the path: "Gracism: the act of extending grace that we have experienced from Jesus to promote living reconciled." Yes! Because "Gracism trumps racism and opens the path to healing." And God's promise is, when we come before Him together like this, "I [the Lord] will instruct

149 Bruce, Sam. A *WisdomSketch of Dr. Sam from Dr. Sam's GreenHouse Dictionary of Spiritual Formation Words.* ©*Come to the Waters Be Refreshed! Ministry & Music Resources,* Sam & Sandie Bruce Ministries. drsambruce@aol.com www.bruceministries.net

you and teach you in the way you should go; I will counsel you with My eye upon you." Psalm 32:8 (AMP) God's GracePortal offers a disconnect with negative, racial thinking, and opens into a connection with possibility Gracism thinking. A portal offers a disconnect with racism, and opens into a connection with Gracism. A portal offers a disconnect with misalignment which is brokenness, separation, strife and bitterness; and opens into a connection with realignment which offers healing, reconciliation, peace and love.

SO! What if . . . we made an intentional commitment and effort – a covenant of love with God and each other – to live in the Power of Gracism instead of the hurt and brokenness of racism; allow the Healing of Gracism to dominate all our relationships? We would discover that the reconciling, restoring, refreshing oil of Gracism could heal hatred, hurts, and hostile relationships. And what an awesome, peaceful, loving, glorious and triumphant community we could build together. It's true and possible! Because through the Word of God, prayer, and worship Gracism trumps racism and opens the path to healing. Gracism trumps racism into love, peace, healing, harmony, caring deeply about one another and to make our state and nation godly and great through the reconciling power of Jesus!"[150]

Bill and Gloria Gaither wrote a beautiful song that expresses this wonderful truth. The chorus says,

I am loved, I am loved, I can risk loving you.
For the One who knows me best loves me most.
I am loved, you are loved, won't you please take my hand.
We are free to love each other, we are loved.[151]

The reason this is true is beautifully articulated in 1 John 4:18, **"There is no fear in love. But perfect love drives out fear, because fear has to do with punishment. The one who fears is not made perfect in love."** When

150 Bruce, *Gracism.*
151 Gaither, W. J. (1978). I Am Loved. Alexandria, IN: Gaither Music.

we, in our relationships with other people, are reconciled to God and begin to move closer to him, we move closer to each other in that *"God-kind-of-love"* relationship. This relationship releases us from fears about what others might do to us, think about us, or say about us.

That *"God-kind-of-love"* relationship enables us to move to new level of love, trust, and appreciation for each other. Paul expresses the joy of our reconciled relationship with God in Romans 5:11, ***"we also rejoice in God through our Lord Jesus Christ, through whom we have now received reconciliation."*** However, it is difficult, if not impossible, to rejoice in our vertical reconciliation with God as long as our horizontal reconciliation with other persons is out of alignment, and vice versa. But living constantly in God's *Portal of Gracism* keeps us settled – safe, secure and steady in alignment in our vertical relationships with God and our horizontal relationships with those He calls us to love and lead.

In Worship We Discover the Lift of Love

One morning as I looked out the window of my upstairs study at the church I pastored, I saw a father taking his son to school in their car. There were two other boys walking along the sidewalk. The father in the car pulled up alongside them, and the son offered them a ride. There were smiles and the exchange of friendly greetings. The boys got into the car, and off they went to school.

I imagined that the son in the car said to his father, "Dad, look, there are a couple of my friends walking to school. Could we stop and give them a lift?"

There was someone in that car who knew the boys' names, and who cared for them. There was warmth and genuine caring, and they gave the boys a lift.

Similarly, before the creation of the world, at the heart of the universe, God the Father and His Son were looking into eternity future and saw a world of people needing a lift. The Son, Jesus Christ, must have said something like, "Father, those people need our love and help. Why don't we go down to the earth and give them a lift?"

They did. Jesus Christ stepped out of eternity to offer His love, consolation, care, and help. He offers us a lift to help with every problem, heartache, and decision that we can ever face. Our greatest need was to be reconciled to God. Paul says that is exactly the reason Christ came into the world, **"If anyone is in Christ, he is a new creation; the old has gone, the new has come! All this is from God, who reconciled us to himself through Christ and gave us the ministry of reconciliation: that God was reconciling the world to himself in Christ, not counting men's sins against them"** (2 Corinthians 5:17-19a).

Geoffrey Wainwright says, "The Church's vision of God is at the origin of its evangelistic mission. The God who revealed himself in Jesus Christ is believed to have a saving purpose for all humanity. His character and purpose need to be proclaimed, because his purpose is to bring human beings to conscious and active participation in the love which characterizes God himself." (Wainwright, 1980, 355)

God's reconciling grace, as we come to Him in worship, shapes our inner lives and relationships with Him so that we are enabled to reach out to others with the same reconciling grace we have received in Christ. Paul says that God **"has committed to us the message of reconciliation. We are therefore Christ's ambassadors, as though God were making his appeal through us. We implore you on Christ's behalf: Be reconciled to God"** (2 Corinthians 5:19b-20). In worship and spiritual formation, we discover the *lift of love* that empowers us to be God's reconciling presence in the world.

PRAYER RESPONSE

Dear God, my Father, You are the God of reconciliation. Thank You for shaping me as a chosen, royal, holy, person of God, that I may declare the praises of You who called me out of darkness into Your wonderful light. As I live in Your presence in worship and in intimate fellowship and communion with You, may I discover that through this relationship You are fashioning my inner life and relationship with You in a way that enables me to live in harmonious relationships with other persons.

As I contemplate who I am in Christ, may I be driven to the Spirit and look into the heart of the Father, into heart of Christ, and see myself accepted, loved, ransomed, healed, restored, forgiven. Enable me to learn to accept other persons for who they are in Christ, and there find a basis for koinonia, acceptance, fellowship, participation. Lord Jesus, You know me with infinite and amazing accuracy. You know my heart, and You say, **"You are . . ."** *You are what you are; you are who you are . . . . If this were all, what tragic hopelessness would defeat me! But in the same breath, and separated only by the briefest pause, You quickly add,* **"You shall be . . . ."**

In that caring, healing, accepting relationship, may I share gladly with You as You fashion my future and my relationships with other persons. Empower me to be a reconciling person through whom Christ breaks down barriers, heals the rifts, mends the fractures, releases persons to worship God freely, and empowers people to be transformed through "spiritual worship."

In all my relationships, keep me aligned with You and your purposes. In worship and spiritual formation, O Lord, please shape my inner life and relationship with You in a way that gloriously transforms my outer life and relationships with other persons. Through me, let Your presence touch others with healing love, mending power, and reconciling grace. In the name of the Prince of Peace I pray. Amen.

Chapter 16

Worship: Key to Spiritual Formation

As I attempt to be more Christ-like, to follow more carefully the paths of worship and spiritual formation, I learn that Satan fights this process tenaciously. It is precisely at the point of worship that Satan launches his most powerful attacks because he knows that he can neither stand against, nor control, nor defeat, nor detour the person, family, church, business, or nation that practices a lifestyle of worship and spiritual formation. Genuine spiritual formation flows out of true worship, as we worship God simply because He is worthy of our worship, praise, adoration, submission, and service. Satan knows that he is a defeated foe when God is the central focus of our worship. He loses control over us when our worship centers on what God has done in Christ and what He continues to do in our lives and relationships through the ministry of the Holy Spirit. Satan has no power over us when we truly practice a lifestyle of worship.

Satan's Basic Sin: Misdirected Worship

Satan's basic sin from the beginning was one of misdirected worship. He desired *to be worshiped as God*, rather than *to submit to God in worship and obedience*. Isaiah says that the following prophecy, which describes Satan's attitude, was made specifically about the king of Babylon. However, the king of Babylon is often used as a symbol, or a type, of Satan; and Babylon is often used as a type of the kingdom of Satan. Certainly, it could be safely said that the statements made by the king of Babylon were satanically inspired, and so, typical of the attitudes of godless rulers.

How you have fallen from heaven, O morning star, son of the dawn! You have been cast down to the earth, you who once laid low the nations! You said in your heart, "I will ascend to heaven; I will raise my throne above the stars of God; I will sit enthroned on the mount of assembly, on the utmost heights of the sacred mountain. I will ascend above the tops of the clouds; I will make myself like the Most High" (Isaiah 14:12-20).

Satan, through the king of Babylon, makes five assertions that reveal his desire to be worshiped rather than to be a worshiper of God:

"I will ascend to heaven."

"I will raise my throne above the stars of God."

"I will sit enthroned on the mount of assembly, on the utmost heights of the sacred mountain."

"I will ascend above the tops of the clouds."

"I will make myself like the Most High."

Satan's Purpose: Seize the Worship that Only God Deserves

Satan's purpose was to take over the throne of God Almighty and to seize the worship that only God Himself deserves. Worship acknowledges the absolute sovereignty of God. Satan, under the facade of the serpent in the Garden of Eden, questioned the sovereignty of God to Adam and Eve. Ever since then, a battle has raged over whom to worship.

Satan's Temptations: The Battle over Worship

Knowing that Jesus came to complete the work of salvation by revealing to men and women the scope, purpose and Person of true worship, Satan once again attempted to seize the position of worship as he tempted Jesus during His forty-day spiritual retreat in the desert. The battle lines were drawn at the point of worship. If Satan had succeeded in his temptations of Jesus, he could have overthrown the Kingdom of God, for the only One worthy of worship would have surrendered His throne, His authority, His dominion, His power, and His Kingship over the world and the universe by becoming a worshiper of Satan rather than continuing as the One who alone is to be worshiped. But God will not share His throne or His worship with any person, power, or principality.

In the Old Testament, worship was the dominant element in the relationship of God's people with God. When their worship was in order, then all other elements of their lives and relationships were right. This did not change in New Testament times, nor has it been changed in the age of the church: worship must be central!

Christ's Conquest: Victory over Satan

Satan did not understand the real purpose of the Cross. If he had, he never would have had Jesus crucified! But, when he crucified Him physically (through the Jewish and Roman leaders), Jesus—through His resurrection, conquered Satan, destroying his grip on the earth, taking the authority over the earth back from Satan to give to the believers. Now Satan only has control over sinners and unbelievers. He has no control over those who trust in the blood and name of Jesus and who use the living and enduring Word of God as the sword of the Spirit to conquer Satan and to thwart his purposes in their lives.

Satan's Tactics: Deception

Since Christ won victory over Satan through His death and resurrection, Satan's main attack against God's people now is deception. He uses it to distract and disrupt the believers' worship of God. He was unsuccessful, both in the beginning and in his temptation of Christ Jesus, in establishing his throne above God's throne and in setting himself up as the one to be worshiped. Thus, he does everything he can to interfere with God receiving the worship He alone deserves.

This is the reason Satan fights our worship, and thus our spiritual formation so persistently. Our spiritual formation grows out of our worship relationship with God through the study of the Word and prayer. In spiritual formation, as we follow Christ in worship, we give ourselves to God: "as a living sacrifice . . . holy and pleasing to God, which is [our] spiritual worship" (Romans 12:1). In response, God gives Himself to us, and begins shaping us into people of God. In spiritual formation, God always has the first word as He takes the initiative in reaching out to us. He speaks to us through His Word and by the Holy Spirit, giving instructions, commands, and challenges. We respond in worship through prayer, by saying, "Yes, Lord, let this happen in me; shape me, mold me, fill me, use me; I am Yours; Your will be done in me. Jesus, be the Lord of my life." As we walk along this path of spiritual formation with our Lord, He gradually, little-by-little, is shaping us into people of God.

Satan's Tactics: Distraction through Diluted Worship

Satan knows this; therefore, he will do everything possible to hinder our worship and our spiritual formation. I understand better now why there are so many distractions and detainments aimed at keeping us from spending time in the Word, in prayer, and in listening to the inner whispers of the Holy Spirit. Satan is still competing for the worship that only God deserves. While he may not succeed in leading us into outright sin, if he can just dilute our worship, then he has succeeded in weakening our effectiveness in ministry, in our personal walk with the Lord, and in our relationships with other people.

Often our worship is diluted when we allow the pressures of work and other involvements squeeze out the time, we should be spending in either personal or corporate worship. When we fail to spend adequate time in worship, our focus turns to pressures, problems, and people rather than on God and His more-than-abundant resources. Geoffrey Wainwright wrote,

Worship may be the sphere in which . . . a renewal of vision and imagery can best take place. Revision of the forms of worship is meant to express and kindle a renewed vision of God. Our vision of God affects, and is affected by, our character and our lives. It is to the pure in heart that the sight of God is promised (Matthew 5:8). It is by beholding the glory of the Lord that we are enabled to reflect it in ourselves (2 Corinthians 3:18). Revision of liturgy and revision of life are mutually conditioning.[152]

Revision of liturgy involves not just changing the kinds of songs we sing, the passages of scripture we read, or the amount of energy we put into a worship service. It involves keeping our focus on who God is, and on what He wishes to change in our thoughts, lives, emotions, and relationships. Thus, as we keep our focus on God in worship, and keep Him in the center of our lives and relationships, then we can visualize Satan as a defeated foe, and confidently, victoriously, triumphantly stand against him and win over any temptation, situation, problem, or obstacle he throws in our way. The Psalm writer understood this when he said,

Those who know your name will trust in you, for you, Lord, have never forsaken those who seek you. I will praise you, O Lord, with all my heart; before the "gods" I will sing your praise. I will bow down toward your holy temple and will praise your name for your love and your faithfulness, for you have exalted above all things your name and your word (Psalms 9:10; 138:1-2).

In worship we learn to trust the Lord who has never forsaken those who trust in Him. Knowing God in this intimate worship relationship gives us great confidence with which to face all the varied circumstances

---

152 Wainwright, G. (1980). *Doxology: The Praise of God in Worship, Doctrine, and Life.* New York, NY: Oxford University Press.

that life, Satan, and people throw at us. According to the above verses, God's "name"—who He is in His character, and His "Word"—what He says to us, give us the courage to live as He directs, for He is dependable in all His ways, completely faithful to all His promises.

John says: **"They will make war against the Lamb, but the Lamb will overcome them because he is Lord of lords and King of kings—and with him will be his called, chosen and faithful followers"** (Revelation 17:14). Because of this confidence, our hearts echo with the hosts of heaven whom John saw in his magnificent vision worshiping around the throne of God, saying: **"Amen, Hallelujah! Hallelujah! For our Lord God Almighty reigns. Let us rejoice and be glad and give him glory!"** (Revelation 19:4b, 6b-7a).

When we truly know and follow God in worship, we can experience the truth of Revelation 12:10, **"Now have come the salvation and the power and the kingdom of our God, and the authority of his Christ."** Worship establishes Christ as the authority of our lives, relationships, and circumstances. Thus, worship becomes the key to our spiritual formation, *the forming of our inner lives and relationships with God in a way that transforms our outer lives and relationships with other persons.* As we willingly place ourselves under "the authority" of Christ (God's anointed One), we are given His protection against the attacks of Satan. The voice from heaven said to John, **"For the accuser of our brothers, who accuses them before our God day and night, has been hurled down"** (Revelation 12:10b). This means that Christ, God's anointed One, has defeated Satan. When we are living in Him in a worship relationship, He protects us from Satan's accusations, intimidations, brow beatings, and harassments. **"Therefore rejoice, you heavens and you who dwell in them! But woe to the earth and the sea because the devil has gone down to you! He is filled with fury because he knows that his time is short"** (Revelation 12:12). When

Christ's rule and power are central in our lives then we can **"overcome by the blood of the lamb and by the word of testimony"** (Revelation 12:11). Certainly, **"this calls for patient endurance and faithfulness"** from us as we **"obey God's commandments and remain faithful to Jesus"** (Revelation 13:10b, 14:12).

Satan's Tactics: Distraction through Division

One of the most painful, difficult, hard-fought, widespread battle-grounds of the church today is not from the outside, but from the inside—distraction through division. It is a battle that happens, not between terrible enemies, but among people who claim to be brothers and sisters in Christ. Its casualties are those who either leave the church or drive others out of the church. Its symptoms are critical spirits, negative comments, hurt feelings, sniper fire backbiting, and head-on attacks—all which grow out of selfish, self-centered, and often self-aggrandizing attitudes. It is a battle over, of all things to fight about, *worship styles*. The most common turf-fight is between those who advocate either so-called *traditional worship* or *contemporary worship*. Usually, neither is willing to change or even allow some kind of balanced or blended worship format. In such battles, the real winner is Satan himself, who has been vying for worship since the Garden of Eden.

Often, if he cannot defeat a church through complacency, lack of evangelism, moral failure, or some other head-on attack, he will distract people, getting them stirred up and quarreling about worship styles. People get angry with one another, sometimes accusing others of being *less spiritual* because of their worship style preferences. Such attacks are usually vicious, and result in unholy attitudes, carnal comments to and about one another, and often tragic church splits. Churches lose their vision, forward momentum, and effectiveness. If Satan can keep churches in an uproar over worship styles, he distracts them from focusing on God as the person and source of true worship, and they miss the whole point of worship. My urgent plea to pastors, musicians, and other precious Christian people is to seek some kind of blended or balanced worship that includes a wide variety of styles that can be inclusive rather than exclusive of those with simply different worship style tastes. Keep the focus on genuine worship rather than on styles. The style of worship is not the goal. The goal of worship is, as *The Apostles' Creed* rightly states, *to worship God and enjoy Him forever!*

Paul elaborated on such attitudes in Galatians 5:15, **"If you keep on biting and devouring each other, watch out or you will be destroyed by each other."** He described some of the ways this happens in his description of the works of the flesh, **"discord, jealousy, fits of rage, selfish ambition, dissensions, factions,"** Galatians 5:20 (I have seen all these exhibited in church worship style battles). Of course, no person who claims to be a Christian would ever admit to acting this way—it is always "the *other person* who acts that way," and "if they were really Christians, they would do worship the way I want it to be done." On the other hand, if a group of Christian people are truly living in vital relationship with the Lord, they ought to be exhibiting the *fruit of the Spirit* in their relationships with other persons, including **"love, joy, peace, patience, kindness, goodness, faithfulness, gentleness and self-control,"** Galatians 5:22-23. Such attitudes will lead to unity rather than division over worship styles. The result will be that God will be honored, churches will be strengthened, worshipers will be blessed, and unsaved people will be brought into the Kingdom of God through Christ-centered rather than style-centered worship.

Worship Is Central in Our Relationship with God and with People

In *The Concept of Worship*, Ninian Smart writes: "God is reached down a certain corridor . . . and this is the corridor of worship."[153] This is a crisp statement of the central role worship plays in both the formulation and the practice of our Christian faith. Worship is vital to both our relationship with God and our life and activity as His chosen people.

"Christian worship is the most momentous, the most urgent, the most glorious action that can take place in the human life,"[154] wrote Karl Barth. Commenting on this statement, Ralph Martin wrote,

> These words of Karl Barth will strike a responsive chord in all who are concerned for the renewal of the church in our day. Yet the truth is that many—if not most—Christians find public worship less than the exhilarating experience Barth wrote about. The situation is a perplexing one. It suggests a deep-seated conviction that the worship of God is indeed a vital part of the church's life and witness. And equally it reflects a wistful yearning that contemporary worship could be vastly improved and given a more satisfying rationale.[155]

If God is going to shape our inner lives and relationships with Himself in a way that transforms our outer lives and relationships with other persons, then worship must be the number one priority for us. *It is the key to our spiritual formation.*

---

153 Martin, R. P. (1982). *The Worship of God: Some Theological, Pastoral and Practical Reflections.* Grand Rapids, MI: William E. Eerdmans.
154 Martin.
155 Martin.

PRAYER RESPONSE

Lord God enable me to be a true worshiper of You, to keep You in Your appropriate and well-deserved place on the throne of my life. As I saturate my mind, spirit, emotions, and relationships with Your powerful and life-transforming Word, establish Your Kingdom within me and in the lives of those You entrust to my care. May I walk in constant obedience to You. May I live in absolute conformity with Your plan for me. Show me any unconquered strongholds in my life, and as I open the gates to my interior world, Lord, cleanse away any wrong motives, attitudes, lack of faith, insurrections, temptations, or sins that might potentially hinder my spiritual formation—the transformation of my inner life and relationship with You in a way that will transform my outer life and relationships with other persons.

Today, Lord, in a new and fresh commitment, I surrender all the kingdoms of my life to Your Lordship. Enable me to worship You in the majesty of Your glory and the splendor of Your holiness. I belong to You, and I enthusiastically await Your further directions. I wholeheartedly yield my life to Your leadership and control. And I praise You for the release, freedom, and joy that come from Your presence in my life. "Hallelujah! For our Lord God Almighty reigns. [I will] rejoice and be glad and give him glory!"[156] Amen.

---

156 Revelation 19:4b, 6b-7a

PART 5

FORMING PEOPLE OF GOD

Chapter 17

Intimacy with God: Key to Transformed Living

Dr. Sam Says . . .

What is the difference between being a Christian and being a *JesusFollower*? I think the biblical principal that answers that question is: *Intimacy with God, which is the Key to Transformed Living*. It is so easy to just be a Christian in name only. You know, "I believe Jesus Christ existed; I believe He was probably the Son of God. I have been baptized; I have joined the church. I give to the church occasionally, or regularly, or even tithe. I am, basically, a good person. I even do things for the church, and I help the downtrodden and needy." And for many, the relationship stops there. The difference between someone who is a Christian in name and someone who is a *JesusFollower* is that a *JesusFollower* is one whose life is in the process of being transformed into a person who is becoming all God created him or her to be, and then accomplishing all God calls him or her to do. Each of us needs to answer for him or herself, "Am I a Christian or am I a *JesusFollower*?"

As we become people of the Word, people of prayer, and people of worship, we discover that we are being shaped into people of God – genuine *JesusFollowers*. Living in the Word, in prayer, and in worship consistently are three keys in the process of cultivating an intimate, personal relationship with God, which is the purpose of spiritual formation—*forming our inner lives and relationships with God in a way that transforms our outer lives and relationships with other persons.* And that is a description of a true *JesusFollower*. This is the Key to Transformed Living!

It is a quest as old as time itself—intimacy with God. Throughout the ages of time, people have desired it, shunned it, feared it, and denied its possibility. Some have spoken of it as a virtue worthy of pursuit, yet unattainable. Others have sought it with all their hearts and have discovered its life-changing realities in a day-by-day, moment-by-moment, breath-by-breath, fulfilling relationship with God.

The Apostle Paul passionately described his personal desire for intimacy with God when he said, **"I want to know Christ and the power of his resurrection and the fellowship of sharing in his sufferings, becoming like him in his death, and so, somehow, to attain to the resurrection from the dead"** (Philippians 3:10-11). The words *to know* mean *to know by experience.* This is more than head knowledge, hear-say knowledge, and book knowledge. This has to do with spiritual formation: *the forming of our inner lives and relationships with God in a way that transforms our outer lives and relationships with other persons.* The Apostle Paul craved intimacy with God above everything else, for he said,

"Whatever was to my profit I now consider loss for the sake of Christ. What is more, I consider everything a loss compared to the surpassing greatness of knowing Christ Jesus my Lord, for whose sake I have lost all things. I consider them rubbish,

that I may gain Christ and be found in him, not having a righteousness of my own that comes from the law, but that which is through faith in Christ—the righteousness that comes from God and is by faith" (Philippians 3:7-9).

Knowing about God or Knowing God Intimately

There is an immense difference between knowing God intimately and knowing about Him historically. A good example of this difference is seen in the difference between my knowledge of birds and my son-in-law Erik's knowledge of birds. I know a few things about birds. I have seen them out in the woods, and in pictures. I have hunted quail, pheasants, doves, and ducks—and I have enjoyed eating them as the result of successful hunting.

Erik knows birds in a more intimate way. He carves birds out of wood, in intricate detail and splendid life-like color. He has carved quail, chickadees, cardinals, and even a full-sized duck, so true-to-life that they look real. In fact, after Erik finished carving the duck (which he sold for $1500 to a man named Nicky Drake, who collects wooden ducks) I was standing in front of a display window in a mall, thinking I was looking at some wooden ducks. In my proud little mind, I was comparing those ducks with the one Erik had just completed, and I said to myself, "Erik can do a much better job of carving ducks than the one who made those in the window." Then I looked up to see the store sign, which revealed that it was a taxidermy shop. Those were real ducks, not humanly carved wooden ducks! I then raised my eyes toward heaven, with an innocent smile on my face, and said, "Sorry, Lord, I didn't intend to insult Your creative skills!"

The point is that when Erik prepares to carve birds out of wood, he studies them intimately to determine their shape, size, colors, shades, little quirks and habits. He carved a little chickadee for Janette's Christmas present. To add to its reality, he carved a sunflower seed and placed it in the bird's little beak. He analyzes the birds so thoroughly that their characteristics are emblazoned in his mind. Then he simply carves out of the wood what he envisions in his mind. He just carves away everything in the wooden block that isn't bird. The result is an exquisite work of art that brings warmth, beauty, and creativity into the eyes and hearts of observers. While I know a few things about birds, Erik knows them so intimately that he can magnificently recreate their likeness out of his heart with wood and paint.

Similarly, Paul's deep inner desire was to know Christ so intimately and personally that he would become **"like Him"** (Philippians 3:10b). Why? Because, Paul said, **"In Christ all the fullness of the Deity lives in bodily form"** (Colossians 2:9). Knowing Christ intimately builds the path to knowing God intimately, for Paul continued, saying, **"You have been given fullness in Christ, who is the head over every power and authority"** (Colossians 2:10). Such intimate, personal, heart-knowledge allows God to shape within us the image of Christ and enables us to become like Him in our innermost being.

Then what we are in the inner chambers of our hearts affects how we relate on the outside to other persons and to circumstances. Paul said, **"You were taught, with regard to your former way of life, to put off your old self** [carving away everything that is not Christlike], **which is being corrupted by its deceitful desires; to be made new in the attitude of your minds; and to put on the new self, created to be like God in true righteousness and holiness"** [*the beautiful JesusFollower person He created you to become*] (Ephesians 4:22-24 NIV). As we become shaped in His image, He cleanses away those things that are not Christ-like – just as Erik carves everything in the block of wood that isn't bird. As He does this, other persons begin to see in us, more-and-more, the likeness of Christ; and this is what it means to be *people of God* – true *JesusFollowers*.

I know from counseling with broken, dysfunctional families, the hurt, frustration, devastation, bitterness, and hopelessness of living in such an environment. Yet I do not know from personal experience what it is like to be trapped in such conditions. However, I do know what it is like from personal experience to live in a home where there is intimacy with God, and where there is deep love, mutual caring, and shared appreciation, for I was privileged to grow up in such an environment from infancy. My parents were godly people who modeled the love of Christ and the comfort of the Holy Spirit. We shared daily in family prayer and Bible reading, and we consistently worshiped together as a family. I also know from personal experience what it is like to be the head of a home where intimacy with God is central.

As our daughters were growing up, we spent our trips to school sharing memorized Scripture passages and praying together. We had family prayer in the girls' room each evening at bedtime. Now those little Christian girls are mature Christian ladies with Christian homes of their own. This is a result of our attempt, both individually and as a family, to cultivate intimacy with God. In spiritual formation we learn to know God intimately, and not to just know about God superficially.

Vision for Ministry: Born in an Intimate Relationship with God

My personal spiritual formation and intimacy with God grows out of a heritage that began many years ago. A few weeks after my dad (Dr. Walter Bruce, former president of Wesley College) went to be with the Lord, Sandie and I stopped by to have an evening prayer time with Mom. We were carrying on a family tradition that Mom and Dad started at the beginning of their marriage. I read the Scripture passage for that day, which was Matthew 9:35-38 which closed with those words, **"Pray ye therefore the Lord of the harvest, that he will send forth laborers into his harvest"** (Matthew 9: 38 KJV). When I closed with those words, Mom told us a special story. She said that when Dad was a young person, just out of high school, he heard his pastor preach on this verse. A few days later, he was reading this passage in the Bible during his own devotional time, which had become a daily practice for him. All who knew him well recognized him as a devoted man of prayer and of the Word. He began praying earnestly, simply out of response to the challenge of the minister, and concern for people who did not know Jesus, **"Lord, send forth laborers into the harvest!"**

As he continued interceding to the Lord, God spoke clearly to his inner spirit, saying, *"Walter, I want you to be a worker in My harvest. I want you to be a minister of the gospel."* God often does humanly surprising things like calling a painfully shy young man from the backwoods of Louisiana into the ministry. In a few days he was hitchhiking from those humble beginnings in Louisiana to God's Bible School, in Cincinnati, Ohio to prepare to fulfill God's calling for his life.

Who would have thought that God had destined him to serve as college president, pastor, General Conference President, and director of foreign missions? Who would have believed that God had planned for him to influence the lives of hundreds of men and women to serve the Lord in ministry as pastors, evangelists, and missionaries? Who could have conceived that he would leave a legacy that would shape the church and people for many years to come? After his retirement as Director of Foreign Missions, at age 71, he pastored the Zion Rest Congregational Methodist church until his death at the age of 82. Only God could have thought such things, for only God could enable such a ministry to happen.

That vision for ministry, born in an intimate relationship with God, continues beyond his lifetime today through Wesley College and the hundreds of Christian ministers that are faithfully working in God's harvest fields. It continues in a son who has served as pastor, Bible college president, president of a national preaching and music ministry, online Christian University professor, and Lead Pastor of a church plant; a daughter-in-law who served as a Director of Children's, Youth, and Adult Ministries, Administrative Assistant, Bible college admissions director; a daughter who is an ordained minister and attorney, and co-pastor; a son-in-law who has been a co-pastor and National Guard chaplain; a son who is a committed Christian layman and concert artist; a daughter-in-law who is a committed Christian layperson and school administrator; a granddaughter who is a minister of worship and music; and several other Christian grandchildren.

Dad's call to the ministry was born in the scriptural mandate to pray for the Lord of the harvest to send forth laborers into the harvest. His lifetime of ministry was bathed in prayer daily. Every decision, every ministry, every service was prefaced by prayer. Every relationship was wrapped in prayer. Dad was recognized by all who knew him as a man of prayer. Is it any wonder that God chose to use a simple, shy young man like him to shape so many lives? The key was not ability, gifts, or boldness—the key was his intimacy with God. That is spiritual formation at its finest.

I remember asking Dad to speak in a chapel service at Wesley College, when I served as president, a couple of years before his death, specifically to give his personal testimony. Among other gems of advice, he told the students:

Some of our older preachers and laity did not know much about *theology*, but they knew much about *knee-ology*. Some of you here have sufficient academic training, but it is going to take much *knee-ology*—praying for our school to survive like we would like to see it do. A word to the students—get all the right kind of education you can, and then, stay with Christ in the School of Prayer . . . . Many times I felt inadequate for the positions I held in our church, but the Lord was very good to help. I was one of the youngest of the preachers in our denomination when I became active in the church, but now I am eighty years young. You staff members, teachers, and students must carry on. You must increase, I am decreasing.[157] Those words indicate that Walter Bruce knew from personal experience the importance of an intimate relationship with God.

Intimacy with God: No Unfinished Business

That intimate relationship was good not only throughout his lifetime, it carried him through death into eternity. On the Thursday night before his death, the intensive care nurses allowed our whole family to gather around Dad's bedside. He had been in a coma since Monday night, so he could not respond to us. We sang some songs, quoted Scripture passages, and told him how much we loved him. I knew that often when people are in comas, the hearing is one of the last senses to stop functioning. I had heard of people waking up and describing beautiful encounters with God and eternity just before stepping out of this life into the next. I said, "Dad, I wish you would wake up for just a few minutes so we could visit with you, and you could tell us what you and the Lord have been discussing during the past few days."

---

157 Bruce, Walter. E. (1991). *Wesley College Chapel Message. Florence, MS.*

Mom quietly responded lovingly and confidently, "Dad doesn't need to come back. He has no unfinished business to settle with God or with anyone else!"

She was right. His intimate, consistent, personal relationship with God across a lifetime carried him gently and faithfully from this life into heaven, to be with God forever. Early the next morning the nurse said that while she was giving him his bath, he simply quit breathing, and he went to be with Jesus.

Although Dad did use the term spiritual formation, he lived it consistently across more than six decades of faithful Christian ministry. That is intimacy with God; and for me, it defines what it means for us, too, to become *people of God – JesusFollowers*. I have known many gifted and talented people who started out in ministry, yet it was short-lived and ineffective because they lacked the main ingredient for a lasting, powerful ministry: intimacy with God. More importantly, it has been thrilling to watch those who lived in covenant relationship of intimacy with God and allowed Him to chart the path of their ministry soar in effective ministry that transformed the lives of those God called them to love and lead, and who were transformed as they stepped into their own *JesusFollower* relationship and ministries.

Intimacy with God: Inner Power Comes through Spiritual Formation

Janet Hagberg believes that "real power" has to do with people becoming more than externally "powerful." It is about people becoming personally powerful. The real power is developed in the context of relationships. "Power is absent," she says, "obviously, if there are not relationships with others; therefore, it is impossible to be powerful in a vacuum."[158] The power she describes is not designed to help people get more by intimidating and manipulating others or by learning the games and maneuvering in our jobs to assure winning or at least to avoid losing. She expands on her thesis as follows:

Personal power is the extent to which one can link the outer capacity for action [forming the outer life][159] with the inner capacity for reflection [forming the inner life] . . . Personal power at the highest stage includes the power derived from external sources represented by organizational and political positions, expertise, titles, degrees, control, material goods, responsibility, and authority but combines with the power that can be derived only from within. Inner power develops from introspection, personal struggles, the gradual evolution of the life purpose, and from accepting and valuing yourself. If you have external power but not internal power, you have very little power. Therefore, some people in the highest positions in organizations are not very personally powerful. And likewise, the most personally powerful people may not have the most prestigious titles or roles in the organization."[160]

Inner power that is real, lasting and effective comes through the disciplines of spiritual formation: becoming people of the Word, people of prayer, and people of worship— which shape us into people of God – JesusFollowers. This is the power that leads through servanthood, service, and modeling rather than by intimidation, manipulating, and maneuvering others.

Again, one of the best models of this leadership style was my father, as described above. By nature, he was an excruciatingly shy, timid, bashful

---

158 Hagberg, J. (1984). *Real Power: Stages of Personal Power in Organizations.* San Francisco, CA: Harper & Row Pub.
159 Brackets mine.
160 Hagberg.

man, but he was a leader among men and women of stature—not because of his eloquence, nor through demands for power. He was known as a man of prayer, a man of the word, and a man of worship—a true man of God – he was a true JesusFollower. Because he daily practiced these spiritual disciplines, people looked to him for guidance, counsel, and wisdom. In difficult and potentially explosive, divisive issues, other leaders often depended on his clear discernment, fair judgment, faithful prudence, and helpful insight. The time he spent in prayer, in the Word, in worship alone with his Lord gave him the spirit of Christ, the mind of God, the leadership and anointing of the Spirit. That is true inner power, the kind gained through intimacy with God, through the disciplines of spiritual formation. That, I believe, is a biblical kind of man of God a true JesusFollower.

An intimate relationship with God through prayer, consistent study of the Word, and worship is the most vital component in the life of a person who desires to be an effective JesusFollower, or to be used in Christian leadership. It is this quality of relationship with God which cultivates the discernment, judgment, prudence, insight, integrity, morals, values, and trustworthiness needed to shape the would-be Christian leader as one who is worthy of being followed. More importantly, a close, intimate relationship with God through the spiritual disciplines is the only true foundation of spiritual formation which leads to becoming women and men of God – true JesusFollowers who point people to the way back home to God. And that is the Key to Transformed Living.

PRAYER RESPONSE

Lord God, I want to be transformed by knowing You more and more in this intimate, close, personal relationship—shaped in my innermost self by the fullness of Christ. "*I want to know Christ and the power of his resurrection . . . that I may gain Christ and be found in him, not having a righteousness of my own . . . but that which is through faith in Christ—the righteousness that comes from God and is by faith.*"[161] Shape within me the image of God, the spirit of Christ, the anointing of the Holy Spirit, and use me as You wish. Enable me to live day by day, moment by moment, breath by breath in such personal intimacy with You that Your will becomes my will, Your desires become my desires, Your way becomes my way. Thank You, Lord, for the high privilege of being "in Christ," which shapes me to be "like Christ." In His wonderful name I pray. Amen.

---

161 Philippians 3:9-11.

Chapter 18

Hangin' Out Around the Campfire with God

Dr. Sam Says . . .

I've been praying lately for God to take me to a deeper level with Him. This, for me, is the purpose of spiritual formation, which I have defined as *forming our inner lives and relationships with God in a way that transforms our outer lives and relationships with other persons.* As we have discovered, spiritual formation is cultivated as we live in the spiritual disciplines of becoming *people of the Word, people of prayer, people of worship* which shape us into *people of God.* One of the best ways I have discovered of illustrating this process of becoming *people of God* through the disciplines of spiritual formation is that it is like *Hangin' Out Around the Campfire with God.*

What comes to your mind if I mention a *hangin' out around the campfire moment?* Do you understand what I mean? Have you ever experienced one? I remember fondly the evening when my eleven-year-old grandson Allen and I were sitting on log stools by our wood pile, splitting pine lighter kindling to start a fire. It was one of those tender, awesome times, as we laughed together and talked about a lot of Grandpa-Grandson kind of "stuff!" Allen said, *"Now Grandpa, this is what I like – just hangin' out with you, splitting firewood, or anything else we do together!"* Did you get that? *Just hangin' out with you . . .* It was one of those *day-maker moments.* We went in our house and built a fire in the fireplace. Later that evening, as the coals were dying down, and His mother had read his devotional book and prayed with him, Allen called for me to come to his room, and said, "Grandpa, would you read my devotional book and pray with me, too?" And I thought, "It doesn't get any better than this!" That's a *hangin' out around the campfire* moment

When I think of *hangin' out around the campfire* kind of moments, I remember affectionately my weekly breakfast and lunch dates with my daughters – one-on-one – every week I was in town, from the time they were about 18 months old. They were really special times we looked forward to – times of fun, laughter, just talking about whatever was on their minds, listening to their thoughts, playing *hang-man* or *dot-to-dot* games on napkins, heart-felt issues, concerns or challenges they were facing and needed some *daddy-thoughts.* Just being silly together. Memory-making times.

Those are *hangin' out around the campfire moment* – with a grandkid, or a daughter, my wife, friends, and most specially, with my Lord Jesus. It's a place where love and intimacy are kindled between us and people that are special to us – a place of warm fellowship, laughter, sharing things that are important among family and friends. A place to hear the deep, personal desires of those that are dear to us.

How do you describe *a hangin' out around the campfire moment?* I have discovered that, in one instance:

Hangin' Out Around the Campfire Was a Place of Regrouping

It's a place to come closer – to family, friends . . . God: *"Lord, bring me closer, closer than I've ever come before to You!"* [162]

One of the most beautiful pictures I have seen of a *hangin' out around the campfire moment* with the Lord is in a story tucked away in 2 Samuel 23:13-17. King David, along with some of his best, most trusted bodyguard platoon – his *mighty men* – was camped out in a cave (when you're camped out, you always need a campfire, don't you?). They were hiding from a garrison of vicious Philistine soldiers who had set up a siege around Bethlehem, David's hometown. David was thirsty, and he just said out loud, **"Oh, how I wish I could have a drink of water from the well at the gate of Bethlehem!"** At that instant, in a dramatic demonstration of loyalty to their king, three of David's finest soldiers set out for the well at Bethlehem. They fought their way through the Philistine garrison and brought a container of water to their king. As they handed him the water – for which they had risked their lives – David was deeply moved by their loyalty, courage, commitment, and strength. And he said, *"I can't drink this water,"* and he poured it out as an offering to the Lord. And suddenly, what began as a simple wish turned into an awesome moment of worship before God.

I can just imagine that David and his men were sitting together in the cave, possibly around a campfire, talking and praying about how they could protect their city, their families, and their belongings. And as David's thoughts drifted toward Bethlehem, which was his hometown, he lamented, **"Oh, how I wish I had a drink from the well by the gate of Bethlehem!"** His words were not a command, or even a request – just a simple wish – a nostalgic desire of his heart.

---

162 Bruce, S. K. (2008). From my song *Glorify Your Name in Me*. Florence, MS: Come to the Waters . . . Be Refreshed! Music, Worship and Ministry Resources; Sam & Sandie Bruce Ministries. drsambruce@aol.com www.bruceministries.net

And because of their total devotion to King David, his wish became their desire, and they fulfilled it, because they loved and respected him. Then as they spent time together in worship, they could regroup and prepare to go out and defeat the enemy that was preparing to attack their city. I think that was one of those *hangin' out around the campfire moments with God*. We need to create more of those moments with our Lord, when we just hang out with Him, listening to His heart's desires, sharing the things that are important to us. It's like taking a timeout – when we break away from the normal (or abnormal!) busyness of life to regroup, refresh, and refocus. I saw this concept illustrated in a football game.

Hangin' Out Around the Campfire with God Is Like Taking a Timeout

My favorite football team is the Dallas Cowboys (Texas-born and raised boy that I am). I remember watching a game on TV several years ago, when Roger Staubach, one of the great players in football history, was quarterback. By the way, Roger is a dynamic Christian. A friend of mine who knows Roger personally sent me an autographed picture of him several years ago. It is on my bookcase near an autographed picture of Tom Landry, former coach of the Cowboys when Staubach was playing, and a committed Christian man.

It was in the final seconds of the game. The Cowboys were behind by four points, several yards from the goal line, fourth down, and one timeout remaining. They needed a touchdown, for a three-point field goal would not be enough to tie, much less win the game. This was nothing new, for the Cowboys have been in that position many times. Staubach called timeout and ran to the sideline to confer with coach Tom Landry. After the timeout, Staubach and the offensive team went back on the field to face the opposing defensive line. Staubach gave the count, the offensive line pushed the defenders back, the receivers ran past the goal line, and Roger fired an absolutely accurate pass into the hands of a receiver, who caught the football and won the game.

The victory isn't so important now, but the principal is important: the timeout is vital, not only in those tense moments toward the end, but all through the game. Whether you are ahead or behind, it is important periodically, to take a timeout, to stop the action, and consult with the coach. Listen to his counsel; be refreshed with a drink of water or Gatorade; regroup your thoughts, your energy; and review the game plan.

This is even truer in life than it is in a ball game. We need to take time out to be with God, to listen to His Word, to pray, and to encourage one another. The very fact that we are so busy, often so desperately driven by responsibilities, worries, demands, makes this timeout more important. Those moments with the Lord God, Who is so much wiser than we are, can give us the guidance we need, the delightful reassurance that He is with us. In that setting we are renewed with a refreshing, revitalizing drink from His powerful, life-transforming Word. We listen to His counsel and encouragement; hear the desires of His heart. Then God gives us the next part of the game plan for our lives. It's time to get off the sidelines, to get back in circulation, and to do the work God has called us to do together. Jesus understood the value of the timeout as Dr. Luke described: **". . . Jesus went out into the hills to pray, and spent the night praying to God"** (Luke 6:12). Amid a heavy, hectic, demanding schedule, Jesus made time to pray . . . to listen to His Father and replenish His spiritual strength for the next day's activities. It was His source of power from God, for His own life and for the people to whom He ministered. If Jesus needed a timeout, how much more important is it for us? That's a *hangin' out around the campfire moment with God.*

Leroy Eims described a *hangin' out around the campfire moment with God* as he said, *"When God finds a person who will place as his first priority a life of intimate, personal, dynamic fellowship with Him, He directs His power, guidance, and wisdom into and through that person. God has found a person through whom He can change the world!"*[163] That's one of those *hangin' out around the campfire moments with God.* We need more of those moments with Him regularly – daily. When we walk away from our time with Him we can accomplish the desires of His heart, not because He has commanded us to do so, but because of our love, devotion, and respect for Him. And because we desire, more than anything else, to walk in unbroken fellowship with Him, and to do what pleases Him. That's where God shapes His *"Change the world"* kind of people.

The timeout is one of those *hangin' out around the campfire moments with God.* It's a time for getting into the Word and prayer. Prayer unleashes the power of the Word to transform our lives, to regroup our thoughts, to reveal God's *game plan,* to replenish our energies, and to move ahead in confidence and victory as we follow the guidance of our Lord. So, *Hangin' Out Around the Campfire Is a Place of Regrouping.*

Hangin' Out Around the Campfire Is a Place of Responding in Prayer

Lord, lead me closer, and deeper, and higher, and farther than I've ever dreamed before with You.[164]

163 Eims, Leroy. Be *the Leader You Were Meant to Be (Wheaton, IL: Victor Books, 1975),* 19.
164 Bruce, S. K. (2008). From my song: *Glorify Your Name in Me. Florence, MS: Come to the Waters . . . Be Refreshed! Music, Worship and Ministry Resources; Sam & Sandie Bruce Ministries.* drsambruce@aol.com www.bruceministries.net

PRAYER RESPONSE

Lord God, thank You for inviting me to hang out around the campfire with You, for being the unifier of my life around Your Word and prayer. Thank You for the supreme privilege of living in close, intimate relationship with You. Amid the busyness, the cluttered schedules, the hectic lifestyles, the noise and chaos, please empower me to create the silent space in which to shape an intimate, prayerful relationship with You through Your Word and prayer. Enable me to take the appropriate time-outs, which are of paramount importance in my relationship with You. Remind me of the necessity of the time-outs — just hangin' out around the campfire with You — to listen to Your directions, to be refreshed in Your presence, and to receive a renewed vision of who You want me to be and what You want me to do. Then take me back into my world a transformed person whom You can use to touch the lives of others with Your love and life-changing power. In the name of the Prince of Peace I pray. Amen.

Hangin' Out Around the Campfire Is a Place of Regrouping and a Place of Responding in Prayer. In this way, God is *forming our inner lives and relationships with Him in a way that transforms our outer lives and relationships with other persons.*

Hangin' Out Around the Campfire Is a Place of Reveling in Delight

Lord, send me farther; farther than I've ever gone before for You! [165]

I believe that David's experience in the cave around the campfire must have influenced his writing Psalm 37: **"Trust in the Lord and do good;**

---

165 Bruce, S. K. (2008). From my song: *Glorify Your Name in Me. Florence, MS: Come to the Waters . . . Be Refreshed! Music, Worship and Ministry Resources; Sam & Sandie Bruce Ministries.* drsambruce@aol.com www.bruceministries.net

dwell in the land and enjoy safe pasture. Delight yourself in the Lord and he will give you the desires of your heart. Commit your way to the Lord; trust in him and he will do this: He will make your righteousness shine like the dawn, the justice of your cause like the noonday sun. Be still before the Lord and wait patiently for him" (Psalm 37:3-7).

"Delight yourself in the Lord" means to revel in delight, to rejoice in just *hangin' out with Him*; to triumph in discovering His plans for us; to celebrate with great joy the privilege of finding and following the desires of His heart for us. Delight also means to be *pliable,* [166] as clay submits to the creative shaping of the potter's hands and our Lord fashions us into vessels He can use to share His love, blessings, and resources with other people. We take pleasure from spending time enjoying His presence and benefitting from His provisions. Peterson, in *The Message,* translates it: **"Keep company with God, get in on the best"** (Psalm 37:4 MSG).

When I first read this passage, my eyes immediately jumped to the part about **"he will give you the desires of your heart."** Isn't that what we all want, *the desires of our hearts*? So, I said, "OK, Lord, where's the key to that treasure chest? Let's get it open!" Then I read again, the first half of that verse, **"Delight yourself in the Lord,"** followed by the little connecting word **and**. That's one of those *If . . . then* statements: *If you do this . . . then I'll do that.* God's fulfillment of the second part is dependent on our fulfilling the first part: *If you* **"Delight yourself in the Lord, [then he] will give you the desires of your heart."**

"So, Lord," I said, "how do I do that, delight myself in You so You can give me the desires of my heart?" He said, "Read the rest of the instructions again!" Here they are: **"Trust in the Lord and do good . . . Commit your way to the Lord; trust in him . . . Be still before the Lord and wait patiently for him . . ."** Then it connected. I began to understand: the

---

166 Strong, J. (2007). *Strong's Talking Greek & Hebrew Dictionary. Austin, TX: WORD-search CROSS E-book.*

Creator God wants to live in a close, personal, intimate relationship with us. That's delighting ourselves in Him – when we commit our way to the Lord – saying, *"Lord, Your will be done in my life, Your plans be fulfilled in my life."* Paul described this kind of *hangin' out around the campfire moment with Jesus* when he wrote, **"we constantly pray for you, that our God may count you worthy of his calling, and that by his power he may fulfill every good purpose of yours and every act prompted by your faith. We pray this so that the name of our Lord Jesus may be glorified in you, and you in him, according to the grace of our God and the Lord Jesus Christ"** (2 Thessalonians 1:11-12).

The words of my song, based on this passage, bring it all together. I think I really ought to name this song: *Sam's Hangin' Out Around the Campfire Song!*

Glorify Your Name in Me [167]

(2 Thessalonians 2:11-12)
Lord, bring me closer, closer than I've ever come before to You.
Lord, plunge me deeper, deeper than I've ever been before in You.
Lord, take me higher, higher than I've ever soared before with You.
Lord, send me farther, farther than I've ever gone before for You.

Lord, glorify Your name in me.
Oh Lord, glorify Your name in me.
Lord, please glorify Your name in me,
And my name in You.

---

167 Bruce, Dr. Sam (2010). *Glorify Your Name in Me Song. Florence, MS: Unpublished, in process. Come to the Waters Be Refreshed! Ministry & Music Resources, Sam & Sandie Bruce Ministries; Demo & music available from* drsambruce@aol.com. www.bruceministries.net

Lord, lead me closer; and deeper; and higher; and farther
Than I've ever dreamed before.

Lord, glorify Your name in me.
Oh Lord, glorify Your name in me.
Lord, please glorify Your name in me,
And my name in You.

Then, as we delight ourselves in Him in this way – just hangin' out around the campfire with Him – He *gives us the desires of His heart*, and as we *commit our way to Him*, we allow the *desires of His heart* to become the *desires of our hearts*. And then, *He can give us the desires of our hearts*. And we can always trust the *desires of His heart* to be what is best and fulfilling for us, for He loves us and wants us to succeed. He expresses this so clearly and beautifully in Jeremiah 29:11, **"I know the plans I have for you . . . plans to prosper you and not to harm you, plans to give you hope and a future."** And as we begin to walk with God in the *desires of His heart* which have become the *desires of our hearts*, we understand Paul's prayer for the Thessalonians Christians, and us as well, that **"God may count you worthy of His calling, and by His power He will fulfill every good purpose of yours and every act prompted by your faith"** (2 Thessalonians 1:11).

Here is the process in a nutshell:

As we delight ourselves in the Lord
in those "hangin' out around the campfire moments,
He gives us the desires of His heart.
Then we allow them to become the desires of our hearts.
Then He can trust us to give us the desires of our hearts

because we are in line with His plan and purpose for our lives.
This is how He can count us worthy of His calling
and by His power fulfill every good purpose of ours
and every act prompted by our faith.
And that is the key to success and fulfillment in every part of our lives.

I Could Have Traded Five Dollars for a Hundred Dollars!

When I was a boy, I had a little dime bank, about the size of a dime coin roll – it would hold five dollars' worth of dimes. It had about two and one-half dollars in it. I had earned those dimes over a period of several months by singing in the services where my dad was preaching as we traveled across the country when he was president of Wesley College. When I was eight years old, Dad made me a member of the worship team, and promised to pay me ten cents each time I sang a solo or duet with my sister. It was his way of helping me feel better about missing little league baseball in the summers due to our travels. I was proud of those dimes, and I enjoyed counting them and stacking them in dollar-size piles and putting them back in the bank.

One day, a lady, in whose home we were having dinner, held out her tightly closed hand toward me. She said, "I'll trade what I have in my hand for your bank!"

Well, I was curious to know what was in her hand, but I also knew what was in my bank and how long it took me to accumulate my treasure. Two and a half dollars – twenty-five dimes – represented twenty-five songs. That's a lot of work, even when you're having fun!

So, after much inner struggle, I decided to keep my dime bank and two and a half dollars.

When the lady opened her hand, I saw a hundred-dollar bill in it, which I could have had for a fifty-cent bank and two and a half dollars! I was so disappointed that I cried. But I learned some lessons that day.

Many people are like I was – holding on to their puny little desires and toys, a few little joys, some happiness, a few fleeting thrills, along with a lot of fears, frustrations, heartaches, and anxieties.

Then Jesus Christ, the great Liberator comes along and offers to trade them eternal life, and a life of inner peace and freedom, purpose and meaning, fulfillment and joy. Yet, they cling to their little empty or partially-full lives because they are afraid to trust Him – afraid to lose that which will not last or satisfy for what is eternal and will satisfy **"immeasurably more than we can ask or imagine"** (Ephesians 3:20). But as you *hang out around the campfire* with our Lord, listening to His thoughts, delighting yourself in Him, getting the desires of His heart, making them the desires of your heart, you learn to trust Him. The Apostle John said, **"There is no fear in love. Perfect love drives out fear . . ."** (1 John 4:18 NIV). And those *hangin' out around the campfire moments with our Lord* enable us to develop that intimate, perfect love relationship of trust with our Lord.

Jesus Christ has proven Himself across the ages of time to be absolutely trustworthy. Millions of changed lives attest to His ability to save and satisfy people, who, in simple faith, trust Him and ask Him to come into their lives and take control.

You see, back in eternity past, God the Father had an offer He wanted to make to us – to trade the gift of eternal life for the brief span of life which we know here on earth: a life which ends in eternal death, separation from God and all that is good. So, He sent His unique Son, Jesus Christ, fully God and fully man, to complete the plan and make the offer.

And as we spend those *hangin' out around the campfire moments with* Him, He gives us the desires of His heart . . . and ours. It's something like *trading two and a half dollars and a fifty-cent bank for a hundred dollars –* only the results of this trade are much more important, with farther-reaching consequences and higher stakes.

Hangin' Out Around the Campfire with God is a place where we cultivate our spiritual formation (*forming our inner lives and relationships with God in a way that transforms our outer lives and relationships with other persons*) as we live in the spiritual disciplines of becoming *people of the Word, people of prayer, people of worship* which shape us into *people of God.*

Hangin' Out Around the Campfire Is a Place of Remaining in Prayer

Lord, lead me closer, and deeper, and higher, and farther than I've ever dreamed before with You! [168]

Prayer Response

My Creator God, I want to spend more moments just hangin' out around the campfire with You. I invite You to live in close, personal, intimate relationship with me. Help me to delight myself in You – to be pliable in Your hands as You shape me into a vessel You can use to accomplish Your purposes for me. Your will be done in my life, Your plans be fulfilled in me. Please give me the desires of Your heart. Enable them to become the desires of my heart. Then give me the desires of my heart. Lord, I pray that you would count me worthy of your calling, show me the awesome plans you have for me, and, by Your power,

---

168 Bruce, S. K. (2008). From my song: *Glorify Your Name in Me.* Florence, MS: *Come to the Waters . . . Be Refreshed! Music, Worship and Ministry Resources; Sam & Sandie Bruce Ministries.* drsambruce@aol.com www.bruceministries.net

fulfill every good purpose of mine and every act prompted by my faith. Set me free to fulfill my God-given potential. Lord, please heal, restore and empower me in my spirit, my mind, my emotions, my body, and all my relationships with other people. I commit my ways to You, and I trust You to prosper me, and to give me awesome hope and a glorious future as I walk with you. Thank You, Lord. I love You! Amen.

Chapter 19

Spiritual Direction

The practice of the discipline of spiritual direction seems to be rare among Christian leaders. The reason for this is, perhaps, that most Christians appear not to understand the purpose, process, or power in spiritual direction. By power, I do not mean that a spiritual director is to have power over another person, but rather to empower another person in his or her own spiritual formation agenda.

Interpersonal Dynamics of Spiritual Direction

Gerald G. May describes the interpersonal dynamics of spiritual direction in this way:

Spiritual direction is generally surrounded by a characteristic atmosphere that is seldom encountered in any other interpersonal relationship. This atmosphere is one of spaciousness and underlying peace; of openness and receptivity; of a kind of quiet clarity in which it is easier to allow and let be. As one person put it, "Being in spiritual direction is just like being in prayer, only there's someone with me in it."[169]

A spiritual director is not, primarily, a counselor, advisor, teacher, or preacher. A spiritual director, in the setting of spiritual formation, is a spiritual friend who asks questions about a person's walk with the Lord. Such questions can help clarify what a person is saying or feeling. A spiritual friend should, rather than giving too much advice, ask questions to help a person work out the answers to his or her struggles and decisions, although, there are times when godly, biblical, prayerful advice are appropriate.

A Sense of the Presence and Resources of God

One of the main contributions a spiritual director should bring to the relationship is a sense of the presence and resources of God. This requires that, as spiritual directors, we continuously cultivate our personal relationships with God. It is difficult to lead other persons on paths we have not personally walked. It is impossible to introduce someone to the presence of God if we are not personally living in His presence. This is why the principles of spiritual formation—*the forming of our inner lives and relationships with God in a way that transforms our outer lives and relationships with other persons*—are imperatives that must be practiced in our lives before we can empower others to practice them. Gerald May quotes a counselor who realized the need to be God's representative to the people who were being counseled:

169 May, G. D. (1982). *Care of Mind, Care of Spirit.* New York, NY: Harper & Row.

My being-in-God is something that I know to be true in my regular counseling work. It exists as a fact, behind all my endeavors, and I can acknowledge it whenever I think about it or when someone asks me about it. Generally, it just hangs around in the background, though, as a kind of underlying principle. But in spiritual direction it comes right up front. It is no longer just background knowledge or inference, but a fully lived and experienced reality. I no longer know it in the usual sense. Instead, I sense it in its lively, loving action—the immediate moment. It's like the difference between thinking about love and being in love, between knowing you are a swimmer and actually diving in and swimming.[170]

The primary task of the spiritual director is to bring to the relationship the presence of God. This underscores "the absolute necessity of personal attention to one's own prayer life and daily awareness of God, and of being in spiritual direction oneself." The spiritual director should come to the relationship out of the personal disciplines of attending to the Master, tending the inner life. May writes: In spiritual direction, one might say, "My prayers are for God's will to be done in you and for your constant deepening in God. During this time that we are together I give myself, my awareness, and hopes and heart to God for you. I surrender myself to God for your sake."[171]

In spiritual direction we accompany those to whom we minister to the throne of grace and mercy to seek God's help, strength, and guidance along the paths of spiritual formation. Eugene Peterson says that

. . . spiritual direction takes place when two people agree to give their full attention to what God is doing in one (or both) of their

170 May, G. D. (1982). *Care of Mind, Care of Spirit*. New York, NY: Harper & Row. 95-96.
171 May.

lives and seek to respond in faith. Three convictions underpin these meetings. (1) God is always doing something: an active grace is shaping this life into a mature salvation. (2) Responding to God is not sheer guesswork: the Christian community has acquired wisdom through the centuries that provides guidance. (3) Each soul is unique: no wisdom can simply be applied without discerning the particulars of this life, this situation.[172]

Be Spiritually Attentive to What God Is Doing

This is the reason why we must be spiritually attentive to what God is doing each time we meet for spiritual direction. Each situation is different; each person has different needs. Those needs vary from day to day. We need to be seeking together to discover what God wants to do currently, for this person, in this situation. Peterson says,

Spiritual direction means taking seriously, with a disciplined attention and imagination, what others take casually. "Pray for me" is often a casual remark. The spiritual director gives it full attention. All those moments in life when awareness of God breaks through the crust of our routines—a burst of praise, a pang of guilt, an episode of doubt, boredom in worship—these take place all the time and are mentioned from time to time in half serious ways while we are on the run to something big or important. Being a director means a readiness to clear space and arrange time to look at these elements of our life that are not at all peripheral but are central— unobtrusive signals of transcendence. By naming and attending

---

172 Peterson, E. H. (1987). *Working the Angles. Grand Rapids, MI: Eerdmans.*

and conversing, we teach our friends to "read the Spirit" and not just the newspapers.[173]

A spiritual friend should be a person to whom you feel close, and with whom you would feel free to be open and vulnerable. Before opening yourself too deeply to that person, be sure to get well acquainted so that you are certain you feel good about your vulnerability with that person. Explore your director's relationship with God, and his or her practice of the spiritual disciplines. Be certain that you are both headed in the same direction in spiritual formation, for "in these moments when we are in conversation with another and spirit touches spirit, 'deep calling to deep,' there is a confirming sense that we are doing our best work. The spiritual director is in charge of attending to these quiet necessities."[174] (Peterson, 1987, 106)

If You Were My Spiritual Friend, You Might Do Things Like These:

1. Make appointments with me to inventory my spiritual life.
2. Counsel and assign me exercises to follow until the next meeting.
   a. Help them understand the *Praying Out of the Word – Journaling* process in chapter 1.
   b. Ask me such questions as:
      i. How is your walk with the Lord?
      ii. How is God active with you in your family? work? church? school?
      iii. What is the next step you need to take to grow in your walk with the Lord?

---

173 Peterson, E. H. (1987). *Working the Angles. Grand Rapids, MI: Eerdmans.*
174 Peterson. 106.

    d.   Give suggestions that have helped with your own spiritual growth such as:

       i.   Spiritual Readings

      ii.   Bible study exercises

     iii.   Prayer Disciplines

     iv.   Answers to Prayers

      v.   Journaling

     vi.   Scripture Memory

    vii.   Other

3.   Establish a time commitment for beginning and ending your spiritual direction. This can be renewed or terminated at the end of that time.

4.   Confidentiality is of utmost importance. **Do not share, without permission, with anyone, not even your spouse or best friend what is discussed in the spiritual direction times.** This requirement cannot be over stressed, it is of absolute importance. Such sharing can break trust, cause embarrassment, destroy friendships, and hinder the whole process of spiritual direction. Once that trust is broken (if you can't trust your pastor, minister, spiritual director, or friend, who can you trust?), it is difficult if not impossible to restore again. Additionally, a ministerial breach of confidence could result in a lawsuit if the damages were serious enough.

5.   Encourage the person to pursue what God has for him or her at this time, not what you feel he or she should be doing. The spiritual director is not to serve as a manager, messiah, or manipulator. Maybe the best way to describe the spiritual director's role is that our responsibility is, as the Holy Spirit works in and through us, to be a *paraclete* (as Jesus described the Holy Spirit

whom He would send to take His place when He ascended back to the Father), one *called alongside* another person to encourage, comfort, guide, help, strengthen, and lead to a safe, quiet harbor. Another way to describe a spiritual director could be that of a spiritual coach or a personal spiritual trainer.

Watchman of the Soul

Mother Perry, who was Sandi Patty's great-grandmother, was a wonderful, saintly lady in the church I pastored. I felt like I was walking on holy ground every time I went to her home for a visit. We always had a special time of prayer together before I left, and she would remind me that as her pastor I was the *watchman of her soul.* To a young pastor just out of seminary, those words startled me the first time she said them, but I learned to understand that they simply meant that she held me responsible both to pray for and with her and to give her counsel and advice in her physically declining years. A few days before her death she reminded me again that I was still the *watchman of her soul.* That is a good description of what practicing the discipline of spiritual direction involves. We are dealing with timely yet eternal issues that affect the well-being and healing of the soul— the spirit, mind, emotions, relationships, and sometimes even the body of another person.

In spiritual direction, Martin Thornton says that we are involved in the

. . . positive development of the man-God relation, which is prayer; this application of the Gospel to human life, and not just to human need, is what pastoral care really means. And it is of the most ultimate social significance because it goes beyond problem solving, either individual or communal, towards redemption; it is not concerned with happiness but with joy, not with mediocrity but with glory.

Prayer—man's continuing relation with God—is neither a sop to make one feel better nor a pious interlude to solve problems: it is the peak of human achievement. Religion is no ally or appendage to philosophy or social science, still less a conventional bulwark to ethics and stability; it transcends all these, piercing the visible and intellectual: it is life more abundant. Spiritual direction is the way forward. It is the positive nurture of man's relation with God, the creative cultivation of *charismata,* the gifts and graces that all have received. It is the opposite of the sort of pastoral care which assumes that religion can only offer little bits of help in emergencies: the ambulance syndrome. And it is the obverse [a counterpart, or complement] of what has come to be called pastoral counseling, or perhaps more fairly the necessary consummation of it; if counseling deals with problems, direction takes over as soon as they are solved.[175]

Another way of looking at this process is to say that spiritual direction is not simply a way of applying a band-aid to a hurt or a problem. It can become an ongoing healing relationship in which the spiritual director leads the mentee into the presence of God and His resources for life with all its varied situations, circumstances, temptations, relationships, and needs. In that setting, spiritual direction becomes, not just a quick fix, but a *continuing ministry in the context of the presence of God in the everydayness of life.*

---

175 Thornton, M. (1984). *Spiritual Direction. Cambridge, MA: Cowley Pub. 10.*

Walking Together in the Presence of Jesus

In such a context, if I am your spiritual director, I might ask you to imagine that we are looking down a path, and we see Jesus coming. I know Jesus, I introduce you to Him. I say something like, "Jesus, this is my friend. Friend, meet Jesus." As your eyes and heart meet His, I say to you, "Friend, tell Jesus what you are feeling, your needs, dreams, joys, heart-aches." Then, as He begins to share His love, wisdom, help, and guidance, the three of us walk down the trail together in a relationship of love and communion that is life-transforming for both of us. In this setting, mine is not the task of solving your problems or planning your life. Instead, it is the privilege of walking with you in His presence and guiding you as you work out the details of your life while we communicate with Him together. In this way, the path of spiritual direction becomes "the journey to heaven, not a trip to the hospital."[176]

C. S. Lewis describes spiritual directors as "those particular people within the whole church who have been especially set aside to look after what concerns us as creatures who are going to live forever."[177] Therefore, Eugene Peterson reminds us, spiritual direction "needs to be practiced out of a life immersed in the pursuit of holiness . . . We prayerfully cultivate an awareness that God has designs on this person, that God is acting in this situation, that God is bringing some purpose long in process to fulfillment right now."[178]

Paul wrote to the Corinthians, **"Even though you have ten thousand guardians in Christ, you do not have many fathers, for in Christ Jesus I became your father through the gospel"** (1 Corinthians 4:15). Whether we are there as pastors, lay ministers, or Christian friends, when we serve

---

176 Thornton, M. (1984). *Spiritual Direction. Cambridge, MA: Cowley Pub. 10.*
177 Lewis, C. S. (1976). *Mere Christianity. New York, NY: MacMillan.*
178 Peterson, E. H. (1987). *Working the Angles. Grand Rapids, MI: Eerdmans. 111.*

in the role of spiritual directors, we are there as guardians and guides in the spiritual growth of other persons. We do so with the caring, listening, helping grace that is characterized by a father's love. In that setting, if people are going to mature in their faith, they need "not only wisdom but a wise person to understand us in relation to the wisdom. A person in need and in growth is vulnerable and readily accepts counsel that is sincerely given. But the help that might be right for someone else, even right for this person at another time, can be wrong for this person at this time."[179]

That is why, as spiritual directors, we need to be spiritually attuned to what God, through the Spirit and the Word, is saying to us at this time, in this setting, for this situation and this relationship. Perhaps one of the roles of the spiritual director is to watch for those times when the embers of spiritual fervor have cooled, the flames of spiritual enthusiasm have died down, and the zeal for spiritual disciplines is lagging. In such vulnerable times, our job is to apply the bellows of prayer, counsel, and encouragement to fan into flames the spiritual disciplines that have become dormant, latent, or lethargic so that our friends—mentees—can glow once again with spiritual fervor and anointing. In those settings, "reputations do not count in spiritual direction. Experience is not enough. Only a life committed to spiritual adventure, personal integrity, honest and alert searching prayer is adequate for the task."[180]

Spiritual direction is not a job, but a calling; not a responsibility, but a privilege; not a chore, but an adventure in helping one of God's children deepen and grow in a vital relationship with Him. I have discovered, thankfully, that in any spiritual director relationship I grow as much or more than those God entrusts into my hands for direction.

179 Peterson. 112.
180 Peterson. 125.

Chapter 20

The Life-Changing Power of Personal Spiritual Retreats

Dr. Sam Says . . .

When I was a pastor, dealing with the rigorous demands of a dynamic, growing church—trying to achieve balance between family, personal prayer and meditation time, ministry, and social opportunities—I discovered a valuable life-renewing, ministry-energizing spiritual discipline. It was what I began to call a *Personal Spiritual Retreat*.

I was fortunate to live close to the awe-inspiring Sierra Mountains where several friends provided me with beautiful cabins in remote spots beside pristine lakes, gurgling mountain streams, and gorgeous wooded seclusions. Armed with my Bible, *Journal*, plenty of food, snacks, and drinks, I would get in my 4-wheel-drive Chevy Blazer, affectionately known as *Bluebird*, and head out for a three-day, three-night quiet place of retreat, alone with my Lord. The *Personal Spiritual Retreat* was a relaxed, yet focused time for meditating on the Word, prayer, listening and speaking with my Lord, writing in *My Journal*, being quiet, resting, singing. Sometimes I would walk in the woods, alongside a stream, stroll beside a lake, or sit quietly on a high rocky point overlooking a great expanse of God's creation in a meadow, a valley, a waterfall or snow-covered peaks. Occasionally I would catch a couple of trout to cook for dinner. All the time, I was soaking up refreshment for my spirit, mind, emotions, and body, as well as renewing my relationship with the Lord. I always returned home from my *Personal Spiritual Retreats* renewed, with fresh energy and vision for my relationships and ministries.

I had the full blessing of Sandie, our daughters, and our congregation for those *Personal Spiritual Retreats* because they knew that they would be the beneficiaries of my alone times with my Lord. It often happened, on the Sunday following one of my *Personal Spiritual Retreats*, after the morning service, someone would remark, "Pastor, you must have been on one of your *Personal Spiritual Retreats*. It shows in your countenance and in your preaching." Remarks like that let me know the value—*The Life-Renewing Power of Personal Spiritual Retreats*. They affected positively not only me, but all those around me as well.

When we were discussing the value of *Personal Spiritual Retreats*, Sandie remarked, "The thing is, pastors, other ministers, and Sunday school teachers often tend to ignore their own personal growth because they are so involved in *doing the work* instead of *being the person*. It is so easy for the Christian workers to get their eyes on *the work* instead of on *the Worker* who can enable them to *do the work*." The purpose of a *Personal Spiritual Retreat* is to *renew the* worker so he or she can *do the work* the Lord calls them to do, and not burn out in the process.

I have learned that *the quality of the effectiveness of my ministry is directly proportional to the quantity of time I spend alone with God*. The *Personal Spiritual Retreat* is similar to the effectiveness of a monthly Vitamin B shot as compared with daily oral Vitamin B tablets over a period of time. The periodic shot gives a concentrated dose that goes directly into the blood stream to provide the nutrients the body needs for effective energy and functions. The *Personal Spiritual Retreat* provides a concentrated time in the presence of God where spirits are renewed, minds are refined, thoughts are regrouped, visions are refreshed, and emotions are restored—and later, often, relationships are rekindled.

Henri Nouwen (*Genesee Diary*) said that people who truly seek the presence of God "are *not* the ones who withdraw from the world to save their own soul, but the ones who enter into the center of the world and pray to God from there."[181] This is my goal, that I continue developing my relationship with my God so that I may live in the center of His power, resources and presence. One wonderful place to develop my relationship with God is in the *Personal Spiritual Retreats*, which empower me, in the words of Nouwen, to "enter into the center of the world and pray to God from there."[182]

Nouwen said, ". . . prayer must be sought with no scant effort: then God, seeing our travail, will give us what we seek. True prayer will not be achieved by human efforts: it is a gift of God. Seek and you will find . . . One must remember that success in any aspect of the spiritual life is the fruit of the grace of God. Spiritual life comes entirely from His most Holy Spirit. We have our own spirit, but it is void of power. It begins to gain strength only when the grace of God flows into it."[183]

I have learned—the more I practice prayer and seeking the presence of God in my life—especially through the *Personal Spiritual Retreats*, that God's grace, strength and power become available to me in direct relation to my consistency in the Word, in prayer, in worship – just spending quiet time alone with Him – and in submission to His control of my life and its affairs.

---

181 Nouwen, H. J. (1976). *The Genesee Diary: Report from a Trappist Monastery*. Garden City, NY: Image Books, Doubleday & Co.

182 Nouwen.

183 Nouwen.

A further confirmation of this concept comes from some comments by Phillip Keller, in *Elijah: Prophet of Power*: "Most of us have never learned the secret of being 'still' before God. We have never come to the maturity that accepts the quiet interludes in life as His provision for our welfare. We have not yet come to see that godly growth and godly attainment can proceed as rapidly in *QuietTimes* and gentle retreats as they can in the heat and fury of action. It is the person who has been in the quiet place, alone with God, who is going to have a message from the Lord. If any person is to have power with men and God, he has to derive that energy and thrust from personal, intimate contact with Christ."[184] A great place to receive that "message . . . and personal, intimate contact with Christ" is in the *Personal Spiritual Retreat*.

PRAYER RESPONSE

Heavenly Father, thank You for not just waiting for me to come to you as the Father did in the story of the prodigal son, but for pursuing me with a relentless love that drew me into Your gracious, life-saving presence. Lord, as I dwell in Your presence, please help me to learn the secret of being still before You in QuietTimes and gentle retreats so that I may receive a message from You to me. And through that message, enable me to have power with men and with God, as I derive energy and thrust from personal, intimate contact with You. As I practice prayer and seek Your plan for my life, please make Your grace, strength and power available to me in direct relation to my consistency in the Word, in prayer, and in just spending quiet time alone with You, and in submission to Your control of my life and its affairs. Thank You for the life I now enjoy in Your presence, living in your **"limitless resources,"** *for the* **"joy of salvation."** *Amen.*

---

184 Keller, Phillip. *Elijah: Prophet of Power*. Waco, TX: Word Publishing Co. 1979.

The two following entries of *My Journal* illustrate the importance of *Personal Spiritual Retreats* in my own life.

Refreshed! An Oasis in a Quiet Place

When I was working on my D. Min. Degree at Fuller Seminary, I took a course in spiritual formation under Eugene Peterson (translator of *The Message, the Bible in Contemporary Language* and author of many books on spiritual formation and pastoral care). It was a personal life-transforming experience for me. As part of the course, I attended a retreat, with 35 other ministers from across our nation and many nations around the world, at the St. Andrews Retreat Center in the high desert above The Mojave Desert. I went for a walk on a desert trail to reminisce, to reflect, to remember times in the past when I sensed God's presence in my life. I came to an oasis, a beautiful little lake in the desert, surrounded by peacefully drooping willow trees and lush green grass. A fountain was springing up in the middle of the lake. Ducks and geese were swimming gracefully across the water. As I sat alone beside the water, soaking up some of the beauty of my Father's creative handiwork, I was reminded that the past year had been one of desert dwelling for me - a time of struggle, pressure. Although I had been in touch with God through His Word and through prayer - and I was certain that these are what had brought me through - I was sensing a barrenness, a tiredness, a weakness.

But I knew God had been faithful. Through His Word and prayer, and coming away from the busyness of life, He had already begun to refresh me at a very deep level of my inner spirit. In Christ I found an oasis in the middle of my desert-dwelling experience. Like my shady retreat there in the desert, my Lord was leading me to the shady green pastures of His presence and love. I welcomed His refreshing power, for it was good!

As I sat there, quietly praying and reading my Bible, I was reminded that we all go through those *desert dwelling times* in our relationships with God, with others, and with ourselves — spiritually, mentally, emotionally, physically, relationally, vocationally, and economically. I realized that moments like these are important times in our lives, for what happens next can set the tone for the next stages of our lives. I remembered the words of Ralph Carmichael's song *A Quiet Place*, which expresses the power of the *Personal Spiritual Retreats* in our lives.

A Quiet Place[185]

There is a quiet place, far from the rapid pace,
Where God can soothe my troubled mind,
Sheltered by tree and flower,
There in my quiet hour with Him,
My cares are left behind.
Whether a garden small or on a mountain tall,
New strength and courage there I find;
Then from this quiet place I go prepared to face
A new day with love for all mankind.

It was in that *Quiet Place* of refreshment and renewal that my gracious Lord introduced me to the value of the *Personal Spiritual Retreat*, not only for me but for all servants of God who wish to be refreshed in their inner beings and to take their relationship with Him to a much deeper level.

Several years later, in another remote *Quiet Place of Refreshment and Renewal* my gracious Lord, when I was seeking clear direction about leaving

---

185 Ralph Carmichael, *A Quiet Place*. © *Lexicon Music. CCLI #2542096*

the presidency of Wesley College to go full-time with Bruce Ministries, gave me the words and music for the theme song of our ministries:

Come to My Waters[186]

Come to the waters that flow from My Springs.
Come to My waters that never run dry.
Come to My waters and you'll thirst no more.
Come to My waters, be refreshed in My Grace!
I'll refresh you; I'll renew you; I will cleanse you right now.

Bring all your sorrows, heartbreaks, your hurts.
Bring all your sicknesses, sighs, and sins.
Taste of My waters, and I'll cleanse you today.
Bring them all to My waters, I'll refresh you within.
I'll refresh you; I'll renew you; I will cleanse you right now.

Bring to Lord Jesus your family and friends.
Bring them to My waters that never run dry!
Bring all the hurting, the wounded and sad.
Bring them all to My waters, I'll refresh them today.
I'll refresh you; I'll renew you; I will cleanse you right now.

Come, Holy Spirit, purify me right now.
Come, precious Comforter, empower me within.
Touch those around me with Your healing grace.

---

186 _© Bruce, S. K. (2010). *Come to the Waters*. Florence, MS: Come to the Waters Be Refreshed! Ministry & Music Resources, *Sam & Sandie Bruce Ministries*; Music & Soundtrack available from drsambruce@aol.com 601.845.8693

Make me free like Lord Jesus, and wholly transformed.
Come, refresh me! Come, renew me! Come and cleanse me today.

Come taste My waters, I'll refresh you right now.
Oh, come to My waters, And drink from My springs.

Prescription for Peace and Power

I am on a *Personal Spiritual Retreat* at Central Camp, alone in a cabin in the beauty of the Sierra Mountains. This morning, as I sat on a log in the middle of a mountain stream, soaking up the beauty of God's creation, I received some new spiritual insights that I felt were from the Lord. It was in a time of prayer, before my Lord, reconfirming my commitment to Him, seeking His guidance, asking Him to refresh my inner spirit and to give me some definite direction for my life and ministry. My thoughts began to focus on some discomfort I felt in my lower back. I began to see some spiritual parallels to a properly aligned spinal column. When the vertebrae in the spinal column slip out of adjustment, they put pressure on various nerves that send messages to different organs and body parts. Not only does the maladjustment cause excruciating pain, but it also often impairs, or hinders, the proper function of various parts of the body.

For instance, a vertebra out of alignment in the lower back can cause terrible shooting pain down the leg and make it difficult for a person to walk. In the neck area, it can make it painfully difficult for you to turn your head. This type of pain can make a person irritable, edgy, tense, and just plain hard to live with. It can affect one's appetite and work productivity, as well as one's ability to function in the normal routines of life.

This is a good picture of the effects of allowing other areas of life to go out of proper adjustment – for instance, moral and ethical standards, our relationship with the Lord, or husband and wife relationships.

When things in the moral or ethical realm are out of order, a person experiences the pain of a guilty conscience, the loneliness of being separated from God, the disappointment of, not only failing God, but of failing ourselves.[187]

Heart specialists say that one of the major causes of heart-failure is clogged arteries, caused by the build-up of cholesterol. The cholesterol stops the proper flow of blood throughout the body. This can slow a person down; hamper his or her ability to think clearly or to function properly. And it can cause physical death. The doctors are learning more and more about this, and they teach that a major cause of cholesterol buildup is improper diet – too much greasy, fatty food, primarily. We have become "junk food junkies," they say. And they are learning that by following proper diet, a person can lower the cholesterol level, thus lowering the risk of a heart attack.

In the spiritual realm, when our relationship with God is out of alignment, or when we allow something to clog the flow of communication between God and us, these are things that take their toll, not only on our bodies, but, more tragically, on our spirits, minds, emotions and relationships. Scripture advises, "Above all else, guard your heart, for it is the well-spring of life" (Proverbs 4:23). That is God's Prescription for Peace and Power. A Personal Spiritual Retreat is a great time to put our lives back in proper alignment with God's plans for us. It can be a time to clear the channel of communication between us and God, to restore strained or even broken relationships with Him. It is a time to gain strength and refreshment in His presence, and then we can go back into our worlds of

---

187 Psalm 51 gives a good prayer for putting a person's life back in line with God's plan.

family, ministry, work, and social interaction with renewed vision, purpose, and effectiveness.

A good way to ask God for this kind of renewal is through a prayer song I wrote in a time of meditation on 2 Thessalonians 1:11-12 (NIV), "With this in mind, we constantly pray for you, that our God may count you worthy of his calling, and that by his power he may fulfill every good purpose of yours and every act prompted by your faith. We pray this so that the name of our Lord Jesus may be glorified in you, and you in him, according to the grace of our God and the Lord Jesus Christ. Later, as I was praying the prayer, it became a song as the Lord gave me the melody."

Glorify Your Name in Me [188]

(2 Thessalonians 2:11-12)

Lord, bring me closer, closer than I've ever come before to You.
Lord, plunge me deeper, deeper than I've ever been before in You.
Lord, take me higher, higher than I've ever soared before with You.
Lord, send me farther, farther than I've ever gone before for You.

Lord, glorify Your name in me;
Oh Lord, glorify Your name in me;
Lord, please glorify Your name in me,
And my name in You.

---

188 ©Bruce, S. K. (2010). *Glorify Your Name in Me*. Florence, MS: Come to the Waters
Be Refreshed! Ministry & Music Resources, *Sam & Sandie Bruce Ministries*; Music &
Soundtrack available from drsambruce@aol.com www.bruceministries.net

Lord, lead me closer; and deeper; and higher; and farther
Than I've ever dreamed before.

Lord, glorify Your name in me;
Oh Lord, glorify Your name in me;
Lord, please glorify Your name in me,
And my name in You.

Finally, *The Life-Renewing Power of a Personal Spiritual Retreat* is discovered as we realize that it is a safe place to bring our brokenness, our failures, our poor judgment, our bad decisions, ruptured relationships, wounded hearts, and yes—our sins! And like that holy ground beside a burning bush that was not being consumed, we encounter the reconciling and healing presence of our God lavishly outpoured. And like Moses discovered, a *Personal Spiritual Retreat* can be a safe and exciting place to explore and receive God's plans for our dreams, visions, and hopes and ask Him, in *The Place of Stillness and Receptivity in His presence* . . . speak to me in your still, small voice; your gentle whisper; that I may listen, hear, understand, accept, and act as you say: **"This is what the Lord says . . . This is the way, walk in it . . . I'll be with you as you do this . . .!"** (2 Kings 9:3 NIV, Isaiah 30:21 NIV, Genesis 26:3 MSG/DSP[189] Matthew 28:20 MSG. During our daily, hectic, over-packed lives, Nouwen said, "God's presence is often a hidden presence. The loud, boisterous noises of the world make us deaf to the soft, gentle, and loving voice of God. A Christian leader is called to help people to hear that voice and so be comforted and consoled"190 And I would add, so we can be a comforting and consoling presence to those to whom God calls us to minister.

---

189 DSP: Dr. Sam's Paraphrase of a Scripture Passage
190 Nouwen, Henri. (1989). *In the Name of Jesus: Reflections on Christian Leadership. New York, NY: The Crossroad Publishing Co. 89.*

I have often discovered deep spiritual formation involving the whole person—spirit, mind, emotions, body, relationships, ministries, and vocations—in The Life-Renewing Power of a Personal Spiritual Retreat. My counsel to all who are involved in any kind of ministry—the highest calling anyone can receive from God—is that they make a covenant with God to regularly go on Personal Spiritual Retreats, for there they too will discover deep spiritual formation involving the whole person—spirit, mind, emotions, body, relationships, ministries, and vocations in The Life-Renewing Power of a Personal Spiritual Retreat. Whether that Personal Spiritual Retreat is on a mountaintop, in a remote cabin in a wooded place, beside a gurgling stream, placid lake or campfire, or wherever else we and the Lord decide to be together, it can be a special quiet place. It is a place where God and we can meet to listen and hear, reflect and speak, be still and rest. The spiritual disciplines of meditating on the Word, prayer, and worship can enable us to create that inner quiet space where God and we can communicate unhampered by the outer clamor and confusion that seek to destroy relationships that are deep and fulfilling. Just Hangin' Out around the Campfire, we can create that inner quiet place where His peace permeates all we do. Again, in that place we discover The Life-Renewing Power of a Personal Spiritual Retreat.

Finale-Prelude

Dr. Sam Says . . .

You have arrived at the *Back of the Book*, but hopefully, not the end of *Your Book!* Whether you arrived here by reading through the whole book, or you jumped here to see how it ends like I sometimes do, I hope this will not be the end of your quest in personal spiritual formation. In *Spiritual Formation: Forming Our Inner Lives and Relationships with God . . . Transforming Our Outer Lives and Relationships with Other People,* I have attempted to plant some seeds in your mind that will grow to bear the awesome fruit of spiritual formation. I wanted to introduce you to some of the *Keys to Spiritual Formation* that will unlock the corridors of your spirit, mind, emotions, and relationships to the life-renovating, life-transforming possibilities of intimacy with our precious Lord that will lead you *closer, deeper, higher, and farther*[191] with Him than you ever dreamed attainable.

I hope that the Finale of this book will be just the Prelude of writing your own story of discovering and using the Keys to Spiritual Formation in your life, relationships, and ministries. The way this can happen most effectively is by applying the Firewall principle I mentioned in the Prelude at the beginning.

---

191 Bruce, *Glorify Your Name in Me. (See Bibliography for ordering information.)*

When the Norton Antivirus Technician was trying to help me solve some issues, she asked me to connect to a website called Remote Access, and to allow her to take over the controls of my computer. As I surrendered my computer to her control, I watched my cursor move across the screen as she made all the necessary changes, downloaded and installed the latest version of Norton Protection System. When I disconnected from Remote Access my computer was working better than ever before. As you study the Word, pray, journal, and worship – learn and practice the disciplines of Spiritual Formation: Keys to Transformed Living – allow God, through His Holy Spirit, to have unconditional access to the control room of your life to make whatever changes are needed. Allow Him to install in your spirit a new Operating System that will be empowered by the spiritual disciplines which are keys to spiritual formation. This relationship will provide the Firewall Protection of our Lord Jesus Christ from all inner and outer forces that would seek to destroy your relationship with God and weaken your witness to other persons. As you do this, your inner life will be empowered and your ministries will be energized in ways you have never yet dreamed possible! And remember, always listen to the small voice of God! That is the Number One Firewall Key to Spiritual Formation.

The words of my songs Come to My Waters, Lord, I'll Be What You Want Me to Be, and Glorify Your Name in Me reflect God's invitation and our response to give Him Total, Unconditional Access to the control room of your life.

God's Invitation:

Come to the waters that flow from My Springs.

Come to My waters that never run dry.

Come to My waters and you'll thirst no more.

Come to My waters, be refreshed in My Grace!

I'll refresh you; I'll renew you; I will cleanse you right now.[192]

Our Response:

Come, Holy Spirit, purify me right now.
Come, precious Comforter, empower me within.
Touch those around me with Your healing grace.
Make me free like Lord Jesus, and wholly transformed.
Come, refresh me! Come, renew me! Come and cleanse me today.[193]

Our Commitment:
Lord, I'll go where You want me to go;
Lord, I'll do what You want me to do;
Lord, I'll say what You want me to say;
Lord, I'll be what You want me to be.[194]

Lord, bring me closer, closer than I've ever come before to You.
Lord, plunge me deeper, deeper than I've ever been before in You.
Lord, take me higher, higher, higher than I've ever soared before with you.
Lord, send me farther, farther than I've ever been before for You.

Lord, glorify Your name in me.
Oh Lord, glorify Your name in me.
Lord, please glorify Your name in me,
And my name in You.

---

192 ©Bruce, S. K. (2010). *Come to My Waters. Florence, MS: Come to the Waters Be Refreshed! Ministry & Music Resources, Sam & Sandie Bruce Ministries; Music & Soundtrack available from* drsambruce@aol.com www.bruceministries.net
193 Bruce, *Come to My Waters.*
194 Bruce, *Lord, I'll Be What You Want Me to Be (See Bibliography for ordering information.)*

Lord, lead me closer, and deeper, and higher, and farther
Than I've ever dreamed before.

Lord, glorify Your name in me.
Oh Lord, glorify Your name in me.
Lord, please glorify Your name in me,
And my name in You.[195]

Now, I hope you will covenant with God to walk with Him in a lifetime of Spiritual Formation: Forming Our Inner Lives and Relationships with God . . . Transforming Our Outer Lives and Relationships with Other People. Amen.

---

195 ©Bruce, S. K. (2010). *Glorify Your Name in Me*, based on 2 Thessalonians 1:11-12 NIV. Florence, MS: Come to the Waters Be Refreshed! Ministry & Music Resources, *Sam & Sandie Bruce Ministries; Music & Soundtrack available from* drsambruce@aol.com www.bruceministries.net.

Bibliography of Spiritual Formation Resources

Allen, Ronald and Gordon Borror. *Worship, Rediscovering the Missing Jewel.* Portland, OR: Multnomah Press, 1982.

Berquist, Maurice. *The Miracle and Power of Blessing.* Anderson, IN: Warner Press, 1983.

Bloesch, Donald G. *The Struggle of Prayer,* New York, NY: Harper & Row Publishers, Inc., 1980.

Bonhoeffer, Dietrich. *Life Together.* New York, NY: Harper & Row Publishers, Inc., 1954.

Bruce, Samuel K. *An Accurate Picture of the Fourth Street Church of God,* Course Project paper for Church Growth I, Fuller Seminary, D.Min. program, C. Peter Wagner, professor, Madera, CA, 1987.

Bruce, Samuel K. *Firewall: Keys to Spiritual Formation.* © 2008 Dr. Sam Bruce. Mid-America Christian University drsambruce@aol.com, www.bruceministries.net, sam.bruce@my.macu.edu

Bruce, Samuel K. *Spiritual Formation Through Becoming People of the Word, People of Prayer, People of Worship – People of God,* Doctor of Ministry Dissertation, School of Theology, Fuller Theological Seminary, Pasadena, CA. 1996. ©2008.

Bruce, Samuel K. *Come to the Waters . . . Be Refreshed! -* Song. *Come to the Waters . . . Be Refreshed! Music, Worship and Ministry Resources,* Sam & Sandie Bruce Ministries, Florence, MS, drsambruce@aol.com, www.bruceministries.net, sam.bruce@my.macu.edu ©2008.

Bruce, Samuel K. *Give Ear to My Words, O Lord* - Song. *Come to the Waters . . . Be Refreshed! Music, Worship and Ministry Resources*, Sam & Sandie Bruce Ministries, Florence, MS, drsambruce@aol.com, www.bruce-ministries.net, sam.bruce@my.macu.edu, ©2008.

Bruce, Samuel K. *Glorify Your Name in Me* - song. *Come to the Waters . . . Be Refreshed! Music, Worship and Ministry Resources*, Sam & Sandie Bruce Ministries, Florence, MS, drsambruce@aol.com, www.bruce-ministries.net, sam.bruce@my.macu.edu ©2008.

Bruce, Samuel K. *Lord, I'll Be What You Want Me to Be* - song . *Come to the Waters . . . Be Refreshed! Music, Worship and Ministry Resources*, Sam & Sandie Bruce Ministries, Florence, MS, drsambruce@aol.com, www.bruceministries.net, sam.bruce@my.macu.edu ©2008.

Bruce, Samuel K. *My Journal. Come to the Waters . . . Be Refreshed! Music, Worship and Ministry Resources*, Sam & Sandie Bruce Ministries, Florence, MS, drsambruce@aol.com www.bruceministries.net sam.bruce@my.macu.edu ©2008.

Chapman, J. B. *Holiness Triumphant.* Kansas City, MO: Beacon Hill Press, 1946.

Cho, Paul Yonggi. *Successful Home Cell Groups.* Plainfield, NJ: Logos International, 1981.

Cho, Paul Yonggi. *Prayer: Key to Revival.* Waco, TX: Word Books, 1984.

DePree, Max. *Leadership Is an Art.* New York, NY: Dell Publishing, 1989.

Draper, James T. *Colossians: A Portrait of Christ.* Wheaton, IL: Tyndale House Publishers, Inc., 1982.

Duewel, Wesley. *Revival Fire.* Grand Rapids, MI: Zondervan Publishing House, 1995.

Duewel, Wesley. *Mighty Prevailing Prayer.* Grand Rapids, MI: Francis Asbury Press of Zondervan Publishing House, 1990.

Dunnam, Maxie. *Alive in Christ: The Dynamic Process of Spiritual Formation.* Nashville, TN: Abingdon Press, 1982.

Eastman, Dick. *The Hour that Changes the World.* Grand Rapids, MI: Baker Book House, 1978.

Eims, Leroy. *Be the Leader You Were Meant to Be.* Wheaton, IL: Victor Books, 1976.

Ellul, Jacques. *Prayer and Modern Man.* New York, NY: Seabury Press, 1979.

Foster, Richard J. *Celebration of Discipline: The Path to Spiritual Growth.* New York, NY: Harper & Row, 1978.

Hayford, Jack W. *The Church on the Way.* Lincoln, NE: Chosen Books, 1982.

Hayford, Jack W., John Killinger, Howard Stevenson. *Mastering Worship.* Portland, OR: Multnomah Press, 1990.

Holy Bible, The: New International Version. New York, NY: The New York International Bible Society, 1978.

James, William. Quoted in Kendrick, Graham. *Learning to Worship as a Way of Life.* Minneapolis, MN: Bethany House Pub., 1984.

Kinlaw, Dennis F. *We Live as Christ: The Christian Message in a New Century.* Clinton, TN: Partnership Press, 2001.

Kreider, Eleanor. *Enter His Gates.* Scottsdale, PA., Herald Press, 1990.

Leech, Kenneth. *Soul Friend, The Practice of Christian Spirituality.* New York, NY: Harper & Row, 1977.

Liesch, Barry. *People in the Presence of God: Models and Directions for Worship.* Grand Rapids, MI: Zondervan Pub. House, 1983.

MacDonald, Gordon. *Ordering Your Private World.* Nashville, TN: Oliver Nelson, 1984.

Mains, David. *The Public Reading of Scripture.* Anaheim, CA: Congress on Biblical Exposition, 1986.

Malphurs, Aubrey. *Developing a Vision for Ministry in the 21st Century.* Grand Rapids, MI: Baker Book House, 1992.

Martin, Ralph P. *The Worship of God: Some Theological, Pastoral and Practical Reflections.* Grand Rapids, MI: William E. Eerdmans, 1982.

May, Gerald D. *Care of Mind, Care of Spirit*. New York, NY: Harper & Row, 1982.

Micks, Marianne H. *The Joy of Worship*. Philadelphia, PA: Westminster Press, 1982.

Murray, Andrew. *The Inner Life*. Grand Rapids, MI: Zondervan, 1980.

Nichols, William. *Jacob's Ladder: The Meaning of Worship*. Louisville, KY: Knox Press, 1958.

Nouwen, Henri J. M. *The Genesee Diary: Report from a Trappist Monastery*. Garden City, NY: Image Books, Doubleday & Co., 1976.

Nouwen, Henri J. M. *In the Name of Jesus, Reflections on Christian Leadership*. New York, NY: Crossroad Publishing, 1989.

Nouwen, Henri J. M. *Making All Things New: An Invitation to the Spiritual Life*. New York, NY: Harper & Row Publishers, 1981.

Nouwen, Henri J. M. *The Way of the Heart*. New York, NY: Seabury Press, 1981.

Peterson, Eugene H. *Answering God: The Psalms as Tools for Prayer*. New York, NY: Harper & Row, 1989.

Peterson, Eugene H. *A Year with the Psalms*. Waco, TX: Word Books, 1979.

Peterson, Eugene H. *Reversed Thunder, The Revelation of John & The Praying Imagination*. New York, NY: Harper & Row, 1988.

Peterson, Eugene H. *Spirituality and Ministry* Class Notes, Pasadena, CA: Fuller Theological Seminary, 1988.

Peterson, Eugene H. *Working the Angles*. Grand Rapids, MI: Eerdmans, 1987.

Postema, Don. *Space for God: The Study and Practice of Prayer and Spirituality*. Grand Rapids, MI: Board of Publications of the Christian Reformed Church, 1983.

Richards, Lawrence O. *Expository Dictionary of Bible Words*. Grand Rapids, MI: Zondervan, 1985.

Steere, Douglas V. *Prayer in the Contemporary World.* Wallingford, PA: Pendle Hill, 1966.

Thornton, Martin. *Spiritual Direction.* Cambridge, MA: Cowley Pub., 1984.

Torrey, R. A. *The Power of Prayer and the Prayer of Power.* Grand Rapids, MI: Zondervan, 1924.

Underhill, Evelyn. *Worship.* New York, NY: Crossroad Pub. Co., 1989.

Von Balthasar, Hans Urs. *Prayer.* New York, NY: Ignatius Press, 1955.

Wainwright, Geoffrey. *Doxology: The Praise of God in Worship, Doctrine, and Life.* New York, NY: Oxford University Press, 1980.

Watson, Philip S. *The Message of the Wesley's.* New York, NY: The Macmillan Co., 1964.

Webber, Robert E. *Worship Is a Verb.* Dallas, TX: Word Pub., 1982.

Wesley, John. *The Works of John Wesley.* Grand Rapids, MI: Zondervan Publishing House, n. d.

Wesley, John. *Wesley's Notes on the New Testament.* Peabody, MA: Hendrickson Publishers, Inc., 1986.

Willard, Dallas. *Renovation of the Heart: Putting on the Character of Christ.* Colorado Springs, CO: NavPress, 2002.

Introducing Sam & Sandie Bruce Ministries

In 2003, Dr. Sam & Mrs. Sandie launched, full time, their extensive national speaking and music ministry among churches, conferences, retreats, camps, and civic organizations. They are available for revivals, concerts, leadership training – preaching ministry, music leadership or both. They are also available for short-term interim church ministry. The theme for their services (whether one service or several) is *Come to the Waters – Be Refreshed: a Concert of Renewal!* Since going full time with Sam & Sandie Bruce Ministries in 2003, the Bruces have ministered in 20 states and 17 denominations. Across their lifetime ministries they have ministered in 40 states and 25 denominations, Washington, D.C., and Grand Cayman.

Service Information

Sam & Sandie Bruce Ministries

Their services – whether preaching & teaching or leading music & worship – feature contemporary Christian music as well as traditional songs and hymns, along with some of their own original songs, with lots of congregational participation in the singing. Dr. Sam's messages are always Bible-centered, real-life related teaching to meet the needs of people in all situations and relationships. The worship and praise lift the hearts of people to God for refreshment, renewal and revival.

God's blessing and anointing are evident in their ministry, as lives are changed, marriages are mended, hearts are encouraged, fresh commitments are made to God, and churches are strengthened. In each service of worship and praise, the Bruces blend memorized Scripture, testimonies, congregational singing, trumpet playing, and positive messages of hope and encouragement with their music and teaching.

Recommendations for Sam & Sandie Bruce Ministries

May I encourage you, as people in the church, here is one of the church's sons and daughters that are giving themselves to this ministry. They will bless your hearts. Sam is one of the most gifted preachers you could get. I've heard him quote the whole book of 1 Peter, or some other book of the Bible. And I said, "Lord, why couldn't I do that?" And God said, "You know, you'd better be yourself and not try to be Sammy Bruce." And so, I thank them for their ministry. I've been with them in Madera, California, when they were there. This family – they were singing saints. They had a big fairground there, and they would have the whole Sammy Bruce family out there to sing for the whole fair. They were just tremendous, and God uses them. And I would encourage you as churches to get behind them and use them for ministry. They are great, great people, and I just thank the Lord for them.

— **Dr. Arlo Newell**, *Former Editor-in-Chief, Warner Press, Anderson, Indiana Pastor, Evangelist*

It is with great joy that I take this opportunity to introduce and to recommend Dr. Sam and Sandie Bruce to you. The multiple gifts of Sam and Sandie have blessed the church in so many ways for over 30 years. Sam's gifts of communication are widely embraced throughout the nation. His years of ministry as senior pastor gave him a clear understanding of the needs of local congregations and pastors. Dr. Sam has served as President of Wesley College in Florence, Mississippi from 1991 - 2003 with excellence and skill. This ministry provided him with the cutting-edge opportunity of relating and training the next generation of church leaders. Sam and Sandie are both greatly gifted in the area of music and worship.

Perhaps what has made them so effective in their ministry as a whole has been the gentle spirit and strong faith with which they serve and share. That spirit and faith have been nurtured by deep roots in the church and the word of God and out of life's real pains and joys! They understand and are witness out of both knowledge and life experiences of God's constant faithfulness, even in the darkness.

I know that there are many individuals and ministries offering their services to your congregation. I can promise you without hesitation that you will find none to be more effective or a greater blessing than the *Sam & Sandie Bruce Ministries.*

> **– Rev. Jeannette Flynn,** *Team Director – Church of God Congregational Ministries; Pastor, Evangelist*

Sam & Sandie Bruce Ministries
333 Highway 469 North
Florence MS 39073
601-845-8693; 601-955-3176
<u>drsambruce@aol.com</u> <u>www.bruceministries.</u>
<u>net</u> <u>sam.bruce@my.macu.edu</u>

Believe it! God Is There:
Fore Guard **– Ahead of You, Charting Your Way!**
Rear Guard **– Behind You: Completing What You Could Not Finish!**
Present Guard **– With You Now: Comforting & Sustaining You!**
All-the-Other-Times-Guard **– Covering Your**
Calendar, Clock & iPhone . . . Forever!

Autobiography – Dr. Samuel K. Bruce

(Known to students as Dr. Sam)

Sam & Sandie Bruce Ministries, President 2003 –
Mid-America Christian University, Professor of Spiritual Formation & Leadership 1983 –
Fourth Street Church of God, Madera, CA, Senior Pastor 1970-1991
Wesley College, President, 1991-2003
Mission Mississippi (a racial reconciliation movement) 2002 –
Rotary Club 1993-

Education:
Fuller Theological Seminary, D.Min.
California Graduate School of Theology, D. Min.
Anderson University School of Theology, M.Div.
Mid-America Christian University, B.A.
Wesley College, A.A.
University of Houston, Science Courses.
Southern Nazarene University, Graduate Work.
Nazarene Bible College, E-Learning Course Development & Teaching Courses

My name is Samuel K. Bruce (my students call me Dr. Sam). I was born in Mt. Vernon, Texas, the home of former Dallas Cowboys' quarterback Don Meredith (not that it has anything to do with me, except that I did play a few baseball games against him when I was in junior high and he was in senior high). My parents, Walter and Lois Bruce, met at God's Bible School in Cincinnati, Ohio, and they were married shortly after Dad graduated. I accepted Christ into my life at age 4, was called to preach at age 8, preached my first sermon at age 14, and began pastoring my first two churches (½ time each) at age 19, during my sophomore year of college.

Dad was president of Wesley College (the same college of which I was president for twelve years) during its first nine years. He later served as president for two years. That meant that I spent those years traveling across the country with parents and various ministry groups. When I was eight years old, Dad put me on staff as a singer with the touring groups and paid me ten cents a song. Dad served as a pastor for several years following his ministry at Wesley College. He served as Director of Foreign Missions for the Congregational Methodist Church. Following retirement, he pastored a church for the last ten years of his life. I suppose it could be said that I have been in ministry all my life.

I met and married Sandie Hinderliter in 1964 when we were students at Mid-America Christian University (Gulf-Coast Bible College). When I walked into my first voice lesson, she was playing the piano as accompanist, working her way through college. I saw her and said, "Wow, Lord, I'll take that one, if You'll let me have her!" He graciously granted my request, and we were married a year later!

Sandie and I have two daughters, four grandchildren, and two great grandchildren. They live near us in Florence, Mississippi. Janelle and her husband Tim have Allen and Austin. Janelle is a second-grade teacher. Tim owns Cycle City USA, a cycle repair shop. Janette and her husband Erik have Kelsey and Caleb. Janette is a minister of music and worship, and Erik is a dental lab technician and works in an archery shop. One of my favorite activities is, "hangin' out" with my grandkids. I also enjoy golf, hunting, fishing, camping and hiking in the mountains.

We have ministered in 39 states, 25 denominations, Grand Cayman, service clubs, and 6 countries in revivals, camp-meetings, concerts, leadership training, and various other ministries.

In 1999, we discovered that Sandie had a huge benign tumor (larger than my fist) in the right frontal lobe of her brain. It blinded her right eye. It had been growing, the doctor said, for several years. Since it was benign, she had no pain, seizures, or anything to indicate it was there. When the neurosurgeon took the tumor out, she was in a coma for several days, and when she came out, she was like a newborn baby. Although her memory was intact, she had to relearn everything a baby has to learn: eating, walking, talking, dressing, showering. Today, her doctors call her a *miracle lady*, and their explanation is that, in addition to removal of the tumor, *the Lord has indeed touched you, Mrs. Bruce!* She travels throughout the nation with me in our motorhome, singing, giving awesome testimonies, and blessing people with her Christlike spirit. While she still has some health issues to deal with, when you talk with her, if you did not know her situation, you probably would not realize it. My explanation is, *"it's just a God-thing."*

Speaking of *God-things*, due to Sandie's many physical challenges following her surgery, a businessman friend purchased a new diesel pusher motor-home for us, so we could continue the travel required by our ministries.

SPIRITUAL FORMATION:

Forming Your Inner Life & Relationship with God
Transforming Your Outer Life & Relationships with Other People

- be transformed from a dull, drab, monotonous, nominal Christian into an exciting, radiant, exhilarating, vibrant Jesus Follower! Here's how...

- learn how to incorporate the principles of spiritual transformation—see how one man did it...

- one of the most demanding books you'll read...apply its principles and you will definitely be changed...

- find the path to a balanced, fulfilled, inspiring life...

Sam, your work needs to be published.
Eugene Peterson, Professor of Spiritual Formation, Fuller Theological Seminary; Translator of The Message, The Bible in Contemporary Language

Dr. Sam lets us all in on the secret of his life of devotion and passion for the Lord ... he has given us an amazing visual of a man's life devoted to pursuing a real relationship with the Messiah.
Pastor Mitch Burch; Evangelist & State Pastor/Overseer; West Virginia Ministries of the Church of God (Anderson, IN)

You will find insight, instruction and inspiration within Dr. Bruce's writing that will give you tools for developing intimacy with God.
Dr. Claude Robold; Pastor New Covenant Church, Franklin, OH; College & Seminary Classmate

This is not a book that can be read quickly or casually. You must read it with a desire to be changed from the inside out. The stories reflect the pastor's heart – the pastor who learned to hear what hurting people were unable to say. Read it and allow your mind to be transformed by the Word of God until the Word becomes your life.
Mary E. Fuller, Attorney at Law; Ordained Minister

As a reader of Spiritual Formation, I have learned how to have a more personal relationship with God. A relationship that is not dependent on my good deeds or actions, but one that encourages me to have a more authentic connection. Throughout the book, Dr. Bruce uncovers how to invite God into our daily crises, concerns, and issues instead of only having Sunday rendezvous with God. I am personally honored to have Dr. Bruce as a mentor. Each page of this book is not only an extension of his heart for God, but also his heart for God's people. The Word of God transforms into a refreshing river of life-altering refreshment when you apply the principles of Spiritual Formation.
Dr. Terrence Z. Johnson, Chief Innovation Officer, Licensed Professional Counselor, iProgress, LLC)

Spiritual Formation: Forming Our Inner Lives and Relationships with God . . . Transforming Our Outer Lives and Relationships with Other People is a timely book for our age. Dr. Sam, let me say I have been to combat in the Global War on Terror and witnessed what discipline our young Soldiers exhibit. Discipline keeps them alive on the battlefield. They have been trained in their Warrior Tasks and Drills. Spiritual Formation: Forming Our Inner Lives and Relationships with God . . . Transforming Our Outer Lives and Relationships with Other People describes and illustrates the imperative disciplines of the soul (Warrior Tasks and Drills) that are needed for our combat with the terrorist kind of evil forces that threaten to destroy our faith and witness. We can win this spiritual warfare if we apply your Keys to Spiritual Formation.
Tommy W. Fuller, Chaplain (COL, Ret.), Joint Forces Headquarters Chaplain, Mississippi National Guard. "Pro Deo Et Patria."

Dr. Sam Bruce is President of Sam & Sandie Bruce Ministries (a global preaching, music & worship, teaching and leadership training ministry) and Online Instructor for Mid-America Christian University. Former Pastor of Fourth Street Church of God, Madera CA, and Former President of Wesley College, Florence MS.

333 Highway 49 N, Florence MS 39073. 601-955-3176
drsambruce@aol.com   sam.bruce@my.macu.edu
www.bruceministries.net

9 781648 302749